OXFORD Business English

Business Grammar & Practice

NEW EDITION

Michael Duckworth

OXFORD

UNIVERSITY PRESS

OXFORD
UNIVERSITY PRESS

Great Clarendon Street, Oxford OX2 6DP

Oxford University Press is a department of the University of Oxford.
It furthers the University's objective of excellence in research, scholarship,
and education by publishing worldwide in

Oxford New York

Auckland Cape Town Dar es Salaam Hong Kong Karachi
Kuala Lumpur Madrid Melbourne Mexico City Nairobi
New Delhi Shanghai Taipei Toronto

With offices in

Argentina Austria Brazil Chile Czech Republic France Greece
Guatemala Hungary Italy Japan South Korea Poland Portugal
Singapore Switzerland Thailand Turkey Ukraine Vietnam

OXFORD and OXFORD ENGLISH are registered trade marks of
Oxford University Press in the UK and in certain other countries

© Oxford University Press 2003

The moral rights of the author have been asserted

Database right Oxford University Press (maker)

First published 2003

2014 2013 2012 2011
15 14 13 12

ISBN-13: 978 0 19 457079 4

Printed in China

ACKNOWLEDGEMENTS

**The publishers would like to thank the following for the use of
photographs and copyright material:**

Alvey & Towers p 50; ©Jay Coneyl p 160; CORBIS p 13 (©Firefly
Productions/video conferencing), p 16 (©William Gottlieb/bottling
plant), p 40 (©Simon Warren), p 44 (©John D.Norman/smashed glass,
©The Purcell Team/roof), p 84 (©Bossu Regis/SYGMA/book fair),
p 104 (©Layne Kennedy/airline pilot); Friends of the Earth p 72
(Jennifer Bates/GM trolley); Getty Images p 9 (Taxi/Adastra/shuttle),
p 13 (Taxi/Dia Max/aircraft),p 16 (Stone/Andy Sacks/milking
parlour), 21 (Stone/Thomas Schmidt/lips, Stone/Chris Craymer/face),
p 33 (Taxi/Christopher Wilhelm/microchip, ImageBank/Stephen
Derr/clean room), p 36 (Taxi/Ed Honowitz), p 49 (Stone/Jerome
Tisne/female), p 60 (ImageBank/Jason Homa), p 125 (FOODPIX/Paul
Poplis), p 144 (ImageBank/Will & Deni McIntyre), p 152 (Stone/Joe
Polillio), p 157 (Stone/Davies & Starr/Sushi), p 177 (ImageBank/Marc
Romanelli), p 180 (Stone/Ken Whitmore); ©Hulton Archive p 142;
©ImageState p 57, p 110; ©Morgan Motor Company p 69; ©Médecins
Sans Frontières p 150 (Roger Job/MSF/nurse, MSF/logo); ©2002
Nintendo p 74; ©Nokia p 8; ©PA Photos p 72 (EPA/diamond),
p 121; ©Powerstock p 49 (male), p 88, p 173; ©Rex Features p 72
(Gracelands), p 104 (©Edward Webb/policeman), p 145 (©IXO/
Avantis); Science Photo Library p 9 (Laguna Design/hydrogen atom),
p 149 (©Tom Van Sant/Geosphere Project, Santa Monica); ©Three
Fishes, Shrewsbury p 117; ©World Food Programme p 150 (Mike
Huggins/food distribution, WFP/logo).

Illustrations by:

Kate Charlesworth p 28, 38, 89, 101, 132, 168; Mark Duffin p 24, 48,
49, 59, 60, 76, 92, 145; David Hine p 128; Harry Venning p 26, 68, 80,
97, 154, 184.

**The authors and publisher are grateful to those who have given
permission to reproduce the following extracts and adaptations of
copyright material:**

P 89 'Leadership Questionnaire' by Donald Clark. Reproduced by
permission of Donald Clark. P 117 'There'll soon be no smoke without
fire' by Anthony Browne © The Observer 29 July 2001. Reproduced by
permission of Guardian Newspapers Limited. P 149 'Hunger talks start
with lobster and foie gras' by Richard Owen © Times Newspapers
Limited, London 11 June 2002. P 160 'Console Wars', The Economist
magazine 22 June 2002. Reproduced by permission of The Economist
Newspaper Limited. P 178 Entry taken from the Oxford Wordpower
Dictionary second edition (ISBN 0194315169)

Sources:

P 25 Information from The Times, Tuesday January 29 2002. P 25
Information from The Financial Times, Tuesday January 15 2002. P 33
Information from Business Week, January 21 2002. P 72 Information
from Business Life, December 2001/January 2002. P 74 Information on
Nintendo www.nintendo.com. P 161 Statistics taken from OECD 2000,
2001, 2002. P 165 Statistics taken from The Times, June 25 2002. P 176
Information from news.bbc.co.uk. P 216 Information from
www.dyson.au

**The author and publisher would like to thank everyone who
helped us by piloting and commenting on the original material
for Grammar & Practice, particularly the following:**

David Allerton, The English Institute, Metz; Catherine Butchart,
Linguarama Spracheninstitut, Hamburg; Robyn Christensen,
Schering AG, Berlin; Kate Cowe, Düsseldorf; Patricia Cook, Formation
et Communication, Paris; Ilse De Kerpel, Silly-Hainault; Joséphine
Ezzarouali and Karen Carnet, LOGOS, Grenoble; Eamonn Fitzgerald,
Munich; Simon Gardner and Katy Ryan, LANSER S.A., Bilbao; Guy
Heath, Aximedia Idiomas, Madrid; Clement Laroy, Nivelles; Kate
Monleón, King's College Business English Programmes, Madrid;
Monica Apraiz Pineda and Juan Antonio Rico, Eurostudy, Bilbao;
Beth Schüth, Tim Hill, and Helmut Hunder, Henkel KGaA, Düsseldorf.

Special thanks to Isobel Fletcher de Téllez.

Contents

Glossary of grammatical terms

Here is a short explanation of some of the grammatical terms used in this book.

Adjective

A word like *large, cold, white, American*, etc. It helps to describe a noun or pronoun.

*I work in a **large, modern** office. It's **nice and spacious**.*

Adverb

A word like *carefully, quickly, well, sometimes, yesterday, never*, etc. It is normally used to say how or when something happens.

*My father drives **slowly**. I'll see you **tomorrow**.*

Article

A word that precedes a noun. *A* and *an* are called 'indefinite articles'; *the* is called the 'definite article'.

Auxiliary verb

A verb like *be, do*, or *have* which is used with another (main) verb to form tenses, passives, negatives, and questions.

*I **am** working.*   *She **has** gone home.*

***Do** you like Germany?*

Conditional (or conditional clause)

A clause or sentence constructed with *if, unless*, etc. It is normally used to discuss an event or situation in the future, present, or past, which may or may not be real.

If you are late, we'll start the meeting without you.

If I were you, I would pay the bill now.

If the roads hadn't been so busy, we would have arrived on time.

Continuous form (see Simple and continuous forms)

Infinitive

The infinitive is the basic form of the verb – *to see, to make, to like*, etc. If you look at the list of irregular verbs on pages 188–89 you will see the infinitive form in the first column. For example:

Infinitive	Past tense form	Past participle
to go	*went*	*gone*

The infinitive is usually introduced with the word *to*.

*I want **to leave**, but it's not so easy **to do**.*

Sometimes we use the 'bare infinitive' – this is the infinitive without the word *to*.

*You must **leave** now. You shouldn't **stay** any longer.*

-ing form

When the *-ing* form of the verb is used as a verb or an adjective, it is called the 'present participle'.

*I saw Peter **leaving**.*

*He's a very **annoying** person.*

The *-ing* form is also used as a noun (sometimes called a 'gerund').

***Travelling** light can help you get through customs quickly.*

Modal verb

A word like *can, could, may, might, must, ought, shall, should, will, would*. A modal verb comes before the bare infinitive of another verb, and adds a certain kind of meaning: for example, ability, permission, obligation, probability, or certainty.

*I **can** speak Japanese, but I **can't** write it.*

*The problem **might** be to do with the computer system.*

*You **should** think about taking out a business loan.*

(Modal verbs are also called modal auxiliary verbs.)

Noun

A word like *computer, accountant, information, Martin, America*. It is the name of an object, concept, place, or person. 'Concrete nouns' are things you can see or touch, like *a car, a table*, or *an office*. 'Abstract nouns' are things that you cannot see or touch, like *an idea, a decision*, or *an opinion*. Nouns can be countable: *one book, two pages, three ideas, four days*, etc.; or uncountable: *water, advice, freedom* (you cannot say *two waters, an advice*, etc.).

Object

The object of a sentence (a noun or noun phrase) usually comes after the verb. In these sentences, *the report* and *a new telephone system* are the objects. They follow the verbs *wrote* and *installed*.

*Peter wrote **the report**.*

*We installed **a new telephone system** last week.*

Participle

The *-ing* or *-ed* forms of verb endings. The *-ing* form is called the 'present participle'; the *-ed* form is called the 'past participle'.

Passive and active forms

In an active sentence we say what people or things do, so we use active verb forms like *went*, *explain*, *is developing*, *will increase*. In this sentence, *The police* is the subject, *arrested* is the verb and *Alain* is the object. This is an active sentence.

*The police **arrested** Alain.*

In a passive sentence, we say what happens to people or things. The passive is formed by using the verb *to be* and a past participle. The object of the active sentence (*Alain*) becomes the subject. The subject of the active sentence (*the police*) is called the 'agent', and is introduced by the word *by*. This is a passive sentence.

*Alain **was arrested** by the police.*

Preposition

A word like *to, in, behind, over, through, into, under*, etc. Prepositions are used to give information about things like place, time, direction, and manner.

*I telephoned our office **in** London **at** 7.00 this morning.*

*Last week we drove **through** the Alps **into** Switzerland.*

*We sent them the documents **by** fax.*

Pronoun

A word like *it, me, you, she, they, him, her*, etc. which replaces a noun in a sentence, usually because we do not want to repeat the noun.

*I bought a new fax machine yesterday; **it** was very expensive.*

*Susan's car has been stolen, and **she** is very upset about **it**.*

Relative clause

A clause beginning with a word like *who, where, which, whose,* or *that*. It is used to identify someone or something, or to give more information about them.

*These lenses, **which** cost only a few pence to produce, cost over $200 to buy.*

*Stefan Andersson is the consultant **that** we employed on our last project.*

Short forms

The verbs *be* and *have*, and the auxiliary *do*, can be contracted into a shorter form (e.g., *I'm, we've, don't, didn't*). These short forms are commonly used in speech and informal writing.

Simple and continuous forms

Tenses have both a simple and a continuous form. The simple form carries a sense of completion, or regularity of action. The continuous form carries a sense of continuity, or incompleteness of action. The continuous form ends in *-ing*.

	Simple	Continuous
Present	*he works*	*he is working*
Past	*he worked*	*he was working*
Present perfect	*he has worked*	*he has been working*

Subject

The subject of a sentence (a noun or noun phrase) normally comes before the verb. It is usually the person or thing who does something, or is the main focus of attention. In the following sentences, the subjects are *My brother Peter* and *The sales conference*.

***My brother Peter** works in London.*

***The sales conference** will be held in September.*

Tenses

The forms of a verb which help us to know the time of an action or event (past, present, or future). There are many different tenses. Here are two examples:

*I **work** in the centre of Munich.* (present simple tense)

*I **worked** in the centre of Munich.* (past simple tense)

Some tenses are formed with the main verb and an extra verb such as *be* or *have*. These extra verbs are called 'auxiliary verbs'.

*Antoinette **is working** late this evening.* (present continuous tense)

*Jan **has finished** his report.* (present perfect tense)

Transitive and intransitive verbs

Some verbs are followed by an object, and some are not. If a verb is normally followed by an object, it is called a 'transitive verb'. The verb *to buy* has an object, so in this sentence, *bought* is the transitive verb, and *a car* is the object.

*I **bought** a car.*

If a verb is not normally followed by an object, it is called an 'intransitive verb'. The verb *to travel* does not have an object, so in this sentence, *travels* is an intransitive verb and there is no object.

*She **travels** frequently in Asia.*

Verb

A word like *buy, sell, be, seem, think, break, decide*, etc. A verb describes an action, a state, or a process. In the following sentences, *competed, lies, buy*, and *sell* are the verbs.

*Five companies **competed** for the engineering contract.*

*La Défense **lies** to the west of Paris.*

*We **buy** and **sell** shares on the open market.*

1 Present simple

Presentation

ⓐ Form

The table below shows how to form the present simple tense of the verb *to work*. All verbs except *to be* and the modals (see Units 23–6) follow this pattern.

For negatives and questions we use the auxiliary *do* and the bare infinitive:

I work	*I do not/don't work*	*Do I work?*
You work	*You do not/don't work*	*Do you work?*
He/she/it works	*He/she/it does not/doesn't work*	*Does he/she/it work?*
We work	*We do not/don't work*	*Do we work?*
They work	*They do not/don't work*	*Do they work?*

Note: The short forms of the negative are commonly used in speech and informal writing.

Common mistakes:

1 Forgetting to put the *-s* ending on the *he/she/it* forms.
   All verbs except modals must end in *-s* in the third person singular affirmative:

wrong: * *My new laptop work very well.*
right: *My new laptop works very well.*

2 Adding the *-s* to the *he/she/it* forms of negatives and questions.

We add the *-es* form to the auxiliary (*do*), and not to the main verb (*work*):

wrong: * *I know Karl doesn't works in Accounts.*
right: *I know Karl doesn't work in Accounts.*

ⓑ Permanent situations

The present simple is for actions and situations that are generally or permanently true:

IBM is one of the largest computer companies in the world; it manufactures mainframes and PCs, and sells its products all over the world.

ⓒ Routines and frequency

We use the present simple to talk about routines and things we do regularly:

I usually get to the showroom at about 8.00 and I have a quick look at my emails. The sales reps arrive at about 8.15 and we open at 8.30.

ⓓ Facts

We use the present simple to talk about scientific or other facts:

Superconductors are materials that conduct electricity and do not create electrical resistance.

ⓔ Programmes and timetables

We use the present simple to talk about programmes and timetables. When we use the present simple like this, it can refer to the future:

The fast train to London leaves at 7.39 and gets in to Paddington at 8.45. Then you catch the Heathrow Express to the airport – it goes every fifteen minutes.

Practice

EXERCISE **1**

Form

Complete the dialogue using the verbs in brackets. See the example.

A: Where [1] *do you come* (come) from?

B: I [2] .... *came* .... (come) from Finland.

A: What [3] .... (you/do)?

B: I'm a software engineer. I [4] .... (work) for Nokia.

A: And so where [5] .... (you/live)? In Helsinki?

B: No, well, I [6] .... (not/live) there permanently. I
[7] .... (spend) the week there but every weekend I
[8] .... (go) back to a small town called Turku –
that's where my wife [9] .... (come) from.

A: [10] .... (you/travel) to England often?

B: Yes, I [11] .... (visit) two or three times a year.

EXERCISE **2**

Permanent situations – company activities

Complete the information about the business activities of the Finnish company
Nokia, using the verbs in the boxes. See the example.

NOKIA
CONNECTING PEOPLE

Originally a paper-making business, the Finnish company Nokia is now one of the
world's largest mobile telecommunications companies. There are three main
divisions — Nokia networks, Nokia Mobile Phones and Nokia Ventures Organization.

NOKIA Mobile phones

This division designs and [1] **manufactures** mobile phones for over 130 countries worldwide.
Its very wide product range [2] .... the different needs of different customers; the
simplest phones [3] .... customers to make voice calls, but others [4] ....
video capability, Internet access and other advanced features.

allow	manufacture	meet	provide

NOKIA Networks

Of course, phones [5] .... without a network, and this division [6] ....
systems and infrastructure networks of all kinds. Nokia [7] .... closely with telecom
operators and Internet service providers so that they can serve their customers better.
The networks are modular, so they can start small and then develop as the customer base
[8] ....

grow	not/function	offer	work

NOKIA Ventures Organization

The Ventures Organization [9] .... at new business areas and opportunities for the
future – even if there [10] .... to be a natural connection with the rest of the company.
The organization also [11] .... in new technology businesses and the US-based
Innovent team [12] .... inventors and entrepreneurs to develop their ideas.

help	invest	look	not/seem

Routines and frequency

Complete the dialogue by putting the verbs in brackets into the correct form. See the example.

Brian: I need to speak to Gina about this new publicity brochure. [1] Do you know (you/know) where she is?

Diana: She [2] .... (not/work) on Fridays. She gave up her full-time job and now she [3] .... (work) part-time.

Brian: Right. When [4] does .... (she/come) to the office?

Diana: Well, she [5] .... (come) in from Monday to Thursday, but she [6] .... (not/stay) all day. She usually [7] .... (start) at 9.00 and [8] .... (go) home at about 2.15.

Scientific facts

Complete the passage using the verbs in the boxes. See the example.

Hydrogen is the simplest and most common element in the universe, and [1] has a very high energy content per gram. As it is so lightweight, rockets and space shuttles [2] .... hydrogen as a power source. Hydrogen rarely [3] .... alone as a gas because it is chemically active and usually [4] .... with other elements to form different compounds.

combine	have
stand	use

When an electric current [5] .... through water, the water [6] .... up into two gases – hydrogen and oxygen. When hydrogen [7] .... , it [8] .... back into water.

burn	pass
split	turn

This process [9] .... pollution, and this [10] .... that hydrogen could be a useful fuel for the cars of the future. At the moment, it [11] .... a lot of electricity to produce hydrogen from water, but some researchers [12] .... that new production methods will be found.

believe	mean
not/cause	take

Programmes and timetables

Complete the dialogue by putting the verbs in brackets into the correct form. See the example.

Laura: Have you got the details of the Easyjet flight? What time [1] does it arrive (it/arrive) at Nice?

Claire: It [2] gets (get) in at 10.05. Now there's also a later one that [3] goes (go) from Luton at 19.00 but it [4] .... (not/get) in until 22.05.

Laura: That's a bit late. Did you check Eurostar?

Claire: Yes, there's a train that [5] .... (leave) Waterloo at 8.27 and that [6] .... (reach) Lille at 11.29. Then you have to change trains, but there's no problem because the Nice train [7] .... (not/leave) until 12.17, so you have 45 minutes. Then it [8] .... (stop) at a few stations on the way and [9] .... (arrive) at Nice at 20.06.

Production

Choose a job title from box A and a verb from box B. Describe what people with these jobs do, making any necessary changes to the verbs. See the example.

A

Personnel officers	Management consultants
An architect	A stockbroker
A journalist	An air steward
Venture capitalists	Auditors

B

invest	advise
design	look after
write	arrange
check	buy and sell

1 An air steward looks after passengers on a plane.
2 _A stock broker buys and sells_ stocks and shares.
3 _An architect designs_ houses.
4 _Venture capitalist_ in small, high-risk companies.
5 _Auditors check_ the accounts of a company.
6 _Management consultants_ companies on how they should be run.
7 _A journalist writes_ articles for a newspaper.
8 _Personnel officers_ interviews.

Look at the information about Nokia on page 8. Write down some similar information about the different divisions and business activities of your company.

....

....

....

....

Answer the following questions about your daily routine.

1 How do you get to work in the morning?

....

2 How long does it take to get to work?

....

3 What sort of things do you do in the mornings?

....

4 What do you do for lunch?

....

5 What do you do in the afternoons?

....

6 What time do you usually finish?

....

7 What do you do at the weekends?

....

2 Present continuous

Presentation

a Form

The present continuous is formed by using the present tense of the auxiliary *be* and the *-ing* form of the verb. For negatives and questions we also use the auxiliary *be* and the *-ing* form of the verb:

I am/'m working	*I am not/'m not working*	*Am I working?*
You are/'re working	*You are not/aren't working*	*Are you working?*
He/she/it is/'s working	*He/she/it is not/isn't working*	*Is he/she/it working?*
We are/'re working	*We are not/aren't working*	*Are we working?*
They are/'re working	*They are not/aren't working*	*Are they working?*

Note: The short forms of the positive and negative are commonly used in speech and informal writing. An alternative short form of the negative is also sometimes used: *you're not, he/she/it's not, we're not, they're not.*

For spelling rules, see Appendix 1, page 187.

b Moment of speaking

The present continuous is used to talk about an activity taking place at the moment of speaking:

*I'm afraid Herr Seifert isn't available at the moment. He **is talking** to a customer on the other phone.*

c Current projects

The present continuous is used to talk about actions or activities and current projects that are taking place over a period of time (even if they are not taking place precisely at the moment of speaking):

*Barton's is one of the largest local construction companies. At the moment we **are building** a new estate with 200 houses and we **are negotiating** with the council for the sale of development land in Boxley Wood.*

d Temporary situations

The present continuous is used to indicate that an action or activity is temporary rather than permanent. Compare:

*Janet **organizes** our conferences and book launches.*
(The present simple is used because this is generally true.)

*Janet is away on maternity leave, so I **am organizing** the conferences and book launches.*
(The present continuous is used because this is only true for a limited time.)

e Slow changes

The present continuous is used to describe current trends and slow changes that are taking place:

*The latest economic statistics from the European Central Bank show that both unemployment and inflation **are falling** in the Eurozone countries, and that the economy **is growing** at an annual rate of 2.6%.*

For information about how the present continuous is used to refer to the future, see Unit 13.

Practice

EXERCISE ❶

Moment of speaking

Put the verbs in brackets into the present continuous. See the example.

1 Could I ring you back in a few minutes? I am talking (talk) to someone on the other line.
2 Jamila is upstairs with Alexei and Roy. They .... (have) a meeting about the products website.
3 What .... (you/do) here? I thought you had gone to the airport.
4 Could you tell Mr Gaspaldi that Miss Lee is here? He .... (expect) me.
5 Oh no, the printer .... (not work). I'll call the IT Department.
6 This is a very bad line. .... (you/call) from your mobile?
7 I .... (phone) to say that I'll be home late this evening.

EXERCISE ❷

Current projects

Read these newspaper extracts about various projects that different companies are currently involved in. Match the extracts in column A with the extracts in column B. See the example.

A

1 China's Central Semiconductor Manufacturing Corporation is planning a big increase in output. b

2 The Hotel Sorrento in Seattle is upgrading its rooms and facilities. f

3 Biota is a leading Australian biotechnology company. a

4 Microsoft is anticipating a downturn in PC sales. h

5 Airbus is confident about the long-term future of the airline industry. e

6 EMI is looking at new ways of distributing music. d

7 Bloomsbury publishes fiction and reference books. g

8 HIT Entertainment has bought the rights to Pingu. c

B

a At the moment it is carrying out research into drugs to cure the common cold.

b It is upgrading its manufacturing plants to produce state-of-the-art silicon.

c It is planning to introduce the cartoon character to children's TV shows in the US.

d It is selling songs on-line through MusicNet and Pressplay.

e It is developing a new double-decker jumbo jet which will come into production in a few years.

f It is converting its 154 rooms into 76 luxury suites for business travellers, each equipped with fax machines and data ports.

g It is currently nearing completion of a new dictionary project.

h It is developing new games consoles and other products for the home to compensate for this decline.

Temporary situations

Two colleagues meet in Paris. Read the dialogue and put the verbs into the present continuous. See the example.

Pierre: Hello, Jason. What [1] *are you doing* (you/do) over here?

Jason: Hello, Pierre. I'm just here for a few days. I [2] .... (attend) the conference at the Pompidou Centre.

Pierre: Where [3] .... (you/stay)?

Jason: At the Charles V.

Pierre: Very nice. And how's business?

Jason: Not that good. The recession [4] .... (affect) us. People [5] .... (not/spend) very much and we [6] .... (not/get) many new orders, but it could be worse. How about you?

Pierre: It's much the same over here. Companies just [7] .... (not/buy) new equipment, so our Training Division [8] .... (not/do) very well. Still, our Financial Services Division [9] .... (manage) to get some new customers, because there are still plenty of people who [10] .... (look) for good financial advice.

Slow changes

Read the following passages about changes that are taking place in the travel industry. Fill in the blanks with the verbs in the boxes, using the present continuous. See the example.

Many major airlines [1] *are beginning* to realize that the lucrative business class market [2] *is declining*. This is partly because some of the low-cost airlines [3] *are taking* an increasing share of the market, and partly because companies [4] *are cutting* down on travel costs.

cut	begin
decline	take

hold	[6] improve	[7] start
transform	[8] not/travel	

There is, however, another factor that [5] *is improving* the market even more radically – video-conferencing. The technology [6] *are working* so fast that video-conference meetings [7] *are holding* to feel almost as real as face-to-face contacts. As a result, more and more executives [8] .... international meetings in high tech video-conferencing studios and [9] .... at all.

Production

TASK 1

Continue these sentences using a verb in the present continuous. See the example.

1 I'm afraid the MD is busy.   *He's having a meeting with the auditors.*
2 Could you call the maintenance people? ....
3 The meeting room isn't free.   ....
4 I've just seen Jane in the cafeteria.   ....
5 Shh! Listen!   ....

TASK 2

Answer these questions about yourself and your company's current projects. See the example.

1 What new product or service is your company currently working on?
   We're developing a new vaccine for the common cold.
2 What are you doing at work these days?

   ....

3 What training courses are you doing?

   ....

4 What examinations or professional qualifications are you studying for?

   ....

5 What other aims and objectives are you trying to achieve outside work?

   ....

TASK 3

Write short paragraphs about some temporary problems. Explain what the cause is. See the example.

A problem with the underground: *At the moment they're repairing the escalator at Sloane Square, and the station is shut, so I'm having to get off at the station before and walk. Still, it should be better next week.*

A problem with public transport:

....

....

A problem at work:

....

....

A problem in the news:

....

....

TASK 4

Write about changes currently taking place with the car market, using the prompts. See the example.

1 size   On the whole, *cars are getting smaller.*
2 safety   Nowadays ....
3 efficiency   ....
4 reliability   ....
5 electric cars   ....
6 pollution   ....

3 Present simple vs present continuous

Presentation

The following are examples comparing the present simple and present continuous:

ⓐ Routine vs moment of speaking

1 *Henry **works** for PDQ, a business delivery company. Every day he **collects** and **delivers** packages for local companies.*
2 *The man in the post room **is packing** some parcels. Henry **is waiting** in reception.*

In 1, we are talking about something that Henry does as a routine.
In 2, we are talking about something that they are doing at the moment of speaking.

ⓑ General activities vs current projects

1 *I **work** for a firm of recruitment consultants. We **design** psychometric tests.*
2 *At the moment we're **working** on new tests for the personnel department of a large oil company.*

In 1, we are talking about a general activity.
In 2, we are talking about a specific current project.

ⓒ Permanent vs temporary situations

1 *Peter **deals** with enquiries about our car fleet sales.*
2 *I **am dealing** with enquiries about fleet sales while Peter is away on holiday.*

In 1, this is permanently true.
In 2, this is a temporary situation.

ⓓ Facts vs slow changes

1 *As a rule, cheap imports **lead** to greater competition.*
2 *Cheap imports **are leading** to the closure of a number of inefficient factories.*

In 1, we are making a statement about a general fact that is always true.
In 2, we are talking about a change that is taking place at the moment.

ⓔ Stative verbs

There are a number of verbs which describe states rather than actions. They are not normally used in the continuous form. Common examples are:

Verbs of thinking:	*believe, doubt, guess, imagine, know, realize, suppose, understand*
Verbs of the senses:	*hear, smell, sound, taste, see*
Verbs of possession:	*belong to, have* (meaning: *possess*), *own, possess*
Verbs of emotion:	*dislike, hate, like, love, prefer, regret, want, wish*
Verbs of appearance:	*appear, seem*
Others:	*contain, depend on, include, involve, mean, measure, weigh, require*

These are usually found in the simple form because they do not refer to actions:
*I'm sorry, I **don't understand** what you mean.*

We do not say: * *I'm not understanding what you mean.*

Practice

EXERCISE ❶

Routine vs moment of speaking

Decide if the speaker is talking about routine activities or activities going on at the moment of speaking. Put the verbs into the present simple or the present continuous. See the example.

An interview with Bill Cogges in the dairy business

Interviewer: ¹Do you usually organize (you/usually organize) the delivery of milk to the factory? ²......................... (the farmers/bring) it here themselves?

Bill: No, ³......................... (we/always collect) the milk ourselves, and the tankers ⁴......................... (deliver) it to the pasteurization plant twice a day.

Interviewer: What sort of quality control procedures ⁵......................... (you/have)?

Bill: As a rule we ⁶......................... (test) samples of every consignment, and then the milk ⁷......................... (pass) down insulated pipes to the bottling plant, which ⁸......................... (operate) 24 hours a day. I'll show you round a bit later, but the production line ⁹......................... (not work) at the moment because the employees ¹⁰......................... (change) shifts.

EXERCISE ❷

General activities vs current projects

Decide whether the verbs refer to general activities or current projects. Put the verbs into the present simple or present continuous. See the example.

We set up the company in 2002 with a grant from the local government. We ¹ provide (provide) IT backup and support for a number of small and medium-sized businesses in the area. We also ² .... (design) web sites for local companies, and we ³ .... (look) after them by doing regular maintenance, and so on. When we ⁴ .... (get) a new customer, we always ⁵ .... (spend) a long time talking to them to find out their needs. At the moment we ⁶ .... (set up) a website for a large local travel agency, and in fact our chief programmer is in charge of that project. She ⁷ .... (have) discussions with them to find out what sort of features they ⁸ .... (require).

Permanent vs temporary situations

In the following exercise, decide whether these situations are permanent or temporary. Put the verbs into the present simple or present continuous. See the example.

1 He joined the company 25 years ago and he still **works** (work) for us.
2 We .... (not/send) out any orders this week because we're waiting for the new lists.
3 I .... (deal) with Mr Matsumi's clients this week because he's away.
4 Go down this road, turn right, and the road .... (lead) straight to the industrial estate.
5 Because of the Euro/Dollar exchange rate, EU exports .... (not/do) very well at the moment.
6 The stock market is risky because the price of shares .... (vary) according to economic conditions.
7 I .... (learn) French because I'm going to be based in the Paris office next year.
8 Hello. I'm Heinrich Brandt, I'm German, and I .... (come) from a small town near Munich.

Facts vs slow changes

In the following newspaper article, decide whether the verbs refer to general statements about change, or to changes that are currently taking place. Put the verbs into the present simple or present continuous. See the example.

Governments cannot last for ever. Normally political parties [1] **enjoy** (enjoy) a period of great popularity in their early years, then they [2] .... (go) through a period of stability and [3] .... (put) their ideas into practice. After that, they [4] .... (run) out of ideas, and the opposition [5] .... (take) power. Now it [6] .... (seem) that the present government [7] .... (begin) to run into difficulties, and people [8] .... (start) to criticize the Prime Minister. The newspapers [9] .... (attack) other ministers because of the state of schools, public transport and hospitals, and the government [10] .... (lose) popularity.

Stative verbs

In each of the following sentences, put one of the verbs into the present simple and the other into the present continuous. See the example.

1 We **are interviewing** (interview) people from outside the company for the new post in the export department, but I **think** (think) we ought to give the job to Mr Janousek.
2 At the moment we .... (carry) out a survey to find out what sort of after-sales service our customers .... (want).
3 We've got a competition on at work to find a name for our new range of cosmetics. The marketing people .... (try) to find a brand name that .... (sound) natural and sophisticated.
4 .... (you/know) what Mrs Ericson .... (do)? She's not in her office and nobody has seen her since lunch.
5 Could you help me? I .... (try) to translate this letter from a Spanish client and I don't know what this word .... (mean).
6 I .... (apply) for a transfer to our London office, but I don't know if I'll be successful. It all .... (depend) on whether or not they have any vacancies.
7 Their new 'own brand' instant coffee .... (taste) very good, so it isn't surprising that it .... (become) more and more popular.

Production

Write sentences using the following prompts. The first verb should be in the present simple, and the second verb in the present continuous. See the example.

1 come from/but/live
I come from Austria, but at the moment I'm living in Switzerland.

2 speak/and/learn

....

3 normally/like my work/but/not enjoy

....

4 want to be a consultant/so/do an MBA

....

5 work from 9 to 5/but/stay late

....

6 travel a lot/and/visit Australia

....

7 have several subsidiaries in Europe/and/set up another one in Brussels

....

8 normally/export a lot to Greece/but/not get many orders

....

Write questions to go with the answers. Use either the present simple or present continuous. See the example.

1 Where do you come from?
I come from a little town called Zug, near Zurich.

2 ....
I'm writing to Markson's to ask for an up-to-date catalogue.

3 ....
I think he's a consultant.

4 ....
I usually cycle in, but sometimes I bring the car.

5 ....
Our Sales Director goes abroad about three or four times a year.

6 ....
No, not at all well. In fact, the factory is doing a three-day week.

7 ....
Yes, very well. We met in 1980.

8 ....
No, not at the moment. But we'll start taking on new staff again in May.

4 Past simple

Presentation

a Form

The past simple (positive) is formed by using the past tense form. Regular verbs add *-d* or *-ed* to the bare infinitive to form the past tense. For negatives and questions we use the auxiliary *did* and the bare infinitive:

I worked	*I did not/didn't work*	*Did I work?*
You worked	*You did not/didn't work*	*Did you work?*
He/she/it worked	*He/she/it did not/didn't work*	*Did he/she/it work?*
We worked	*We did not/didn't work*	*Did we work?*
They worked	*They did not/didn't work*	*Did they work?*

Note: The short form of the negative is commonly used in speech and informal writing.

Common mistakes:

Using the past tense form in negatives and in questions.

wrong: *Did you checked the figures? No, I didn't checked them.*
right: *Did you check the figures? No, I didn't check them.*

The verb *to be* follows a different pattern: *I/he/she/it was* and *you/we/they were.*

b Irregular verbs

Some verbs do not add *-ed* to the bare infinitive to form the past simple, but change in other ways. Look at the example of the verb *to go*:

I went	*I didn't go*	*Did I go?*
You went	*You didn't go*	*Did you go?*
He/she/it went	*He/she/it didn't go*	*Did he/she/it go?*
We went	*We didn't go*	*Did we go?*
They went	*They didn't go*	*Did they go?*

There is a list of other common irregular verbs in Appendix 2, page 188.

c Completed actions

The past simple is used to talk about completed actions in the past:
Baring's, the oldest merchant bank in England, collapsed in 1995 when a rogue trader in the Singapore branch lost £800 million on currency deals. Later that year, the Dutch group ING bought the entire bank for the sum of £1.

d Time expressions with prepositions

As in the example above, the past simple is often used with past time expressions:

at 6 o'clock/1.15/the end of the year/Christmas
on Tuesday/15th May/the 21st/New Year's Day
in January/1987/the 1980s/summer

no preposition: yesterday/yesterday morning/last Monday/next April/a few days ago/the day before yesterday/when I was young

Practice

EXERCISE ❶

Form

Use the verbs in the box to complete the sentences. Some of the sentences are positive statements, some are negative, and some are questions. See the example.

accept	complain	hire	place
~~realize~~	study	visit	

1 Oh, I'm sorry to disturb you. I *didn't realize* you had a visitor.
2 .... you .... economics when you were at university?
3 She .... the job because the salary was too low.
4 Last week a number of customers .... about slow service.
5 .... you .... the Acropolis when you were in Greece?
6 I am writing with reference to the order I .... with you last week.
7 At last year's launch party, who .... you .... to do the catering?

EXERCISE ❷

Irregular verbs

A Write in the missing form of each of the irregular verbs below. Each verb can be used with the expressions on the right.

bare infinitive	past tense	expressions
run	ran	… a business, … out of something, … up a bill
do	1........................	… a job well, … your best, … business (with)
make	2........................	… a profit, … a mistake, … a complaint
3........................	went	… abroad, … out for a meal, … bankrupt
write	4........................	… a letter, … a report, … out a cheque
5........................	had	… lunch, … a meeting, … problems
pay	6........................	… by credit card, … cash, … in advance
7........................	sold	… something at a profit, … at a loss, … out

B Choose a past tense form and one of the expressions above to complete the following sentences. See the example.

1 He made some calls from his hotel room and *ran up a large phone bill*.
2 We .... with that company a few years ago, but then we stopped dealing with them.
3 After losing billions of dollars for years, Amazon.com finally .... in the last quarter of 2001.
4 He couldn't find a suitable job in his own country, so he .... to look for work.
5 When the consultants had finished their study they .... for the directors, giving a list of recommendations.
6 The engineers .... with the gearbox, so they made some modifications to it.
7 They didn't want cash or a cheque, so I ....
8 The product was very popular. We .... on the first day and ordered more stock.

Completed actions

Complete the following passage by putting the verbs into the past simple. See the example.

THE ESTEE LAUDER STORY

Estée Lauder was born Ester Mentzer in New York in 1908.

Her parents [1] **were** (be) both immigrants, and she [2] .... (get) her first experience of business by helping her father Max in his hardware shop.

But it was her uncle, John Schotz, who [3] .... (introduce) Ester to the world of cosmetics. He was a chemist and [4] .... (set) up a small laboratory behind the family home where he [5] .... (make) face creams. Ester [6] .... (sell) these creams door-to-door, at parties, clubs and lunches and [7] .... (carry) on developing her business during the depression of the 1920s and 1930s. She [8] .... (marry) Joseph Lauter on January 15 1930, and they [9] .... (have) their first child, Leonard, in March 1933.

At the end of World War II, she [10] .... (found) the company Estée Lauder Inc, and her big break

[11] .... (come) in 1948, when the famous department store Saks in Fifth Avenue New York [12] .... (give) her some counter space. She [13] .... (develop) a whole new style of selling, with in-store demonstrations and free samples, and new outlets soon [14] .... (open).

As her company [15] .... (grow), Estée [16] .... (keep) a close eye on the business, [17] .... (go) to every new store and often [18] .... (train) the salesgirls herself. Over the next few decades, the company [19] .... (bring) out a huge range of perfumes, make-up and toiletries. By the time her son Leonard [20] .... (take) over as CEO in 1982, the company was one of the biggest cosmetics companies in the world – and even today, it still accounts for almost 50% of cosmetics sales in American department stores.

Time expressions with prepositions

Make questions from the prompts and complete each answer by using *in*, *on*, or *at*. See the example.

1 When/Estée Lauder/born? **When was Estée Lauder born?**
   She was born **in** 1908.

2 When/she/marry Joseph Lauter? ....
   She married him .... January 15, 1930.

3 When/they/have/first child? ....
   They had their first child .... March 1933.

4 When/she/set up/company? ....
   She set up the company .... the end of World War II.

5 When/she/get/first big break? ....
   She got her first big break .... 1948.

6 When/Leonard/take over/CEO? ....
   He took over as CEO .... 1982.

Production

In 2001, a small shoe company lost a great deal of money. Then a group of younger managers took the company over and made it profitable. Say what they did, using the past tense. See the example.

1 There were three very old directors on the board.
   They made the directors redundant.

2 Their offices were too small.

   ....

3 The factory where they made shoes used very old machinery.

   ....

4 The workers in the factory disliked their working conditions.

   ....

5 The company had two loss-making subsidiaries.

   ....

6 The company only had two salesmen.

   ....

7 All the company's customers came from the local area.

   ....

8 The company's products were very old-fashioned.

   ....

9 The company had no presence on the Internet.

   ....

10 The Accounts Department did all the book-keeping by hand.

   ....

Write a short paragraph about your career history, giving the dates where possible. See the example.

Dominique Mallarmé went to the Ecole Polytechnique in Paris, where she studied mathematics. She graduated in 1999 and then worked as a trainee at the European Space Agency. In 2001 she moved to Aerospatiale, where she worked with a team designing propulsion systems for the Ariane rocket.

....

....

....

....

....

5 Present perfect (1)

Presentation

ⓐ Form

The present perfect tense is formed by using the present tense of the auxiliary *have* and the past participle. For negatives and questions we also use the present tense of the auxiliary *have* and the past participle:

I have/'ve taken	*I have not/haven't taken*	*Have I taken?*
You have/'ve taken	*You have not/haven't taken*	*Have you taken?*
He/she/it has/'s taken	*He/she/it has not/hasn't taken*	*Has he/she/it taken?*
We have/'ve taken	*We have not/haven't taken*	*Have we taken?*
They have/'ve taken	*They have not/haven't taken*	*Have they taken?*

The past participles of regular verbs end in *-d* or *-ed*, and have the same form as the past simple. For a list of irregular verbs, see Appendix 2, page 188.

Note: The short forms of the positive and negative are commonly used in speech and informal writing.

ⓑ Present result of the past

The present perfect often links a present situation with something that happened at an unspecified time in the past. Therefore we do not use specific time expressions such as *yesterday, last week, in 1998, two days ago,* etc.:

*I **have given** your report to the MD.*
(Past action: *I gave her your report yesterday.* Present result: *She has the report now.*)

*I **have sent** them the samples they wanted.*
(Past action: *I sent the samples this morning.* Present result: *They are in the post now.*)

ⓒ Specific and non-specific time

If we say when something happened, we use the past simple, not the present perfect:

wrong: **I have spoken to her yesterday.*
right: *I spoke to her yesterday.*

Similarly, with expressions such as *on Monday, in 1987, at 3.30,* etc. (see Unit 4), or with questions beginning *When ...?* and *How long ago ...?*, we use the past simple and not the present perfect.

ⓓ *Just*

The present perfect is often used with the word *just* to talk about very recent news or actions that have taken place very recently. Again, the exact time is not mentioned:

*I'm sorry, Mrs Smith is not here. She **has just left**.*

ⓔ *Been* and *gone*

Notice the difference between *has been* and *has gone*:

*I'm afraid Mr Smith is not here at the moment. He **has gone** to a meeting in London.*
(He is still at the meeting.)
*Amanda **has been** to the travel agent. She has your tickets for Hong Kong.*
(She went to the travel agent and has returned.)

Practice

EXERCISE 1

Form

Complete the following sentences by putting the irregular verbs into the present perfect. See the example.

1 I'm going to send them a reminder. They **haven't paid** (not pay) us for their last order.
2 Some of these tech shares .... (fall) by over 80%, and they still look very risky.
3 .... (you/write) to them about that shipment, or do you want me to phone them?
4 We .... (spend) a lot on modernizing the factory, and it is now very well equipped.
5 Unemployment is very high here because all of the coal mines .... (shut) down.
6 The lawyers .... (draw) up the contracts, so we are now ready to go ahead with the deal.
7 I .... (not speak) to the MD about your proposal, but I will soon.
8 .... (you/find) a suitable replacement for Ivan Sloboda, or is the post still vacant?
9 Carmen .... (just/get) back from lunch. Why don't you call her now?
10 Peter, ... (you/meet) Alistair MacFarlane? He's our new Finance Director.

EXERCISE 2

Present results of the past

Look at the notes below the pictures. Write sentences in the present perfect which link the past events with the present results. See the example.

Past event

1	2	3	4

Present result

He/miss/the flight	Euro/fall/against Dollar	They/redecorate/office	We/re-locate/Korea
He has missed the flight.	....	....	....

EXERCISE 3

Specific and non-specific time

Complete the following newspaper extracts with the correct form of the verb in brackets. Then say when these actions took place. If you do not have the information, write *no information*. See the examples.

Virgin Mobile [1] *said* (say) yesterday that it was in talks with 3G license holders in Hong Kong about a possible joint venture. The company [2] *has grown* (grow) rapidly and now has over 1.5 million customers, making it the UK's fifth largest mobile phone service.

Toys R Us [3] .... (announce) a programme of cutbacks last week, when it [4] .... (give) details of the 64 stores that are going to close with the loss of 1,900 jobs. The shares are currently trading slightly higher. Most analysts [5] ....(welcome) the news, particularly as the company [6] .... (state) that it is confident of reaching its targets in spite of 'difficult trading conditions.'

EGYPT yesterday [7]............................ (carry) out a limited devaluation of the Egyptian pound as a way of reassuring international lenders who are concerned about the state of the economy. The country [8] .... (suffer) a great deal from the loss of revenue from tourism, and the unofficial rate for the Egyptian pound [9] .... (fall) to below E£5 to the dollar. Egypt is looking for about $2bn in support, and the US [10] .... (already/ agree) to speed up the annual payment of aid.

1	said	– yesterday	6	....
2	has grown	– no information	7	....
3	....	....	8	....
4	....	....	9	....
5	....	....	10	....

EXERCISE 4

Just – recent actions

Complete the sentences with one of the verbs in the box, using *just* and the present perfect. See the example.

announce	arrive	buy	give
~~leave~~	read	speak	

1 I'm afraid Ms Japtha isn't here. She **has just left.**
2 A: There's an article in the paper about BMW.
   B: Yes, I know. I .... it.
3 He's feeling very pleased. They .... him a pay rise.
4 I .... a new car. Would you like to come and have a look at it?
5 A parcel for you .... in reception. Shall I send it up to you?
6 I .... to the MD about your proposals, and he wants to discuss them.
7 The company .... it is going to close the Glasgow factory next month.

EXERCISE 5

Been and *gone*

Fill in the blanks with *have/has been* or *have/has gone*. See the example.

1 I'm afraid Mr Davis **has gone** to Bali and won't be back for two weeks.
2 Jane will know a good place to stay in New York. She .... there lots of times.
3 I .... to the printers to collect the brochures. They're in my car.
4 Mr Lund .... to Oslo. Would you like the phone number of his hotel?
5 I don't know where their new offices are. I .... not .... there.

Production

TASK 1

Complete these sentences. Use a verb in the present perfect to explain why the present situation has occurred. See the example.

1 Our sales are improving because ...
we have introduced some new product lines.

2 Our agent wants the brochures delivered urgently because ...

....

3 Maria is off work for three months because ...

....

4 We are having a very successful year because ...

....

5 At the moment the government is very unpopular because ...

....

6 This year's coffee crop in Colombia will be very small because ...

....

7 I think it would be a good time to buy shares now because ...

....

TASK 2

'The office isn't the same as it was when you were here.'

Write short paragraphs about the changes that have taken place. See the example.

1 The new supermarket is attracting a lot of new customers.
The new managers have refurbished the building completely and they have put in a new delicatessen section. They have improved their range of fresh foods and have added a cafeteria.

2 The office isn't the same as it was when you were here.

....

....

3 The company has spent a great deal on new technology.

....

....

TASK 3

Complete or continue these sentences using the present perfect. See the example.

1 Indira's definitely here today. I've just spoken to her on the phone.

2 He isn't coming in to work today. ....

3 Yes, the report is ready. ....

4 Boeing's financial future now looks very secure. ....

5 Why don't we have lunch in that new restaurant that ....

6 I think she must be out. ....

7 No, I won't have a coffee, thank you. ....

6 Present perfect (2): *ever, never, already, yet*

Presentation

ⓐ *Ever* and *never* + present perfect or past simple

The present perfect is often used with the words *ever* and *never* to talk about general life experience:

Have you ever worked abroad?   (i.e., In all your life up to now?)
I have never been to South America.   (i.e., Not in all my life up to now.)

The present perfect with *ever* is often followed by the past simple. We use the past simple to give more information about a completed action, when referring to a specific time or context:

Have you ever been to Hong Kong?
Yes, I have. I worked there when I was with Coopers and Lybrand.

ⓑ *Already* and *yet*

The present perfect is often used with *already* and *yet*:

They are getting on well with the new building. They have already modernized the warehouse, but they haven't decorated the reception area yet.

Already is used in positive sentences. It often indicates that something has taken place slightly earlier than expected. Notice its position in the sentence (between the auxiliary and the verb):

*She has already shown me the figures. (not: *She has shown me already ...)*

Yet is used in questions and negatives. It shows that we expect that an action will take place if it has not happened up to now. Notice the position of *yet*, and *not yet*:

wrong: *Have you talked yet to Peter?*
right: *Have you talked to Peter yet?*
wrong: *I haven't talked yet to him.*
right: *I haven't talked to him yet.*

ⓒ Finished and unfinished periods of time

The present perfect is often used with words or phrases indicating periods of time that have not finished yet. Common examples are: *today, this morning, this month, this year, so far, to date, over the last few weeks, up to now, recently,* etc.:

This month we have received a lot of complaints about late deliveries.
(The month has not finished, and there may be more complaints.)

If we are speaking after one of these time periods, we use the past simple because we are referring to a period of time that has finished. Compare:

Have you seen John this morning?
(It is now 11.15 in the morning; the morning has not finished.)

Did you see John this morning?
(It is now 2.30 in the afternoon; the morning has finished.)

Practice

Ever and *never* + present perfect

Delegates at an international sales conference in Tokyo are getting to know each other. Write questions using the prompts. See the example.

1 you/ever/be/one of these conferences?
Have you ever been to one of these conferences?

2 you/ever/be/Japan before?

....

3 you/ever/learn a foreign language?

....

4 you/ever/organize a conference like this?

....

5 you/ever/work for a Japanese company?

....

6 you/ever/eat/sushi?

....

Ever + present perfect and past simple

Read the following dialogues. Put the verbs into the present perfect or the past simple. See the example.

1 A: *Have you ever been* (you/ever/be) to Kyoto?
   B: Yes, I have. I *went* (go) there last year.
   A: How long *did you stay* (you/stay)?
   B: I *was* (be) only there for a couple of days for a meeting.

2 A: .... (you/ever/be) to Europe?
   B: Yes, I have. We .... (have) a skiing holiday in the Alps last year.
   A: Which resort .... (you/go) to?
   B: We .... (go) to Wengen.

3 A: .... (you/ever/be) to one of Karl Mason's seminars?
   B: Yes, I have. I .... (go) to one a couple of months ago.
   A: What .... (it/be) like ?
   B: I .... (think) it .... (be) very interesting.

4 A .... (you/ever/visit) the Frankfurt office?
   B: No, I .... (never/visit) Germany, but I .... (be)
   to France.
   A: Really. When .... (you/do) that?
   B: I .... (give) some talks there a couple of years ago.

EXERCISE ③

Already and *yet*

Complete the dialogue by putting the verbs into the present perfect. See the example.

A: Good afternoon, Mr Heinriksen here. How are you getting on with the car I brought in this morning? ¹Have you finished it yet (you/finish it/yet)?

B: Nearly. We ².......................... (already/do) most of the work on it. We ³.......................... (not/find any major problems/yet), but we ⁴.......................... (already/fix) the things you mentioned.

A: ⁵.......................... (you/check) the headlights? I think they need adjusting.

B: Yes, we ⁶.......................... (already/alter) them. The only other thing is that you need two new tyres, but I ⁷.......................... (not/order them/yet), because they're €140 each.

A: That's fine, go ahead with that. Do you know what the bill will be?

B: No, I ⁸.......................... (not/work it out/yet), but it'll be about €380. Are you coming to get the car now?

A: No, I ⁹.......................... (not/finish work/yet). I'll be there in about an hour.

EXERCISE ④

Unfinished periods of time

Read this passage about the performance of a manufacturer of DVDs and digital TVs. Fill in the blanks with the verbs in the box, using the present perfect. See the example.

~~be~~	go	grow	have
manage	already/reach	open	

This ¹ has been an excellent year so far, and we ² .... most of our sales targets. Worldwide unit shipments ³ .... up to 2.5m over the last eight months, and every region ⁴ .... to set new records. In North America, we ⁵ .... sales of $1.1 billion, and sales in Europe and the Pacific Rim ⁶ .... by 38% and 94%. Our international expansion plans are going well. We ⁷ .... a new office in Beijing and are planning to open five more next year.

EXERCISE ⑤

Finished and unfinished periods of time

Match each of the sentences from column A with a suitable context from column B.

A

1 I hope you enjoyed the launch party.
2 I hope you have enjoyed the launch party.
3 Has the post come this morning?

4 Did the post come this morning?
5 Has Max rung this week?
6 Did Max ring this week?

7 Has Mary finished that report?
8 Did Mary finish that report?

B

a Mary has gone home. It is 6.00 p.m.
b The launch party is about to finish.

c Max rings on Monday or Tuesday. It's Friday at 6.00 p.m.
d Mary is still at the office. It is 2.30.
e It is 10.00 in the morning.
f Max rings on Monday or Tuesday. It's Tuesday.
g It is 3.00 in the afternoon.
h The launch party was last week.

Production

Complete these sentences using *never* and the present perfect. See the example.

1 I'm feeling rather nervous.
   I have never given a presentation to so many people.

2 I don't like taking unnecessary risks with money, so …

   ....

3 ....

   but I would like to go there for a holiday one day.

4 What are Nigel Seymour's books on management like?

   I don't know. ....

5 I can definitely recommend Hewlett Packard printers. I've had one for years, and …

   ....

6 Their record of industrial relations is excellent.

   ....

Write a short paragraph saying what you have already done and what you haven't done yet. See the example.

1 The new model is almost ready for production.
   We have done a lot of research and we have finalized the design. We have solved the problems we had with the prototype and we have already set up a production unit in Cambridge. We haven't decided who will lead the project yet, but we are interviewing three possible candidates.

2 I am nearly ready to start my own business.

   ....

   ....

   ....

Complete the sentences, using the present perfect to make it clear that the periods of time have not finished yet. See the example.

1 I must get a new alarm clock. *I have been late three times* this week.

2 Our new website is getting a lot of hits. So far this month …

   ....

3 The clothing company fizz.com is cutting its workforce dramatically. So far this year …

   ....

4 I think they must have put the wrong phone number on the advertisement because up to now we …

   ....

7 Present perfect (3): *for* and *since*

Presentation

ⓐ Stative verbs + *for* and *since*

The present perfect is often used with *for* and *since* and stative verbs (see Unit 3e) to talk about things that began in the past and have continued up to now:

I have known about the takeover bid for several weeks. (And I know now.)
She has owned shares in GM since she started work there. (She owns them now.)

ⓑ For or *since*?

We use *for* to talk about the duration of periods of time and *since* to talk about when a period started. Look at the time line and the examples:

since 7.00   *10.00*
← *for 3 hours* →
PAST   NOW   FUTURE

for   *ten minutes/five days/three months/two years/a long time/ages/etc.*
since   *10.15/Monday/the 18th/last week/June/1989/I left school/etc.*

I have been with this company for six years.
I have been in advertising since the beginning of 2001.

ⓒ How long ...?, *for* and *since*

To ask questions about periods of time up to the present, we can use *How long ...?* + the present perfect:

How long have you been in England? I have been here since August/for six months.

Common mistakes:
We do not use the present simple tense with *for* and *since* to talk about something that began in the past and has gone on up to the present:

wrong: **I am here since December.*
right: *I have been here since December.*

ⓓ Negatives

We can use the present perfect negative to talk about the amount of time that has passed between now and the last time something happened:

We haven't had any large orders from them for several months.
I'm not sure if his trip is going well. I haven't heard from him since Monday.

ⓔ Completed actions over a period of time

If we talk about a completed action, (particularly if we give details about how much, how many, etc), we can use the present perfect and *since* (but not *for*). We can also use other phrases of duration such as *to date, recently, over the past five years*, etc. The action itself is finished, but the period of time extends right up to the present:

We have opened six new branches since July. (From July until now.)

Practice

EXERCISE **1**

For and *since* with stative verbs

Some of these sentences are right and some are not. Put a tick [✓] next to the ones that are right, and correct the ones that are wrong. See the example.

1 ~~I am here~~ since last week. *I have been here ...*
2 I've had the same company car for two years. ....
3 I know Mia since we were at INSEAD together. ....
4 How long are you with Microsoft? ....
5 We have had an office in Adelaide for several years. ....
6 She has an account with HSBC bank since 1998. ....
7 CPT is in financial difficulties for several months. ....
8 How long has the office been vacant? ....

EXERCISE **2**

For or *since*?

Fill in the blanks with *for* or *since*. See the example.

1 They have operated as joint directors *since* the company started.
2 Orders have risen .... the start of the new TV ad campaign in June.
3 Our sales executives have used the same hotel .... over 20 years.
4 I can't get hold of Erik. He has been in a meeting .... 8.30.
5 When I joined the company, I worked in the LA branch .... six months.
6 Car prices have fallen .... the introduction of the new EU directive.
7 We have done all our business in Euros .... 2002.
8 It isn't a new Mercedes. He has had it .... several years.

EXERCISE **3**

How long ...?, *for* and *since*

Make questions and answers, using the prompts. See the example.

1 How long/you/be/in charge of the Finance Department?
   A: How long have you been in charge of the Finance Department?
   B: (I/six months) I have been in charge of it for six months.
2 How long/you/have a website for investors?
   A: ....
   B: (We/three months) ....
3 How long/the property/be on the market?
   A: ....
   B: (It/six months) ....
4 How long/you/have an office in Spain?
   A: ....
   B: (We/2000) ....
5 How long/Jason/be in the States?
   A: ....
   B: (He/the 18th) ....

Negatives

Rewrite the sentences using the negative form of the present perfect, with *for* or *since*. See the example.

1 The last time I saw Mr Ng was in September.
  I haven't seen Mr Ng since September.
2 The last time the company made a profit was three years ago.
  ....
3 The last time I had a pay rise was two years ago.
  ....
4 The last time we looked at their proposal was in July.
  ....
5 The last time we raised our prices in real terms was in 2002.
  ....
6 The last time we played golf together was three months ago.
  ....
7 The last time there was a fall in unemployment here was in 2001.
  ....
8 The last time I went on a sales trip abroad was in January.
  ....

Completed actions over a period of time

Read the following article about recent developments in China. Put the verbs in brackets into the present perfect tense. See the example.

CHIPS IN CHINA

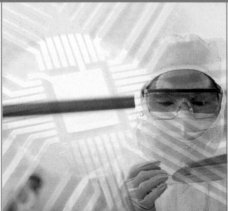

SINCE 1997, there ¹ has been (be) a high-tech revolution in China. The once struggling state-owned factories ² .... (become) mass producers of made-to-order chips. Enthusiasm for the new industry ³ .... (spread) across the country, and the government ⁴ .... (help) investors with special tax deals.

Some analysts are worried about investing so much in a single industry. Back in 2001, when there was a big slowdown in demand, many chip factories from Malaysia to South Korea sat unused and thousands of workers lost their jobs.

In spite of these fears, companies ⁵ .... (make) huge investments in China's new plants in the last year or two. Semiconductor Manufacturing International

⁶ .... (spend) $1.5 billion on a factory in Shanghai, and Huaxia ⁷ .... (announce) a $1.3 billion project in Beijing. Western companies ⁸ .... (join) in as well – Motorola ⁹ .... (build) a plant in the north-eastern city of Tianjin, and Intel and Fairchild ¹⁰ .... (add) new facilities to their existing plants.

Over the last few decades, China ¹¹ .... (transform) all sorts of global industries, from clothing to electrical goods and ¹² .... (drive) prices down around the world. Now, it looks like chips are going to follow this trend.

1 Which paragraphs use mainly the present perfect tense? ...., ... and ....
2 What time periods are mentioned in these paragraphs? ....,
   .... and ....
3 What finished time period is mentioned in paragraph two? ....

Production

Read the following notes. In each pair, decide which sentence should be in the simple past and which should be in the present perfect. See the example.

1   a   I/meet/Mr Christiansen/1998
        I met Mr Christiansen in 1998.
    b   I/know/Mr Christiansen/1998

    ....

2   a   Dyson/build/a factory in Malaysia/2002

    ....

    b   Dyson/have/a factory in Malaysia/2002

    ....

3   a   Austria, Finland and Sweden/join/the European Union/1995

    ....

    b   Austria, Finland and Sweden/be/members of the European Union/1995

    ....

Continue these sentences, using a verb in the present perfect negative (e.g. *I haven't done ...*) and a time expression with *for* or *since*. See the example.

1   I'm not sure what my bank balance is.
    I haven't had a statement for several weeks.

2   I don't know how my investments are doing.

    ....

3   I am not sure how the negotiations are going.

    ....

4   They used to be one of our major clients, but ...

    ....

5   I used to be quite good at Japanese, but ...

    ....

Write a short paragraph about the recent trends or general changes that have taken place in your company or industry over the last few years. See the example.

Over the last two or three years there has been a big increase in demand for our catalogue clothing, and this has affected our business a great deal. We have developed several new lines and taken on more than 50 new employees. We have opened two new call centres in the North East. Sales have risen by 40% over the past two years, and demand for children's clothing in particular has gone up sharply.

Over the last two or three years ....

....

....

....

....

8 Present perfect (4): continuous and simple

Presentation

ⓐ Form

The present perfect continuous is formed with the present perfect of *be* (*have been*) and the *-ing* form of the verb.

I have/'ve been working	*I have not/haven't been working*	*Have I been working?*
You have/'ve been working	*You have not/haven't been working*	*Have you been working?*
He/she/it has/'s been working	*He/she/it has not/hasn't been working*	*Has he/she/it been working?*
We have/'ve been working	*We have not/haven't been working*	*Have we been working?*
They have/'ve been working	*They have not/haven't been working*	*Have they been working?*

Note: The short forms of the positive and negative are commonly used in speech and informal writing.

ⓑ Ongoing activities

The present perfect continuous is used with *for*, *since*, *How long …?* and other expressions of duration (e.g., *all day*), to talk about activities starting in the past and still happening now. The activity may have been going on continuously or repeated several times:

*They **have been producing** cars here **for ten years**.*
(They started producing cars ten years ago. They are still producing cars.)
*I **have been trying** to ring them **all day**.*
(I started trying to ring them this morning. I am still trying to ring them.)

However, we normally use the present perfect simple with stative verbs or for situations we consider permanent (see Unit 3):

*Ken **has been** in London since 9 o'clock this morning.* (not: **has been being* …)
*I **have lived** in London all my life.* (not: **have been living* …)

ⓒ Finished and unfinished activities

We use the present perfect simple if we are talking about an action completed recently, particularly if we give details of how much or how many. We use the present perfect continuous when something is still going on:

*I've **written** a report for the Director.* (It is finished.)
*I've **been writing** a report for the Director.* (I am still writing it.)

ⓓ Negatives

In the negative, the present perfect simple focuses on the amount of time that has passed since something happened. The present perfect continuous focuses on the verb itself:

*I **haven't had** a holiday for two years.* (The last time was two years ago.)
*I **haven't been feeling** well recently.* (This has been continuing for days.)

ⓔ Recently finished activities

We can use the present perfect continuous to talk about an activity that has just finished. Often there is something you can see that shows the activity has just finished.

*Look – the ground is very wet. It **has been raining**.*

Practice

EXERCISE ①

Form

Complete the sentences by putting the verbs into the present perfect continuous.
See the example.

1 I didn't realize you had moved to Novartis. How long have you been working
(you/work) for them?

2 We .... (export) a lot of high technology equipment to China since
the government relaxed export regulations.

3 The price of new cars fell when the EU introduced new laws, and it
.... (fall) ever since.

4 Because of the recession, many businesses .... (not/invest) in capital
equipment over the last couple of years.

5 We .... (not/fly) in Business Class because we are trying to keep our
costs down.

6 They .... (try) to sell their dotcom business, but so far there has been
very little interest in it.

7 I .... (make) contributions to my pension for the last five years.

8 How long .... (you/use) psychometric tests in interviews?

EXERCISE ②

Ongoing activities

Phoenix Media Inc. publishes books, makes educational software and produces TV
programmes. Using the notes, continue the interview with Alex Brander, the CEO of
the company. See the example.

1996 – Alex Brander starts running Phoenix Media

1997 – Phoenix Media starts selling children's books

1999 – Phoenix moves into education and starts producing books for schools

3 years ago – Phoenix starts making educational software

2 years ago – Phoenix starts joint venture with InterSat TV to produce children's TV programmes

6 months ago – Phoenix launches new children's online book club

1 you/run/company

Q: How long have you been running the company?
A: I have been running the company since 1996.

2 you/sell children's books

Q: How long ....
A: We ....

3 you/produce/books for schools

Q: ....
A: ....

4 you/make educational software

Q: ....
A: ....

5 you/work with InterSat TV

Q: ....
A: ....

6 you/run/online book club

Q: ....
A: ....

Finished and unfinished activities

Put the verbs in brackets into the present perfect simple or the present perfect continuous. See the examples.

1 We are thinking about opening an office in Warsaw, so I have been learning (learn) Polish at evening classes for the last two months.
2 By the way, I have worked (work) out those figures. They are on your desk now.
3 So that's where the order form is! Peter .... (look) for it all morning.
4 I'm sorry, I didn't know that you were here. .... (you/wait) long?
5 Since January, our turnover .... (increase) by 18%.
6 The film company is a reasonable investment. They .... (make) four very successful films.
7 The lawyers .... (look) through the contract, but they say they need another day to read it all.
8 We .... (visit) potential sites for the new workshops, but we haven't found anything suitable yet.

Negatives

Rewrite these sentences, using the present perfect simple or the present perfect continuous. See the example.

1 I didn't feel well on Monday, Wednesday, Thursday, and Saturday.
(not feel/recently) I haven't been feeling well recently.
2 The last time I had a meeting with them was two weeks ago.
(not have/two weeks) ....
3 My computer crashed on Monday, Tuesday and yesterday.
(not work/properly/recently) ....
4 The last time they gave their workers a pay rise was three years ago.
(not give/three years) ....

Recently-finished activities

Match the questions in column A with the replies or explanations in column B. See the example.

A	B
1 Why is your office in such a mess?	a They've been travelling so much that they never have time to do any.
2 Why has the wages bill been so high recently?	b We've been losing a lot of stock because of shoplifting.
3 Why have you got three new store detectives?	c I've been having a lot of problems with it recently.
4 Why are they so behind with their work?	d I've been looking for that letter from Graylings, but I can't find it.
5 What's your car doing at the garage?	e Yes, but I've been interviewing people all day.
6 You look tired, Annick. Are you OK?	f Because everyone's been doing a lot of overtime.

Production

Write short paragraphs answering the questions, giving details about the activities that have been going on. See the example.

1 Why do you think Peter should be dismissed?
He has been coming in late and he hasn't been doing any work. He's been spending hours every day talking to his friends on the phone and he's been upsetting the customers.

2 Why do you think you deserve a pay rise?

....

....

....

3 What have you been doing to improve your English?

....

....

....

4 What have you been doing at work recently?

....

....

....

....

Reply to the following questions using a verb in the present perfect continuous. See the example.

1 Is it wet outside?
Yes, it's been raining.

2 You look terrible. What have you been doing?

....

3 Look at your hands – what is that? Ink or oil?

....

4 How come your golf has improved so much?

....

5 Why do you think she's been having so many days off?

....

6 Why are you under so much stress at the moment?

....

7 Why is your expenses claim so high this month?

....

9 Past simple, present perfect and present perfect continuous

Presentation

ⓐ Past simple

We normally use the past simple to talk about actions that took place at a time in the past that is separated from the present. It is used with expressions like *yesterday, on Monday, last week, in 1997, at 6.30, How long ago ...?*, etc.:

*Hans Behrmann **did** an MBA at Harvard **in 2000**.*
*He **joined** IBM **in 2001**.*

We can use the past simple and *for* to talk about something that happened during a period that has now finished:

*I **lived** in Ecuador **for three years**, then I came back to England.*

ⓑ Present perfect

The present perfect is used to talk about the present result of past actions and recent events. It is often used with words like *ever, never, just, already, yet,* and phrases of unfinished time such as *so far*:

*NTL **has just announced** that it is cutting the price of broadband Internet access by 20%.*
*Have **you ever tried** Chilean wine?*
*We have exchanged emails, but we **have never met**.*
*Don't worry about the order form. I **have already dealt** with it.*
*I'm afraid I **haven't written** that report **yet**. I'll do it tomorrow.*
*The CD was released two weeks ago and **so far** it **has taken** $1.5m.*

ⓒ Present perfect simple with *for* and *since*

The present perfect can be used with *for* and *since* and stative verbs, or to refer to actions that are seen as long term or permanent. We use *for* to talk about the duration of a period of time and *since* to talk about the starting point of an action or state:

*I **have been** with the company **since 1996**.*
*I **have lived** here **for 15 years**.*

It is also used in the negative with *for* and *since* to talk about the last time something took place:

*I **haven't seen** her **since Monday**.*
*I **haven't seen** her **for three days**.*

It is used with *since* to talk about completed actions:

*Property prices **have risen** by 8% **since the beginning of the year**.*

ⓓ Present perfect continuous

The present perfect continuous can be used with *for* and *since* to talk about:

a) actions or activities that have gone on repeatedly or continuously for a period of time, and are still going on:

*I've **been trying** to get through to Technical Support, but the line's always engaged.*

b) actions or activities that are ongoing but temporary:

*I've **been working** from home because they're re-decorating my office.*

Practice

EXERCISE ❶

Past simple or present perfect?

Read these reports by a financial adviser and put the verbs into the past simple or present perfect. See the example.

Matrix Media

Matrix Media is a small film company that ¹ *has produced* (produce) a number of profitable films in the last few years. Their last success ² .... (be) in 2002 with Blue Moon over the Water, which ³ .... (make) over $40m in its first six months. The latest news is that Oscar-winning director Ben Loach ⁴ .... (join) the company as a director and ⁵ .... (agree) to make three films. At $1.88 the shares look undervalued. Recommendation: BUY

TRL Engineering

TRL Engineering ⁶ .... (perform) steadily over recent years, but in the last few months, the share price ⁷ .... (be) very volatile. In May the company ⁸ .... (announce) that it had lost a major motorway maintenance contract and in July it ⁹ .... (issue) a profits warning. Recently the shares ¹⁰ .... (recover) from a two-year low, but prospects do not look good. Recommendation: SELL

EXERCISE ❷

Past simple or present perfect?

Complete the dialogue by putting the verbs into the past simple or the present perfect. See the example.

A: Can I have a word about your trip to Dubai?

B: Yes, of course. Is everything OK?

A: Yes. Your tickets ¹ *have arrived* (arrive) and they're in my office now. And I ² .... (just/had) an email from the hotel confirming your reservation.

B: Which hotel ³ .... (you/book) me into?

A: The Burj Al Arab.

B: Thank you. What about money?

A: I ⁴ .... (already/order) some Dirhams for you. I ⁵ .... (ring) the bank yesterday, and they'll have them tomorrow. And I can get some traveller's cheques as well if you like.

B: No don't worry, I ⁶ .... (never/need) traveller's cheques before. I normally use a credit card and cash machines.

A: Really? Are you sure you can use your card in Dubai as well?

B: Yes, I think so. I ⁷ .... (be/to) quite a lot of countries in the Middle East and I ⁸ .... (never/have) a problem.

A: OK, but have a word with Alison Morgan in Production. I know she ⁹ .... (go) to Dubai a couple of months ago, so I expect she would know.

Present perfect simple or present perfect continuous

Underline the correct form of the verb in *italics*. See the example.

1 I've *stayed*/<u>*been staying*</u> in a hotel for the last ten days, but I hope to find an apartment of my own soon.
2 I wonder how Hussein is getting on. I haven't *heard/been hearing* from him for nearly a week.
3 Roberto is a natural salesman. He has *sold/been selling* eight cars since the beginning of the week.
4 I didn't realize that you and Ismail were friends. How long have you *known/been knowing* him?
5 This report is a nightmare. I have *written/been writing* it for two weeks, and it still isn't finished.

Review

Read the following email. Put the verbs in brackets into the past simple, present perfect, or present perfect continuous. See the example.

To: ken.smith@agreen.co.uk

Subject: Marketing trip

Dear Ken

I'm just writing to let you know how I'm getting on with the marketing trip. Sorry I ¹ **haven't been** (not/be) in touch for so long, but I ² .... (be) very busy since I ³ .... (arrive) here on the 18th.

There is lots of interest in the new organic fertilizer. Last week I ⁴ .... (go) to Sydney, where I ⁵ .... (meet) a number of farmers and ⁶ .... (see) a couple of agents. I ⁷ .... (leave) Sydney last Sunday and ⁸ .... (be) here in Darwin since then, making a few useful contacts.

So far the feedback at all my meetings ⁹ ....(be) very positive and I can say that I ¹⁰ .... (never/have) such an enthusiastic response to a new product. I keep hearing the same thing – that interest in organic farming ¹¹ .... (grow) for the last few years; more and more consumers ¹² .... (buy) organic food, and it looks as if this will continue.

Last night I ¹³ .... (have) dinner with Barry Thomas – you may remember him – he ¹⁴ .... (work) for Agrichem London for a couple of years in the 90s, and then ¹⁵ .... (come) over here to set up on his own. For the last year or so he ¹⁶ .... (act) as a distributor for some of our agricultural machinery, and he is interested in becoming a distributor for the fertilizer. I ¹⁷ .... (not/give) him an answer yet, but I think he could be a good choice.

I'd better send this off to you now – I ¹⁸ .... (just/have) a phone call from another farmer who ¹⁹ .... (hear) about the fertilizer on a radio programme that ²⁰ .... (go) out this morning.

I'll be in touch soon.

Best wishes
Jim

Production

TASK 1

Write a short paragraph about one of your or your company's current projects. Talk about what is happening now, what you have already done, and what you haven't done yet. See the example.

We're going to the Frankfurt Book Fair next week. We've reserved a 20-metre stand, so the display will be quite impressive. We have sent most of the stock on ahead, but there are one or two books that haven't come out yet, and we're going to take them with us. We have already arranged a lot of meetings, but there are still a few people that we haven't contacted yet.

TASK 2

Write a paragraph from a covering letter applying for a job. You should give details of your general experience, and mention some specific dates when you did something. See the example.

As you will see from the enclosed CV, I have worked in the financial services sector for several years. I spent two years with Allied Dunbar as a pensions salesman, and then moved to Sun Alliance, where I have been working in the Life Assurance division. I have had considerable managerial experience, and I recently became Area Manager.

TASK 3

Complete each of the following sentences in two ways. In one sentence, use the present perfect to say what these people have done, and in the other use the present perfect continuous to say what they have been doing. See the example.

1 I got into trouble for not working hard enough last week. Since then ...
   I have stayed late three times.
   I have been working very hard.

2 I handed in my resignation a month ago. Since then ...

3 We got a new manager a few weeks ago. Since he arrived ...

4 The new product is going to be a big success. Since its launch ...

10 Past continuous

Presentation

a Form

The past continuous is formed with *was/were* + the *-ing* form of the verb:

I was working	*I was not/wasn't working*	*Was I working?*
You were working	*You were not/weren't working*	*Were you working?*
He/she/it was working	*He/she/it was not/wasn't working*	*Was he/she/it working?*
We were working	*We were not/weren't working*	*Were we working?*
They were working	*They were not/weren't working*	*Were they working?*

Note: The short forms of the negative are commonly used in speech and informal writing.

b Points of time in the past

We use the past continuous to talk about an action or activity that was in progress at a particular moment of time in the past:

*At 3.15 yesterday afternoon, Signor Antinori **was travelling** to Florence.*

c Interrupted past action

We can use the past continuous to talk about an action or activity that was already in progress, and which was interrupted by another action:

*He **was checking** the accounts when he spotted the error.*

We can rephrase this sentence using *while* + the past continuous:

***While** he **was checking** the accounts he spotted the error.*

The activity may or may not continue after the interruption:

*Amélie **was writing** a report when her boss asked her to fetch an invoice.*

(Amélie fetched the invoice and then probably carried on writing the report.)

*Amélie **was writing** a report when the fire broke out.*

(Amélie stopped writing the report and left the office.)

d Sequence of tenses

With a time clause like *when the phone rang*, we can use either the past continuous or the past simple.

The past continuous tells us what was happening up to the point when the phone rang:
*When the phone rang, I **was talking** to a client.*

The past simple tells us what happened afterwards:
*When the phone rang, I **answered** it.*

Practice

Points of time in the past

David's colleague Jack (who doesn't have enough work to do) has tried to phone him several times without success. Complete their conversation by putting the verbs in brackets into the correct form of the past continuous. See the example.

Jack: I rang at 9.15 and again at 9.30 but the phone was engaged. Who ¹ *were you talking* (you/talk) to?

David: Oh, I ² .... (call) some clients.

Jack: And I tried again at 10.15, but there was no reply.

David: At 10.15? I think I ³ .... (discuss) the new catalogue with Sue Tims.

Jack: And then I rang back again at 11.10.

David: Yes, I was out. I ⁴ .... (have) a coffee in the canteen.

Jack: I thought so, so I rang again at 11.30.

David: I was out again. The new designer and I ⁵ .... (organize) the artwork for some adverts.

Jack: What ⁶ .... (you/do) at 1.30, then? I called again, and tried to leave a message but even the answering machine ⁷ .... (not/work)!

David: I'd better have a look at it, but the designer and I ⁸ .... (have) lunch. Anyway, what did you want to talk about?

Jack: Oh, nothing special. I just wanted to try out my new mobile phone.

Interrupted past action

Complete the text with the past simple or past continuous form of the verbs in brackets. See the example.

Accidental discoveries and inventions

Although companies spend billions of dollars on research and development, new products sometimes come about just by chance.

SAFETY GLASS – The idea of safety glass came to a French scientist, Edouard Benedictus, in 1903. He ¹ *was working* (work) in his laboratory one night when he suddenly ² .... (knock) over a glass jar containing celluloid. The glass broke, but did not shatter because it stuck to the celluloid, and this led to the idea of safety glass – two sheets of glass with a central sheet of celluloid.

TEFLON – Roy Plunkett ³ .... (make) the first batch of Teflon while he ⁴ .... (work) for Du Pont. He ⁵ .... (carry) out research into coolant gases when he ⁶ .... (leave) one batch in a container overnight. He came back the next day to find that the gas had turned into Teflon, the slipperiest substance in the world.

PFIZER'S LUCKY BREAK – Scientists at Pfizer's laboratory in England ⁷ .... (test) a new heart drug called Viagra when they ⁸ .... (realize) that, although it was of little use in treating heart problems, it had some unexpected side-effects. The result was a hugely successful new product that has probably done more to save the rhinoceros than anything else in history.

Sequence of tenses

Read each set of information. Decide the order in which things happened. Then write two new sentences based on the information. Begin each one with the same words. See the example.

1 His car broke down. He went the rest of the way by taxi. He was driving to Bonn for a conference.
   a When his car broke down, he was driving to Bonn for a conference.
   b When his car broke down, he went the rest of the way by taxi.

2 We left the building. We were having a meeting. The fire alarm went off.
   a When ....
   b When ....

3 They took our company over. We were losing a lot of money. They made a lot of people redundant.
   a When ....
   b When ....

4 My secretary went to meet him. I was having lunch in the canteen. Mr Takashi arrived.
   a When ....
   b When ....

5 Herr Streibel arrived at the airport. He came straight to the office. The chauffeur was waiting.
   a When ....
   b When ....

Review

In the following sentences, put one of the verbs in brackets into the past continuous, and the other into the past simple. See the example.

1 (walk, notice) The security guard noticed the broken window while he was walking round the warehouse.

2 (go, meet) I first .... Mr Rodriguez when I .... round Mexico on a marketing trip.

3 (interrupt, give) When she .... her presentation, someone at the back of the room .... to ask a question.

4 (finalize, ring) While my PA .... arrangements for my trip to Brazil, the clients .... up to cancel the visit.

5 (notice, look) The auditors .... a large unauthorized withdrawal while they .... through the accounts.

6 (happen, clean) The accident .... when one of the workers .... the chemical tank.

7 (drop, bring) One of the removals men .... my computer while he .... it into my office.

8 (approach, work) A headhunter .... her while she .... for ICI.

Production

Complete each sentence in two ways. In a, use the past continuous to say what was happening at the time. In b, use the past simple to say what happened next. See the example.

1 When I got to the airport …
   a the company driver was waiting for me.
   b I went straight to the meeting.

2 When I got to work this morning …
   a ....
   b ....

3 When the accident happened …
   a ....
   b ....

4 When they decided to close down the factory …
   a ....
   b ....

Explain what was happening up to the point when the following events took place. Use *because* + past continuous. See the example.

1 He decided to see a doctor because he wasn't feeling well.
2 Peter handed in his resignation ....
3 They gave Miss Ling a new company car ....
4 We offered our agents an extra 5% discount ....
5 Hélène phoned the service engineer ....

Write a short paragraph about one of the following events. Say what you were doing when it happened, and what you did next.

You won some money.
You got your present job.
You were stopped by the police.
You first met your partner.

....
....
....
....

11 Past perfect

Presentation

ⓐ Form

The past perfect is formed with *had* + the past participle of the verb:

I had/'d worked	*I had not/hadn't worked*	*Had I worked?*
You had/'d worked	*You had not/hadn't worked*	*Had you worked?*
He/she/it had/'d worked	*He/she/it had not/hadn't worked*	*Had he/she/it worked?*
We had/'d worked	*We had not/hadn't worked*	*Had we worked?*
They had/'d worked	*They had not/hadn't worked*	*Had they worked?*

Note: The short forms of the positive and negative are commonly used in speech and informal writing.

ⓑ Previous and subsequent events

The past perfect is used to refer back to completed actions that happened before other events in the past. Compare:

1 Past simple: ***When I got to the hall**, the presentation **started**.*
    (I arrived at the hall, and then the presentation started.)

2 Past perfect: ***When I got to the hall**, the presentation **had started**.*
    (The presentation started before I got to the hall. I was late.)

In 1, it is also possible to use *As soon as* and *After* in place of *When*.
In 2, it is also possible to use *By the time* in place of *When*.

ⓒ Present perfect and past perfect

The past perfect acts as the past form of the present perfect (see Units 5–9). It is often used with adverbs like *just, already, never*. Compare:

*I am nervous because I **have never had** an interview.* (I am about to have an interview.)
*I was nervous because I **had never had** an interview.* (I was about to have an interview.)
The past perfect is often used in reported speech structures (see Units 31–32) and in 3rd conditionals (see Unit 22).

ⓓ Past perfect continuous

The past perfect continuous is formed by using the auxiliary *had been* + the *-ing* form of the verb *(I/he/you/etc. **had (not) been working**)*.

We use the present perfect continuous to talk about how long an activity has been going on up to the present (see Unit 8). We use the past perfect continuous to talk about the duration of an activity up to a point in the past. Compare:

*I **have been working** here for nine months.*
(I am still working here now.)

*When I left my last job, I **had been working** there for six years.*
(I started in 1995 and I left in 2001.)

We do not use the past perfect continuous with stative verbs like *know, like*, etc. (see Unit 3). Instead, we use the past perfect:

*I recognized my old boss at once even though I **hadn't seen** him for over 20 years.*

Practice

Form

Compare these two pictures of a small town as it was 20 years ago and as it was last year. Then complete the sentences using the past perfect form of the verbs in brackets. See the example.

Twenty years ago

Last year

1 When I returned to Waverton after 20 years, the High Street looked very different. They **had built** (build) a lot of new offices near the river.
2 The old sweet shop .... (close).
3 They .... (turn) the street into a pedestrian area.
4 The traffic lights and zebra crossing .... (disappear).
5 The butcher .... (not/change) at all.
6 A large new supermarket .... (open) next to the bank.
7 The trees by the bank .... (grow) taller.
8 I was pleased to see that they .... (not/cut) the trees down.

Previous and subsequent events

Complete each of the following sentences in two ways, using *because* + past perfect and *so* + past simple. See the example.

1 When I left the office, the building was empty ...
   (everyone/go home) **because everyone had gone home.**
   (I/lock the doors) **so I locked the doors.**
2 When I arrived at the office the next morning, the place was in a terrible mess ...
   (I/phone the police) ....
   (someone/break in) ....
3 The chairman was in a very good mood ...
   (we/win/a major contract) ....
   (we/open/a bottle of champagne) ....
4 The negotiators realized another meeting would be necessary ...
   (they/not reach an agreement) ....
   (they/get out/their diaries) ....
5 I didn't know their phone number ...
   (I/call/Directory Enquiries) ....
   (they/move/to new premises) ....
6 The Marketing Manager's flight from Japan arrived late ...
   (she/go/straight home from the airport) ....
   (there/be/a security alert in Tokyo) ....

Present perfect and past perfect

Change the following sentences into the past perfect. See the example.

1 'I don't want lunch because I've already eaten.'
   I didn't want lunch because I had already eaten.

2 'We can't give him the job because he hasn't had enough experience.'
   We couldn't give him the job because ....

3 'I'm phoning Jocelyne to say a fax has just arrived for her.'
   I phoned Jocelyne to say that ....

4 'I can't give Armando a lift because I haven't finished work.'
   I couldn't give Armando a lift because ....

5 'I'm looking forward to my trip because I've never been to Russia.'
   I was looking forward to my trip because ....

6 'He is calling a press conference because we've just closed a major deal.'
   He called a press conference because ....

Past perfect continuous

Look through the notes about the history of Pharmogen, a genetic engineering company that specializes in producing medical products. Write sentences about the company's activities until it went public in 2003. See the example.

1 When the company went public, (they/produce/auto-injectors/six years)
   they had been producing auto-injectors for six years.
2 When the company went public, (they/market the auto-injectors/USA/five years)
   ....

3 When the company went public, (Dr Pierce/run it/four years)
   ....

4 When the company went public, (Dr Warner/be the Medical Director/three years)
   ....

5 When the company went public, (they/manufacture cholesterol test kits/two years)
   ....

6 When the company went public, (they/operate/a production unit in Spain/a year)
   ....

Production

TASK 1

Complete the following sentences using the past perfect. See the example.

1 She found working from 9.00 to 5.00 very difficult because ...
she had never had a full-time job before.

2 The company decided to take legal action because ...

3 The company was forced to pay a fine to the tax authorities because ...

4 My trip to the airport to collect Mr Olivera was a waste of time. When I got there I found that ...

5 She was not worried when the stock market fell because ...

TASK 2

Continue the paragraph below. Use the past perfect to describe the changes, and the past simple to describe the results of the change. See the example.

1 When BMW's new Mini Cooper S was launched at the Tokyo Motor Show, it was an instant success. *The exterior had been re-designed to give it an eye-catching look, and the interior had been upgraded with high-quality materials. The engineers had added a supercharger to the four-cylinder engine, and had added a new six-speed gearbox.*

2 When the management consultant went back to see the company, she found that it had followed her advice.

TASK 3

Continue the sentences. Say what activities had been going on. See the example.

1 He felt very tired at 4.30 because *he had been working at the VDU all day.*

2 They realized that none of their confidential information was safe because ...

3 She felt that a change of job would be good for her because ...

4 The accountant finally discovered why the phone bill was so high. One of the night security guards ...

5 There was a very long delay at the airport. When we finally left, we ...

12 The future (1): *will*

Presentation

a · Spontaneous decisions

We can use *will* (or the short form *'ll*) + bare infinitive to refer to the future when we make an instant or spontaneous decision to do something:

A: *I haven't seen the minutes of the last meeting yet.*
B: *Sorry – I'll email them to you now.*

We often use the *will* future after *I think* and *I don't think*:

A: *I don't think I'll stay on in Geneva after the conference.*
B: *Nor will I. I think I'll get a flight back home straight afterwards too.*

The negative of *will* is *won't* (*will not*):

I won't stay long. I've got a meeting at 2.15.

Common mistakes: We don't use *won't* after *I think*.

wrong: **I think I won't come to the conference.*
right: *I don't think I'll come to the conference.*

b · Predictions

We can use *will* to make predictions and to state facts that will be true in the future:

*Over the next few years, there **will be** a massive increase in TV channels because of the growth in cable, broadband and satellite services.*

c · Future time words

We use a present tense (not: **will*) to refer to the future with time words like: *if, when, before, as soon as, after,* etc:

*I will contact you **as soon as** I **get** the information.* (not: **will get*)
(See also Unit 19, Conditionals)

d · Offers, promises, requests

Will can also be used to ask if someone is willing to do something, to make requests, promises, and threats, and to offer help:

*I'm afraid the line is busy. **Will you hold**?*	(asking if they are willing)
A: ***Will you give** me a hand with these boxes?*	(making a request)
B: *Of course – **I'll take** the big one.*	(offering help)
*Don't worry about the meeting. I **will support** you.*	(making a promise)

The word *won't* can mean *is not willing to* or *is refusing to*:

*There's something wrong with the printer. It **won't print** copies in reverse order.*

Practice

Spontaneous decisions

Match the responses in the box to the comments in the speech bubbles.

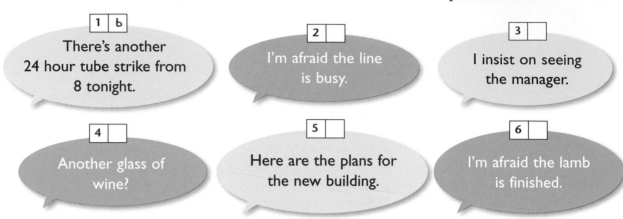

| 1 | b |
There's another 24 hour tube strike from 8 tonight.

| 2 | |
I'm afraid the line is busy.

| 3 | |
I insist on seeing the manager.

| 4 | |
Another glass of wine?

| 5 | |
Here are the plans for the new building.

| 6 | |
I'm afraid the lamb is finished.

> **a** Very well madam, I'll go and call her.
> **b** Is there? I think I'll work from home tomorrow then.
> **c** No thanks, I'm driving. I'll have an orange juice.
> **d** OK, I'll have the lasagne.
> **e** Thanks, I'll have a look at them later.
> **f** Don't worry – I'll call back later.

EXERCISE 2

Predictions

A government committee is looking at various experts' predictions for the economy next year. Match the notes to the graphs and forecast the changes using *will*.

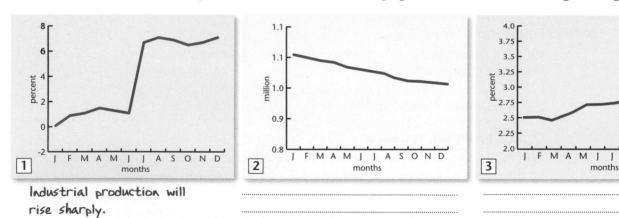

1 Industrial production will rise sharply.

2 ....

3 ....

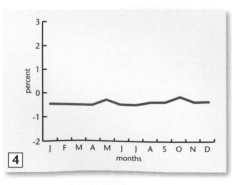

4 ....

5 ....

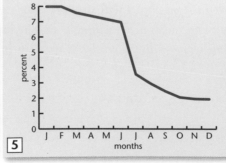

Consumer prices/remain stable

Inflation/rise slowly

Industrial production/rise sharply

Interest rates/fall sharply

Unemployment/fall slowly

Future time words

Put the verbs in brackets into the *will* future or the present simple.

1 Sally's working on the sales forecast at the moment. I will give (give) you the figures as soon as I get (get) them.

2 Most people expect that there .... (be) trouble when the G7 meeting .... (take) place next month.

3 The shipment isn't in yet, but the agent .... (phone) us as soon as it .... (arrive).

4 Give me the report and I .... (show) it to the lawyers before they .... (leave).

5 Because of the bad publicity, I expect our share price .... (fall) when the Stock Market .... (open) again on Monday.

6 When the company .... (move) production to Malaysia, most of the workers here .... (lose) their jobs.

7 I .... (give) you a ring next time I .... (come) to Helsinki and maybe we can arrange dinner.

8 When the strike .... (be) over, everyone .... (feel) happier.

9 We can't avoid a rise, but our sales .... (fall) when we .... (put) our prices up next year.

10 Don't worry about the office. I .... (tidy) it up before Mr Kosser .... (get) back.

Offers, promises, requests

Rewrite the following sentences using *will* or *won't*.

1 Has anyone offered to collect you from the airport?
Will anyone collect you from the airport?

2 I promise not to be late again.
....

3 The finance group 3i has agreed to loan us $18m for the project.
....

4 The company has offered a 5% pay rise in return for a no-strike deal.
....

5 I promise not to discuss this information with anyone.
....

6 They have refused to increase our discount.
....

7 The company has offered to pay my relocation expenses.
....

8 The cash machine is refusing to take my card.
....

9 Let me give you a hand with those boxes.
....

Production

TASK 1

Make spontaneous decisions using _I'll..._ based on the comments below.

1 You won't be able to get to Paris. The air traffic controllers are on strike.
   Really? Then I'll take Eurostar.

2 I'm sorry. The wine waiter says we have no more Chateau-Lafite '64.

   ....

3 I'm afraid Mr Howard's line is busy.

   ....

4 The BA flight is fully booked, but there is still availability with Lufthansa.

   ....

5 One of your clients – Mrs Mason – just rang. She sounded very upset about something.

   ....

TASK 2

Look at the topics below. Write three short paragraphs predicting what the world will be like in 20 years' time. See the example.

1 Medical developments
   In 20 years' time, there will be new ways of curing disease. People will live longer, and transplants will be very simple and effective. On the other hand, there will also be new diseases, and some common bacteria will become resistant to drugs.

2 The Internet and e-commerce

   ....

   ....

   ....

3 The world of work in 2100

   ....

   ....

   ....

4 My life and career

   ....

   ....

   ....

TASK 3

Complete the sentences using a verb in the present tense.

1 Don't worry, I'll go and see the lawyer before I _sign the contract._
2 I think our Sales Director will leave as soon as ....
3 You needn't wait for Mr Takashi. I'll stay here until ....
4 My boss will be delighted if ....
5 Everyone is very stressed, but things will get better when ....
6 I am fairly sure that I will get promoted as soon as ....

13 The future (2): present continuous and *going to*

Presentation

ⓐ Present continuous – arrangements

The present continuous (see Unit 2) is often used to talk about appointments or things we have arranged to do in the future. We generally use it with a future time phrase:

*Are you **doing** anything this weekend?*
(Have you arranged to do anything?)

*Yes, I**'m playing** golf with Barry on Saturday.*
(I have arranged to play golf with him.)

We do not use the present continuous with stative verbs (see Unit 3).

ⓑ *Going to* – decisions

We use the auxiliary ***be* + *going to*** + bare infinitive to talk about something we intend to do, or have already decided to do:

*According to the papers, Richard Branson **is going to buy** a second island in the Caribbean.*

ⓒ *Going to* – predictions

We can also use ***going to*** for making firm predictions when there is some physical evidence that an event will take place:

*Can you get some more paper for the printer? It**'s going to run out** any minute.*

In many cases, however, it is possible to predict future events using either ***going to*** or ***will***. There is little difference in meaning, but ***going to*** usually suggests that the event will happen soon. Compare:

*The present government **will win** the election (next year).*
*The present government **is going to win** the election (next week).*

ⓓ *Will*, present continuous, or *going to*?

The most important differences between the present continuous, ***going to***, and ***will*** are as follows:

We use the present continuous for arrangements (except with stative verbs):
*I**'m having** a meeting with the Export Manager on Thursday at 2.15.*

We use ***going to*** for decisions and intentions:
*I've made up my mind. I**'m going to buy** a BMW 730i.*

We use ***going to*** for firm predictions:
*It's already 28°c. It**'s going to be** very hot today.*

We use ***will*** for spontaneous decisions:
*I wonder if Peter is back from his marketing trip? I**'ll give** him a ring.*

We use ***will*** for promises, offers, and requests:
*I**'ll give** you a hand with those boxes if you like.*

We use ***will*** for general predictions:
*In the twenty first century computers **will play** a vital role in everyone's life.*

(For details of when the present simple is used to refer to the future, see Unit 1.)

Practice

EXERCISE **1**

Arrangements

Two managers of an engineering company are trying to arrange a meeting. Put the verbs in brackets into the present continuous.

Peter: Amelie, Peter here. Could we arrange a time tomorrow to talk about the new freight schedules? Say, er … 9.15?

Amelie: I'm a bit busy first thing because I ¹'m having (have) a meeting with one of the new drivers. But would 10 o'clock suit you?

Peter: I'm afraid not. I ²............................. (go) over to the factory, and after that I ³............................. (see) Mr Henderson for lunch.

Amelie: What time ⁴ .... (you/come) back?

Peter: At about 2.30 I suppose, but I ⁵............................. (not/do) anything special after that. Would you be free then?

Amelie: No, I don't think so. I ⁶............................. (see) a sales rep from Mercedes from 2.00 until about 3.30. So shall we say 3.45?

Peter: Fine. I think Janet ought to be there too. She ⁷............................. (come) along to lunch with me and Henderson tomorrow, so I can tell her about it then.

EXERCISE **2**

Decisions and intentions

Re-write these sentences using *going to*.

1 I have decided to accept the job.
   I'm going to accept the job.

2 You have heard my complaint. What do you intend to do about it?
   ....

3 We have decided to go ahead with clinical trials of the new drug.
   ....

4 They have decided not to go abroad this year.
   ....

5 This is where we are planning to build the new offices.
   ....

EXERCISE **3**

Predictions

Use the words in brackets to make predictions with *going to*.

1 These dotcom stocks are ridiculously over-valued.
   (they/crash) They're going to crash.

2 Demand for tin is rising, but supply is falling.
   (price/rise) ....

3 The company is in serious financial difficulty.
   (it/go bankrupt) ....

4 My boss is looking for another job.
   (she/leave the company) ....

5 We should have left much earlier.
   (we/be late) ....

EXERCISE **4**

Will or present continuous?

The export manager of an agricultural machinery company is talking to his PA about a sales trip. Put the verbs into the *will* future or the present continuous.

Kati: I've booked your flight and hotels for your trip to Ethiopia. You [1] **'re leaving** (leave) on the 18th at 6.30 a.m., and that means you [2] .... (be) in Addis Ababa late afternoon.

Marcus: What about hotels?

Kati: You [3] .... (stay) at the Addis Ababa Hilton, and you [4] .... (have) to get a taxi there from the airport. Your first meeting is on Monday, and you [5] .... (see) Mr Haile Mariam from the Ministry of Agriculture at 10.30.

Marcus: [6] .... (I/need) any vaccinations?

Kati: I'm not sure, but leave it with me. I [7] .... (phone) the travel agent right away, and I [8] .... (let) you know what she says.

EXERCISE **5**

Will or *going to*?

Fill in the blanks with the correct form of the future, using *will* or *going to*.

1 A: I'm afraid the fax machine isn't working.
   B: Don't worry, it's not a very urgent letter. I'll **post** (post) it.

2 A: We've chosen a brand name for the new biscuits.
   B: Really? What .... (you/call) them?

3 A: Why are you taking the day off on Friday?
   B: I .... (look) at a new house.

4 A: I'm afraid there's no sugar. Do you want a coffee without any?
   B: No, I .... (not have) one, thanks.

5 A: Have you decided what to do about improving the circulation of the magazine?
   B: Yes, we .... (cut) the cover price by 10% as from October.

6 A: I'm afraid I can't take you to the airport. Something important has just come up.
   B: Never mind. I .... (take) a taxi.

7 A: Do you need any help?
   B: Oh, yes please. .... (you/carry) the display stand for me?

8 A: Could you make sure Mr Wilson gets my message?
   B: Yes, I .... (tell) him myself when he gets in.

Production

TASK 1

Write a short paragraph about the arrangements that have been made for the CEO of a major American bank to open the new European HQ in London.

The CEO is arriving at Heathrow at 9.00, and ....

....

....

....

....

18 June	9.00	Arrive at Heathrow
	10.15	Meeting with Executive Vice-Presidents
	1.00	Lunch with officials from Department of Trade and Industry
	3.00	Official opening of new office in Threadneedle Street
	7.00	Speech: 'Financial Deregulation in the EU'
	8.00	Dinner at the Guildhall
19 June	11.30	Return flight to New York

TASK 2

Look at the following subjects. Write sentences about any definite plans you or your company have. Use *going to* and/or *not going to*.

1 training and courses   3 new equipment   5 holidays
2 new products and services   4 staffing changes   6 marketing campaigns

1 *I'm going to do a course in business Japanese in September, but I'm not going to take any exams.*

2 ....

3 ....

4 ....

5 ....

6 ....

TASK 3

Add comments to the sentences. Use the present continuous, *going to*, or *will*.

1 I'm afraid that I can't meet you for lunch on the 30th.
   I'm seeing Mr Karlssen in Oslo.

2 The management have announced how they intend to reduce costs.

....

3 I'm sorry, I didn't realize you were busy.

....

4 Our Sales Manager has finally chosen the new company car he wants.

....

5 I need some time to think about this proposal.

....

6 Our Export Manager is in Peru at the moment looking at new offices.

....

14 The future (3): other future tenses

Presentation

ⓐ Was going to

We can use *was going to/were going to* when we talk about plans or intentions that have changed. Look at the following example:

We intended to launch the model in July, but because of technical problems there was a three-month delay.

We can re-phrase this as:

*We **were going to launch** the model in July, but because of technical problems there was a three-month delay.*

ⓑ Was doing /were doing

When we talk about an arrangement that has been changed, we can use the past continuous (*was/were doing*):
*I **was flying** to Amsterdam last Friday, but I was needed at the office this weekend, so I'm travelling next Wednesday instead.*

This is similar to *was going to*, but the past continuous is normally used to report changed arrangements rather than changed plans or intentions.

ⓒ Will be doing

The future continuous (*will be doing*) is used to talk about an activity that will be in progress at a particular moment in the future:

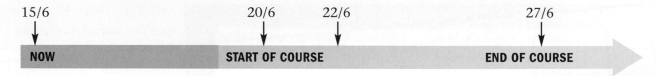

*I'm afraid I can't see you on the 22nd because I **will be attending** a training course in England.*

ⓓ Will have done

We use the future perfect (*will have done*), and a time phrase with *by*, to talk about something that will be completed before a particular time in the future:

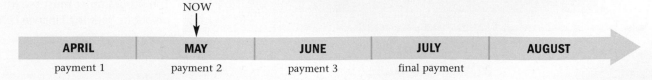

*We **won't have repaid** the loan by the end of May.*

Practice

EXERCISE 1

Was going to – changed plans

Look at the information. Using the notes, write sentences about the changed plans.

1 # CELEBRITY HOTEL
Opening ~~November~~
March

they/open hotel/November
they/open it/March
They were going to open the hotel in November, but now they're going to open it in March.

ADVERTISING BUDGET
3 original proposal – $240,000
amended proposal – $180,000

we/have/$240,000/for/advertising budget
now/only have/$180,000

....
....

2 TRX 3000 Proposed models:
Saloon, ~~Estate~~

they/produce/saloon and estate versions
they/only produce/saloon

....
....

4  IMPROVING **SALES** TECHNIQUES

Presentation by
Jill Lawson

~~Tuesday 4.30 pm~~
Friday 10.00 am

Jill/give presentation/Tuesday
now/give it/Friday

....
....

EXERCISE 2

Changed arrangements – problem solving

Look at schedule A for a programmer's visit to a client. All these appointments must be rearranged because of certain problems – see the notes in the box. Work out a new schedule B and write sentences about the changes.

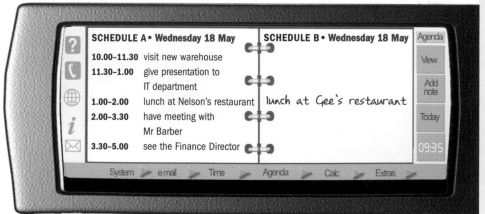

SCHEDULE A • Wednesday 18 May

Time	Activity	SCHEDULE B • Wednesday 18 May
10.00–11.30	visit new warehouse	
11.30–1.00	give presentation to IT department	
1.00–2.00	lunch at Nelson's restaurant	lunch at Gee's restaurant
2.00–3.30	have meeting with Mr Barber	
3.30–5.00	see the Finance Director	

Nelson's is closed on Wednesdays.

Gee's restaurant is only shut on Mondays.

The IT Department is busy all morning.

Mr Barber is not free at 2.00.

The Finance Director is busy all afternoon.

The warehouse shuts at 3.30.

The programmer must see Mr Barber before he sees the Finance Director.

1 ....
2 ....
3 He was having lunch at Nelson's, but now he's having lunch at Gee's.
4 ....
5 ....

Will be doing and *will have done*

Look through the notes about the building of a new hotel and leisure complex. Say what will be happening and what will have happened at each of the times below.

April – June	clear site and lay foundations
July – Sept	build central hotel
Oct – Dec	put up the 20 guest cottages in grounds
Jan – Mar	finish golf course and other sporting facilities
April 5 –	first guests arrive

1 In May, we will be clearing the site and laying the foundations.
2 By the end of June, we will have cleared the site and laid the foundations.
3 In August, we ....
4 By the end of September, ...
5 In November, ...
6 By the end of December, ...
7 In February, ...
8 By the end of March, ...
9 By the middle of April, ...

Will do, will be doing and *will have done*

Look at the information. Then put the verbs into the right tense.

1a The talk (start) will start at 10.00.
 b Mr Wright (give) will be giving his seminar at 10.23.
 c The talk (finish) will have finished by 11.15.

2a The plane (take off) .... at 18.00.
 b At 19.35, Miss Wilson (travel) ....
   to Athens.
 c Miss Wilson (arrive) .... in Athens
   by 22.30.

3a The first exam (start) .... at 10.00.
 b We (have) .... a break at 1.30.
 c We (finish) .... by 6.00.

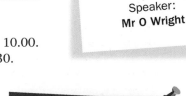

1

BUSINESS SEMINAR

How to be a High Flier

10.00–11.00

Speaker:
Mr O Wright

2

ITINERARY FOR MISS WILSON:
Dep. London Heathrow 18.00
Arr. Athens 22.00

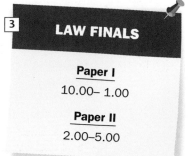

3 **LAW FINALS**

Paper I
10.00– 1.00

Paper II
2.00–5.00

Production

Complete these sentences using *was/were going to* or *was/were doing*.

1 I was going to accept a job in Qatar

    ... but in the end I decided that I probably wouldn't enjoy it.

2

    ... but I couldn't get a flight until the 18th.

3

    ... but in the end we felt it was too expensive.

4

    ... but she was ill, so we had to cancel.

5

    ... but in the end we decided that three was enough.

6

    ... but it was fully booked.

Answer the following questions about yourself in 20 years' time.

1 Who will you be working for, 20 years from now?

2 What position will you have in the company?

3 What sort of things will you be doing as part of your job?

4 What will you have achieved by then?

5 What changes will have taken place in your family life?

Continue these sentences using *will be doing* or *will have done*.

1 I hope that, by the time I am your age, ...

2 This time next week, ...

3 There's no point trying to get to the meeting now. By the time you do, ...

4 By the way, they've changed the venue for the sales conference. ...

5 This time tomorrow, ...

15 The future (4): possibility and probability

Presentation

a Definitely, probably, etc.

Definitely, *probably*, and *perhaps/maybe* show how probable we think a future event is. Notice that *won't* normally comes after *probably* and *definitely*:

Degree of chance:	In the next 10 years …
100%	computers will **definitely** become faster and more powerful.
75%	computers will **probably** get much smaller.
50%	**maybe/perhaps** computers will be able to recognize speech better.
25%	computers **probably** won't be able to translate perfectly.
0%	computers **definitely** won't start having feelings or emotions.

b Likely to, certain to

We can also use the verb *be* + *(un)likely/certain* + infinitive to refer to the future. We use the present tense of the verb *be* (*is certain to*) and we do not say: * *will be certain to*. We use *certain to* to refer to things that we think are certain, *likely to/expected to* to refer to things that are probable, and *unlikely to* to refer to things that are improbable:

*You'll meet Jane at the Sales Conference next week. She **is certain to** be there.* (definite)

*The final cost of the project **is likely to** be higher than the current estimates.* (probable)

*The European Central Bank **is unlikely to** lower interest rates again this year.* (improbable)

c I think, I doubt, etc.

Various verbs and expressions show how probable we think a future event is. For example:

High probability	I'm quite sure that …	
↑	I'm confident that …	
	I expect that …	
	The chances are that …	they will give you a pay rise.
	I should think that …	
	I shouldn't think that …	
	I doubt if …	
↓	I doubt very much whether …	
Low probability	I'm quite sure that + (won't) …	

d Modal verbs

We can use *may, might,* and *could* + bare infinitive to refer to the future:

*The latest statistics suggest that house prices **may/might/could fall** over the coming year.*

(For further information on modal verbs, see Units 23–26.)

Practice

EXERCISE **1**

Definitely, maybe, probably

A leading newspaper interviewed a selection of financial experts and business people and asked them to predict what would happen to the economy in the coming 12 months. Look at the results below and write sentences about the predictions using *definitely, probably,* or *maybe + will/won't*.

1 Maybe interest rates will fall in the Eurozone countries.
2 _____
3 _____
4 _____
5 _____
6 _____
7 _____
8 _____

▬	Y = yes
▬	N = no
▬	? = don't know

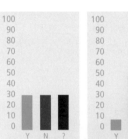

1 Will interest rates fall in the Eurozone countries?

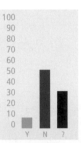

2 Will the euro rise against other leading currencies?

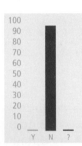

3 Will there be a recession in Europe?

4 Will the stock market in Japan recover?

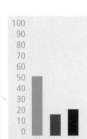

5 Will there be a fall in unemployment?

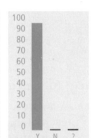

6 Will overall taxation rise?

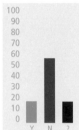

7 Will exports to the US go up?

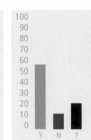

8 Will imports from the Far East increase?

EXERCISE **2**

Certain to, likely to, unlikely to

Complete the sentences with the correct form of *be certain to, be likely to,* or *be unlikely to.*

1 I will offer them a 10% discount, but they are likely to ask for more because they are sometimes very tough negotiators.
2 She _____ get the job. She has the experience and the qualifications, and none of the other applicants are any good.
3 They have very little experience of the entertainment industry, so they _____ get finance for their broadband video-on-demand network.
4 Of course the stock market goes up and down, but you _____ lose all your money in such a safe investment.
5 I can give Harriet the message. She _____ be here at some stage tomorrow, because she usually comes in to the office on Thursdays.
6 The consortium _____ need some extra finance for the bridge; they have spent all of their money and the project is only half-finished.
7 We are relocating to a site that is quite close, so most of the staff _____ stay with the company.
8 I have booked a hotel room in London for the 18th, because the dinner _____ finish before 11 p.m., and then it will be too late to get a train back to Liverpool.
9 The new manager _____ make a number of changes in the department; the only question is exactly what those changes will be.

I think, I doubt, **etc.**

A **Arrange the expressions in the box in the appropriate columns.**

I'm quite sure + (won't) ...	I'm confident that ...	~~I doubt if~~ ...
I should think that ...	The chances are that ...	I'm quite sure that ...
I expect that ...	I shouldn't think that ...	I doubt very much whether ...

Definitely	Probably	Probably not	Definitely not
		I doubt if ...	

B **Match the sentences in column A with sentences in column B that have a similar meaning.**

A

1 I'm quite sure they will sign the deal.
2 The chances are that we'll win the contract.
3 I doubt if they will sign the deal.
4 We will definitely win the contract.
5 I should think they will sign the deal.
6 I'm quite sure they won't sign the deal.
7 I doubt if we'll win the contract.
8 I doubt very much whether we'll win the contract.

B

a They are unlikely to sign the deal.
b They definitely won't sign the deal.
c We probably won't win the contract.
d We're very unlikely to win the contract.
e We'll probably win the contract.
f We are certain to win the contract.
g They are likely to sign the deal.
h They are certain to sign the deal.

Review

Rewrite the sentences, using the words in brackets.

1 He says we are certain to get the contract.
   (confident) He is confident that we will get the contract.
2 I shouldn't think that their new store will attract many customers.
   (unlikely) ....
3 I don't imagine they will give us better terms.
   (probably) ....
4 I'm likely to be very busy early next week.
   (probably) ....
5 They are unlikely to deliver the equipment this month.
   (think) ....

Production

TASK 1

Reply to the following questions about your future in two different ways.

In the next few years, what are your chances of ...

1 ... working abroad?
   a I should think I'll work abroad in the next few years.
   b Perhaps I'll work abroad in the next few years.

2 ... changing jobs?
   a ....
   b ....

3 ... getting rich ?
   a ....
   b ....

4 ... getting promoted?
   a ....
   b ....

5 ... marrying someone English?
   a ....
   b ....

6 ... taking over control of your company?
   a ....
   b ....

7 ... having to spend some time doing military service?
   a ....
   b ....

TASK 2

Make predictions about what changes will happen in the next few years.

1 New technologies I should think we will see a great deal of research into nanotechnology (technology on an atomic or molecular scale). It probably won't lead to any instant results, but I am confident we will find out much more about its potential.

2 Your company ....
....
....

3 New Internet services ....
....
....

4 The countries of the Pacific Rim ....
....
....

5 Scientific developments ....
....
....

16 The passive (1): actions, systems and processes

Presentation

a Form

The passive is formed by using the verb *be* and the past participle (e.g., *broken, driven, used*). For example, the present tense passive is formed with *am/is/are* + past participle:

I am driven	*I am not driven*	*Am I driven?*
You are driven	*You are not driven*	*Are you driven?*
He/she/it is driven	*He/she/it is not driven*	*Is he/she/it driven?*
We are driven	*We are not driven*	*Are we driven?*
They are driven	*They are not driven*	*Are they driven?*

b Focus on actions

We often use the passive to focus on something that happens to someone, when we do not want to focus on the person who does the action:

About 85% of the world's rubber is produced in the Far East.

(We use the passive here because we do not know, or need to say, who produces it.)

c Systems and processes

The passive is often used to talk about systems and processes:

On most rubber plantations, the latex is collected from the rubber trees every day. It is mixed with water and then formic acid is added. This process creates crude rubber, which is then rolled into sheets.

d Active or passive?

If it is important to say who performs an action, we can use the active or we can use the passive and the word *by*:

active: *Peter Franks runs the Marketing Department.*
passive: *The Marketing Department is run by Peter Franks.*

Both of these sentences are correct. If we were already talking about Peter Franks, we would probably use the active:

Peter Franks is an old colleague of mine. He works for Butterfield International, and he runs the Marketing Department.

If we were talking about the Marketing Department, and don't want to change the subject in the second sentence, we would probably use the passive:

The Marketing Department is a large and very successful division that employs over 100 people. It is run by Peter Franks.

Practice

Form

Read this interview with a taxi driver. Put the verbs in brackets into the present simple passive.

A: [1] *Are you employed* (you/employ) by a taxi company or is Pet Taxi your own business?

B: Pet Taxi is all mine – and I started it because there are lots of drivers who don't like it when [2] _____ (they/ask) to drive cats and dogs in their cars.

A: Is that a problem?

B: Yes, it can be, because every time you have a cat or a dog, dust and hairs [3] _____ (leave) behind. And these days there are lots of passengers who [4] _____ (not/allow) to go anywhere near animals because of allergies.

A: So what does your taxi look like?

B: It's a bit like a van, but it [5] _____ (fit) with a big cage where the animals [6] _____ (keep), and in the roof there are vents so that the air [7] _____ (let) in – which is important for long journeys.

A: So what sort of animals [8] _____ (you/ask) to carry round?

B: Well, mostly, [9] _____ (I/contact) by people who want me to take their cats and dogs to the hairdresser's or vet's. But I do some work for a film studio too, so sometimes [10] _____ (I/give) more unusual creatures – I once had a huge snake – a python!

Focus on actions

Many of the following sentences sound unnatural because they are in the active. Rewrite them in the present simple passive, but do not mention the agent (e.g., *by workers, by people***).**

1 Workers in China make these telephones.
  These telephones *are made in China.*

2 Employers pay many manual workers weekly.
  Many manual workers _____

3 They keep a large amount of gold at Fort Knox.
  A large amount of gold _____

4 Workers build a lot of the world's supertankers in South Korea.
  A lot of the world's supertankers _____

5 Farmers grow a third of the world's cocoa on the Ivory Coast.
  A third of the world's cocoa _____

6 Countries store most nuclear waste underground.
  Most nuclear waste _____

7 Scientists test most new drugs extensively before they go on sale.
  Before they go on sale, most new drugs _____

8 Printers print a lot of our books in Hong Kong.
  A lot of our books _____

Systems and processes

Read this information about the Morgan Car company, a privately-owned family firm that makes classic sports cars. Put the verbs into the present simple passive.

THE MAKING OF A MORGAN

Every Morgan ¹ is ordered (order) in advance and each one ² _____ (build) to the customer's specifications.

Body shop – The first stage of production involves the construction of the frames. The frames ³ _____ (make) of wood, and they ⁴ _____ (put) together carefully by expert craftsmen.

Sheet metal shop – This is where the panels of steel or aluminium ⁵ _____ (cut) out. The sheet metal shop is the main supplier for the assembly shop.

New Assembly shop – This is where the wooden frame ⁶ _____ (bolt) to the steel chassis. Afterwards the aluminium panels ⁷ _____ (attach) to the frame. Then the wings, bonnets and wheels ⁸ _____ (fit) and the car ⁹ _____ (prepare) for painting.

Chassis erection shop – Here is where the engine ¹⁰ _____ (assemble) to the chassis – most of the engines that ¹¹ _____ (use) come from Rover, Ford or BMW. This is also where the gear boxes and other parts ¹² _____ (add) to the car. This part of the process takes a day.

Finishing shop – Here the final operations ¹³ _____ (carry) out. The leather seats, electrical wiring, dashboard and windscreens ¹⁴ _____ (fit) to the cars. Afterwards the cars ¹⁵ _____ (take) for a road test.

Despatch department – It is here that the cars ¹⁶ _____ (check) against a quality list. Then they ¹⁷ _____ (clean and polish) and ¹⁸ _____ (despatch) to the customers.

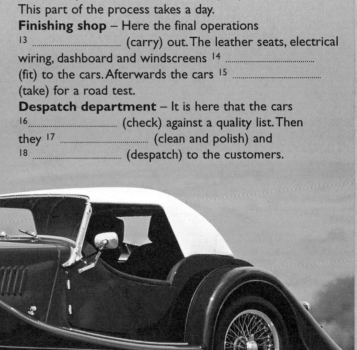

Active or passive?

Read each of the following statements. Then say if it would most probably be followed by sentence a or sentence b. Underline the best answer.

1 Roche Inc. is one of the world's leading pharmaceutical groups.
   a It manufactures vitamins, perfumes, and antibiotics.
   b Vitamins, perfumes, and antibiotics are manufactured by it.
2 Qantas is Australia's largest airline.
   a A fleet of 145 aircraft is operated by it.
   b It operates a fleet of 187 aircraft.
3 Our most successful department by far is Research and Development.
   a It is run by Dr Stein and her colleagues.
   b Dr Stein and her colleagues run it.
4 News Corporation is a global media and entertainment empire.
   a As well as publishing newspapers and books, 20th Century Fox is owned by it.
   b As well as publishing newspapers and books, it owns 20th Century Fox.

Production

A person who works in the Personnel Department is explaining how they select candidates in her company.

1 — If there's a vacancy, I usually advertise it in-house first of all.

2 — If I don't find any suitable candidates, then we advertise the job in the papers.

3 — We ask applicants to send in their CVs.

4 — We invite some of the candidates to an interview.

5 — After that, we draw up a shortlist.

6 — We ask some of the applicants back for a second interview.

7 — We choose the best candidate.

8 — Then I check his or her references.

9 — If everything's OK, we offer the applicant the job.

Complete the sentences below to give a general description of the recruitment process. Use the passive in your answer.

1 The vacancy is advertised in-house.
2 If there are no suitable in-house candidates, the job ....
3 Applicants ....
4 Some candidates ....
5 A shortlist ....
6 Some applicants ....
7 The best candidate ....
8 The references ....
9 The successful applicant ....

Write a short paragraph describing a system or process you know well, using the present simple passive. You may find the following linking words helpful:

First of all, ... Then, ... Next, ... After that, ... Finally, ...

....
....
....
....
....

17 The passive (2): other tenses

Presentation

a Other tenses

The examples below show how to form the passive with other tenses.

Present continuous passive: ***am being***, ***is being***, or ***are being*** + past participle:

*Our website **is being re-designed** at the moment.*
*Apparently some quite major changes **are being made**.*

Past simple passive: ***was*** or ***were*** + the past participle:

*Our company **was founded** in 1848 in London.*
*In 1849, three other branches **were set up** in Oxford, Cambridge and Edinburgh.*

Note the passive form ***be born***:

A: *When **were you born**?*
B: *I **was born** in 1968.*

Past continuous passive: ***was being*** or ***were being*** + the past participle:

*I couldn't use the company car yesterday because it **was being serviced**.*
*We only noticed the mistakes when the brochures **were being printed**.*

Present perfect passive: ***has been*** or ***have been*** + the past participle:

*A small design fault **has been found** on our latest chip.*
*All of the chips **have been recalled**.*

Past perfect passive: ***had been*** + the past participle:

*They emailed us to say that the shipment **had been delayed**.*
*None of their orders **had been fulfilled**.*

Future passive: ***will be*** or ***going to be*** + the past participle:

*The shipment **is going to be delayed**.*
*It **will be delivered** next Tuesday.*

b Personal or impersonal?

The passive is also often used in business correspondence, because it is less personal than the active. Compare:

*Amanda Mason, who opens our post at this branch, **received** your letter yesterday. She **has forwarded** it to Head Office.* (active)

*Thank you for your letter, which **was received** at this branch yesterday. It **has been forwarded** to Head Office.* (passive)

The present perfect passive is often used when we are describing changes that have taken place, and we are more interested in the changes than who has made them:

*The factory is completely different. The whole place **has been modernized** and **computerized**, and most of the shop floor workers **have been made redundant**.*

Practice

EXERCISE ❶

Tenses in the passive

A Put the verbs in brackets into the present continuous active or passive.

The environmental group Friends of the Earth [1] is encouraging (encourage) members of the public to take action and protest about the testing of genetically modified (GM) crops. At the moment there are about 30 sites where large scale trials [2] .... (carry out). Many environmentalists fear that plants and animals near the sites [3] .... (affect) because proper safety measures [4] .... (not / take). The government, however, insists that researchers [5] .... (do) everything possible to make the trials safe.

B Put the verbs in brackets into the past continuous active or passive (*was/were doing* or *was/were being done*).

At the Old Bailey yesterday, five men were found guilty of planning the most ambitious jewel robbery in history. The gang had tried to steal the De Beers Millennium diamonds (worth over $200 million) which [1] .... (display) at the Millennium Dome. Four of the men smashed into the Dome early one morning with a JCB digger, but over 200 policemen [2] .... (wait) for them because they knew about their plans. They first arrested the two men who [3] .... (stand) outside, and then arrested the others who [4] .... (smash) the glass case where the jewels [5] .... (keep). While the men [6] .... (take) away, the police picked up the driver of the getaway boat who [7] .... (wait) on the river next to the Dome.

C Put the verbs in brackets into the past perfect active or passive (*had done/had been done*).

Elvis Presley was one of last year's highest earners, thanks mainly to his widow Priscilla and the CEO of Elvis Presley Enterprises, Jack Soden. When he died in 1977, Elvis's financial affairs were in a mess. The rights to all his records [1] .... (sell) to RCA Records in 1973 in a deal in which Elvis [2] .... (pay) about $5 million and his manager [3] .... (receive) $7 million. Priscilla decided to keep their home, and to open it as a tourist attraction, even though she [4] .... (advise) to sell it. It was a good move, and within a year, more than 300,000 visitors [5] .... (visit) Graceland, and today it generates $15 million annually in admission fees alone.

Future passive

Put the verbs in brackets into the *will* future active or passive.

Janet: I've booked you on the 8.30 Olympic Airways flight, so you [1] ´ll arrive (arrive) at 2.30 Athens time. You [2] .... (meet) at the airport by one of their chauffeurs, and you [3] .... (drive) straight to their Head Office.

Helen: Fine. Have you organized a hotel?

Janet: Yes, you [4] .... (be) at the Inter-Continental.

Helen: OK. Do they know how long the meeting [5] .... (last)?

Janet: They expect that you [6] .... (be able) to finish at about 7.30 in the evening, and then you [7] .... (take) to the hotel. I've told the hotel you probably [8] .... (not arrive) until 8.30. They say that's fine – the room [9] .... (keep) for you, and it [10] .... (not/give) to anyone else.

Present perfect: change

Some staff changes have taken place at a small UK engineering company. Complete the dialogue between a company employee and a friend who used to work there. Put the verbs in brackets into the present perfect active or passive (*has/have done* or *has/have been done*).

John: Are things different now?

Sara: Yes. What has happened is that the Sales and Marketing Department [1] has been turned (turn) into three separate divisions – there is now an International Division, a UK Division, and a new office that [2] .... (just/set up) in the US.

John: Is Peter still in charge?

Sara: No, they [3] .... (make) him Senior Director, so he doesn't have much to do with the department now. Laura [4] .... (promote) to Sales Director, so they all report directly to her. Ben Warner and Katie Lang [5] .... (put) in charge of the International Division and the UK Division.

John: Is Ken still there or [6] .... (they/send) him to the US?

Sara: No he's still there – but he doesn't get on with Laura, basically, so he [7] .... (demote) to UK Sales Assistant, and now he works for Katie. Obviously he's not very happy about it and he doesn't think that the company [8] .... (treat) him fairly. I don't expect he'll stay long.

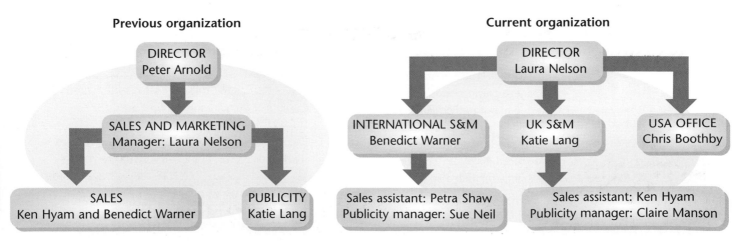

Previous organization	Current organization
DIRECTOR Peter Arnold	DIRECTOR Laura Nelson
SALES AND MARKETING Manager: Laura Nelson	INTERNATIONAL S&M Benedict Warner — UK S&M Katie Lang — USA OFFICE Chris Boothby
SALES Ken Hyam and Benedict Warner — PUBLICITY Katie Lang	Sales assistant: Petra Shaw Publicity manager: Sue Neil — Sales assistant: Ken Hyam Publicity manager: Claire Manson

Production

TASK 1

Write sentences from the prompts using one of the verbs from the box.

build	discover	elect	found
invent	destroy	open	

1 The Berlin Wall/1961
   The Berlin Wall was built in 1961.

2 The Channel Tunnel/1994

   ....

3 Radium/Marie and Pierre Curie

   ....

4 The wireless/Marconi

   ....

5 Fiat SPA/1899

   ....

6 The World Trade Center/11 September 2001

   ....

7 President George W Bush/2000

   ....

TASK 2

Add a response to each of the following questions.

Have you heard what ...

1 ... has happened to their Spanish subsidiary? *It has been sold.*
2 ... is happening to the department? ....
3 ... happened to the chairman at the meeting? ....
4 ... has happened to the strikers? ....
5 ... is happening to the price of petrol? ....
6 ... happened to our office in Singapore? ....
7 ... has happened to the Euro? ....

TASK 3

Read the information about Nintendo. Then write a similar short paragraph about the history of your company.

....

....

....

When Nintendo was founded by Fusajiro Yamauchi in 1889, it manufactured Japanese playing cards. The company started making other games in 1963. The first video games were introduced in the 1970s, and the first Game Boy was introduced in 1989. The products were constantly upgraded and improved, and the Nintendo GameCube of 2001 became the fastest-selling hardware system in the world.

The passive (3): passive verbs and infinitives, *have something done*

Presentation

ⓐ *Have something done*

We can use the structure *have something done* to talk about things we pay or employ other people to do for us. We use the verb *have* + object + past participle:

have +	object +	past participle
We have	*our books*	*printed in Singapore.*

Common mistakes:

We put the object before the past participle, not after it:

wrong: **We have serviced our cars by a local garage.*
right: *We have our cars serviced by a local garage.*

ⓑ **Get something done**

In most cases we can also use *get* instead of *have*. This is slightly less formal:

We get our brochures printed in Hong Kong.

ⓒ **Different tenses**

We can use *have something done* or *get something done* in different tenses. To do this, we use the correct tense of the verb *have* (or the verb *get*). Look at the following examples:

present simple:	*We have the machines cleaned regularly.*
present continuous:	*He is having the letter typed out.*
past simple:	*They got the order sent by courier.*
present perfect:	*Have you had your accounts checked?*
going to:	*We're going to have an ADSL line installed.*
modals:	*You must have your office repainted.*
infinitive:	*I want to get the air conditioning repaired.*
-ing forms:	*Would you be interested in having your house valued?*

ⓓ **Managing people**

When we talk about what we ask other people to do, we can use *have* + object + bare infinitive:

I'll have my secretary book a meeting room.

We can also use *get* + object + *to* infinitive:

I'll get my secretary to book a meeting room.

Practice

Have something done

Read the magazine article about mass customization. Using the structure *have something done*, fill in the blanks with the missing information.

MASS CUSTOMIZATION

Thanks to the Internet and new technology, mass customization is becoming more common.

1 Some computer companies don't sell their computers in stores – they only start assembling the computer after they get your order, which means you can 1 **have your computer made** (computer/make) the way you want. For example, if you are going to use it a lot for artwork or video, you can 2 .... (a powerful graphics card/add) to the computer. If you need special software, you can 3 .... (the programs/ load and test) before the computer is

sent to you. If you need a lot of storage, you can 4 .... (a bigger hard disk/fit), and anyone who needs to use big programs can 5 .... (extra memory/ build) in.

2 After choosing your system, you can think about accessories. If you want internal devices like modems or extra drives, you can 6 .... (them/install) in the machine. If you need external devices such as scanners or printers, you can 7 .... (them/deliver) with your order.

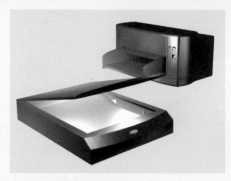

3 Finally, you may choose the kind of after-sales service you want. If the machine goes wrong, you may want to send it back to the factory to 8 .... (it/repair), or you may prefer to 9 .... (it/fix) on-site by a technician.

This is just a very early example of mass customization, but there's no doubt that even bigger changes in manufacturing and services are on the horizon, and soon we will be able to 10 .... (other things/customize) to suit our needs. We have come a long way since Henry Ford's famous words about the Model T: 'You can have any colour you want, as long as it's black.'

Get something done

Read what the manager of a maintenance department says about her work. Re-write the sentences using the structure *get something done*. See the example.

1 People come and clean the office every evening.
 We get the office cleaned every evening.
2 Someone sweeps the floors every night.
3 Someone services the air conditioners twice a year.
4 Someone changes the indoor plants once a month.
5 Someone cleans the windows every six weeks.
6 Someone checks the central heating system once a year.
7 In the winter, someone delivers oil every week or so.

Tenses

Rewrite the following sentences using the structure *have something done*.

1 Someone makes my suits in London.
   I have my suits made in London.

2 Someone is going to print 5,000 new catalogues for us.
   We ....

3 When is someone going to redecorate my office?
   When ....

4 Someone is designing a new office for them.
   They ....

5 Someone has checked these figures for me.
   I ....

6 Has someone done your hair?
   Have ....

7 Someone should mend the photocopier for you.
   You ....

8 Someone delivered the new furniture for us yesterday.
   We ....

9 Nobody has repaired my car yet.
   I ....

10 Where did someone make those t-shirts for you?
   Where ....

Managing people

Read through the problems or situations below. Using the words in brackets, suggest solutions. See the example.

1 'Casco have phoned again to complain that we still haven't paid that invoice.'
   (get/accounts department/send them/cheque immediately)
   I'll get the accounts department to send them a cheque immediately.

2 'We really need to discuss this face to face.'
   (have/my PA/set up/meeting)
   ....

3 'My plane won't be getting back until 3 a.m.'
   (get/driver/come and collect you)
   ....

4 'We won't have time to stop for lunch.'
   (get/canteen/send up/sandwiches)
   ....

5 'The printer doesn't seem to be working.'
   (get/Barry/come and have a look)
   ....

6 'I'd be very interested in working for you.'
   (have/personnel manager/arrange an interview)
   ....

7 'I'd like details of your full range of products.'
   (have/my secretary/send you/catalogue)
   ....

8 'I'm worried about one or two bits of this contract.'
   (get/lawyer/check/carefully)
   ....

Production

TASK 1

Look at these advertisements from a local business directory. For each advertisement, write down three things that you can *have done* or *get done* by these companies.

1

TYPOGRAPH
Premier
Printers
and
Stationers

business and
personal stationery

in-company magazines
and brochures

colour photocopying

2

BUSBY AND WALLACE
Office Decoration and Maintenance
- interior and exterior painting
- wallpaper hanging service
- regular office maintenance contracts available

HARRINGTON PHOTOGRAPHIC

instant passport and driving licence photographs

colour or black and white portraits

3

photo restoration

1 ....

....

....

2 ....

....

....

3 ....

....

....

TASK 2

Think about how mass customization is affecting, or will affect these areas, and what you *can have done* for you now or what you *will be able to have done* in the future.

1 Photography: If you've got a digital camera but no printer, you will soon be able to go to a photo booth at the airport and have all your holiday photos printed out before you pick up your baggage.

2 Music and CDs: ....

....

3 Clothes: ....

....

4 Home shopping: ....

....

5 Cars: ....

....

TASK 3

Using the structure *get someone to do something* or *have someone do something*, say who you call in these situations.

What do you do if ....

1 ... there is something wrong with the central heating?

I get the maintenance department to have a look at it.

2 .... you want to travel abroad?

....

3 ... your computer breaks down?

....

4 ... your car breaks down on the motorway?

....

5 ... you are unsure about something in your tax bill?

....

6 ... your office needs redecorating?

....

19 Conditionals (1): *if you go ...*

Presentation

ⓐ Zero conditional

We can talk about general facts or things that are always true using an *if* sentence. This kind of sentence has the present tense in both parts:

If + present tense	Present tense
If the price of a product falls,	*demand for it usually rises.*

In statements like this, *if* means the same as *when* or *every time*. This is sometimes called the 'zero conditional'.

ⓑ First conditional

When we talk about the results of future events that are reasonably likely, we can use an *if* sentence. The *if* clause states the condition, and the other clause states the result.

Condition	Result
If + present tenses	*will* + bare infinitive
If you give me an extra day's holiday,	*I'll work this weekend.*

The *if* clause can come in the first part of the sentence or the second:

If the government raises taxes in the next budget, consumer spending will fall.
Consumer spending will fall if the government raises taxes in the next budget.

Common mistakes: We do not use *will* in the *if* part of the sentence:

wrong: **If the shipment will arrive tomorrow, I will collect it.*
right: *If the shipment arrives tomorrow, I will collect it.*

ⓒ *If* or *when*?

When we talk about events that will take place in the future, we can use *if* or *when*, but there is an important difference in meaning.

I'm flying to the States today. I'll give you a ring if I get in at a reasonable time.
(The speaker is not sure if he will get in at a reasonable time or not.)

I'm flying to the States tonight. I'll give you a ring when I get there.
(The speaker has no doubt that the plane will arrive safely.)

ⓓ Variations

We can use the imperative, or a modal verb (see Units 23–6), instead of *will* + infinitive:

Imperative: *If you hear from Susan today, tell her to ring me.*
              If Mr Duval comes in, get him to sign that contract.

Modal: *If the traffic is bad, I may get home late.*
              If we sign the contract today, we can start production at the end of next month.

We can use the present continuous or the present perfect in the *if* clause:

Present continuous: *If they are still considering Peru, I shall suggest Lima.*
Present perfect: *If you have placed the order, the goods will arrive in ten days.*

Practice

EXERCISE ❶

Zero conditional

Complete the first part of the sentences in column A with the right endings in column B.

A		B	
1	Governments expect something in return	a	when I go on a long haul flight.
2	Every time Peter chairs a meeting	b	it normally arrives in seconds.
3	People are usually more productive	c	I usually look after them.
4	If you send someone an email,	d	if they give aid.
5	If inflation rises,	e	whenever we launch a new model.
6	When you have a high staff turnover,	f	it always goes on for a long time.
7	If anyone from our Hamburg office visits,	g	if they work in pleasant surroundings.
8	We spend a great deal on promotion	h	the value of people's savings goes down.
9	I always fly Club Class	i	something is wrong with the management.

EXERCISE ❷

First conditional

Look at the notes about each situation. Then write *if* sentences using the present simple and *will* + infinitive.

1 a motorway may be very busy – we/miss the flight
   If the motorway is very busy we'll miss the flight.
 b traffic may be OK – we/get to the airport on time

   ....

2 a weather may be good – they/have the party in the garden

   ....

 b it may rain – they/hold the reception in the marquee

   ....

3 a the play may do well – it/open on Broadway

   ....

 b the play may do badly – it/close after a week

   ....

If or when?

Fill in the blanks with *if* or *when*.

1 I don't think you'll have any problems, but call me .... you do.
2 Mrs Barton is coming this afternoon. Could you send her up .... she arrives?
3 We won't be able to compete .... we don't adopt a better Internet strategy.
4 Put that on my bill please, and I'll pay .... I check out.
5 I'll be disappointed .... I'm not promoted this year.
6 Sales are low this spring, but they will improve .... summer starts.

Variations

Read the following dialogue, and choose the best option from the words in *italics*.

Hans: I'll be at a meeting this afternoon, so if Pierre [1] *will call/calls*, [2] *tell/you'll tell* him
          I'll give him a ring later.
Claudia: OK, but there's one other thing. You've got a meeting with Mr Sachs at 5.00.
          Will you be back by then?
Hans: It depends, really, but I'll call you. If the meeting [3] *will go on/goes on* after 4.30,
          you [4] *will/can* cancel my appointment with Mr Sachs. But if it has already
          finished by then, I [5] *may/am able to* get back in time.
Claudia: Anything else?
Hans: Yes, if you [6] *will manage/manage* to get hold of Kevin, you [7] *must/will* get the
          October sales figures from him. I need them today. The Chairman [8] *may/can*
          come to the sales meeting tomorrow, and if he does, he [9] *will want/must want*
          to see them.

Right or wrong?

Some of the following sentences are right and some are wrong. Put a tick (✓) next to the ones that are right and correct the ones that are wrong.

1 If you finish everything that needs to be done before five, ~~you are able to go home.~~
  If you finish everything that needs to be done before five, you can go home.
2 Mr Lo probably won't want to go out for dinner if he has had a meal on the plane.

   ....

3 If it will be their first visit to England, I expect they might want to do some sightseeing.

   ....

4 I may go and visit their headquarters if I will go to London next week.

   ....

5 Please don't hesitate to contact me if you require any further information.

   ....

6 What should I do if everyone will be still talking when I want to start my presentation?

   ....

7 If you will go to Paris next week, I can give you the name of a good hotel I know.

   ....

Production

Explain the meaning of these sentences using a first conditional sentence with *if*.

1 For further information call us on 0800 726354.
If you ring 0800 726354, we'll give you some more information.
2 We've got these products on a 'sale or return' basis.

3 Subscribe to *Business Age* before 30 September and save up to 33%.

4 The Ford Ka comes with a money-back guarantee.

Complete these sentences.

1 If I have time this weekend, ...
2 If I go on holiday this year, ...
3 If I can afford it, ...
4 If I carry on learning English, ...
5 If I stay in my present job, ...
6 If I feel tired this evening, ...
7 If I finish work early, ...
8 If I move house at some stage in the future, ...

You have been asked to speak on these topics at a meeting. Write short paragraphs about what you think will happen during the next two or three years, and what you or your company will do.

1 Interest rates
I think that interest rates will rise again during the next two or three years.
If they do, we will have to try to reduce our costs and the amount we borrow as much as possible, and we will not be able to expand.

2 Your market share

3 New competitors

4 Technological changes

20 Conditionals (2): *if, unless,* etc.

Presentation

ⓐ *If* and *unless*

Unless means the same as *if ... not*. It always refers to the conditional part of the sentence and not the result part of the sentence:

If sales **don't improve** soon,	we'll have to cut production.
(condition)	(result)
Unless sales **improve** soon,	we'll have to cut production.
(condition)	(result)

We often use *not* + *unless*, which means *only ... if*, when we want to emphasize a condition:

*The bank will **only** lend me the money **if** I can give them some kind of security.*
*The bank **won't** lend me the money **unless** I can give them some kind of security.*

ⓑ *In case* and *so that*

We use *in case* to talk about precautions and safety measures we will take *before* a problem happens. These precautions, however, will not prevent the problem from happening.

*I'll reserve the meeting room from 3.00–9.00 **in case** the meeting goes on a long time.*
(I'll reserve the room for 6 hours to be on the safe side – the meeting may or may not go on for a long time.)

We use *so that* to talk about the purpose of a decision or a safety measure. Usually these safety measures are designed to achieve a benefit of some kind or to prevent a problem from happening in the first place.

*I'll reserve the room from 3.00–5.00 **so that** the meeting doesn't go on for a long time.*
(We will only have the room for 2 hours. That will prevent the meeting from going on for a long time – we will have to stop at 5.00.)

ⓒ *Provided that, as long as,* etc.

We can use *provided that/providing, as long as,* and *so long as* when we want to emphasize a condition. These mean *if* and *only if.*

*I will sign this contract **provided that** you guarantee me a commission rate of 15%.*
(I will not sign it if you do not give me this guarantee).
*The strike will be successful **as long as** we all stay together.*
(It will only succeed if we all stay together.)

Providing and *so long as* mean the same as *provided that* and *as long as,* but they are a little less formal. Note that we use the same sentence pattern as with other *if* sentences.

Practice

EXERCISE ❶

If and unless

Match the first part of each sentence in column A with the right ending in column B.

A	B
1 There's going to be a train strike tomorrow	a unless we give her the salary she wants.
2 The union won't go on strike	b we will not make a loss this year.
3 She will accept the job	c we will make a loss this year.
4 She won't accept the job	d they will not take legal action.
5 Unless sales improve dramatically	e unless we agree to their demands.
6 If sales improve dramatically	f if we agree to their demands.
7 Unless we pay them immediately	g they will take legal action.
8 If we pay them immediately	h if we give her the salary she wants.

EXERCISE ❷

Unless

Rewrite the following sentences using *unless*.

1 If nothing goes wrong, we will sign the deal tomorrow.
   We will sign the deal tomorrow unless something goes wrong.

2 We're not going to get that contract if we don't improve our offer.
   We're not going to get that contract ....

3 Only phone me if it is an emergency.
   Please don't phone me ....

4 If demand doesn't increase soon, we're going to have a bad year.
   We're going to have a bad year ....

5 This project will only be viable if you can cut your overheads.
   This project will not be viable ....

6 I'll accept an overseas posting if I can have my job back when I return.
   I won't accept an overseas posting ....

EXERCISE ❸

In case

A manager is going to Frankfurt to attend a book fair. Complete the sentences about what he is going to do using *in case* + present tense.

Possible problems that may or may not happen:

~~The hotels may be busy.~~
It might be cold.
He might want to hire a car.
The office might need to phone him.
He might have to see a doctor.
He may lose his passport.

1 He's going to book a room in advance in case the hotels are busy.
2 He's going to photocopy his passport ....
3 He's going to take his driving licence ....
4 He's going to take his mobile ....
5 He's going to take out medical insurance ....
6 He's going to take some warm clothes ....

EXERCISE **4**

So that

A colleague is also going to the same book fair. Look at her decisions and at the list of the benefits she will achieve or the problems she will avoid. Write sentences about these using *so that*.

Benefits/Problems she will avoid:
1 She won't have to spend hours looking for a hotel.
2 She won't have to find a bank.
3 She will be able to change her flight times if necessary.
4 People will be able to phone her.
5 She won't end up with a large hospital bill.
6 She will be able to do some work on the plane.

1 She'll book a room well in advance *so that she doesn't have to spend hours looking for a hotel.*
2 She'll take plenty of euros in cash ....
3 She'll buy a full business class fare ....
4 She'll take her mobile ....
5 She'll take out medical insurance ....
6 She'll take her laptop ....

EXERCISE **5**

In case or so that?

In each of the following sentences, fill in the blanks with *in case* or *so that*.

1 The building has smoke alarms *so that* we can detect fires immediately.
2 Keep the insurance documents safe .... we need to make a claim.
3 I'll send you a fax .... you get all the information you need today.
4 I'm going to hold a meeting .... everyone can say what they think.
5 I'll phone you later .... you have any problems with the program.
6 I've left the answering machine on .... anyone calls.

EXERCISE **6**

Provided that, as long as, etc.

Underline the best option from the words in *italics*.

1 We'll sign the contract today *provided that/unless* there aren't any last minute problems.
2 The banks will support us *unless/as long as* the company is profitable.
3 I won't call you *unless/providing* I have a problem I can't deal with.
4 *So long as/Unless* we continue to order in bulk, they will go on giving us free delivery.
5 *Unless/Provided that* we solve the problem now, the situation is going to get worse.
6 We will be able to start this project in two months *as long as/unless* the board think it is a good idea.

Production

TASK 1

Complete the following sentences.

1 I'll probably stay in my present job unless …

....

2 The economic situation will continue to improve as long as …

....

3 I won't be able to go to the interview on Thursday unless …

....

4 Provided that Boeing get the safety certificate for their new aeroplane, …

....

5 Unless I have to change the time of the meeting for some reason, …

....

6 We will allow you to become the sole distributor of our product providing …

....

TASK 2

Finish each of the sentences in three ways, using *if*, *in case*, and *so that*.

1 I'm going to leave early …
   a … if my boss lets me.
   b … in case the traffic is bad.
   c … so that I get to the airport on time.

2 I'll take some local currency with me …
   a … if ....
   b … in case ....
   c … so that ....

3 I'll take my address book with me …
   a … if ....
   b … in case ....
   c … so that ....

4 They haven't paid the invoice yet. I'll send them a reminder …
   a … if ....
   b … in case ....
   c … so that ....

5 You'd better take your driving licence with you …
   a … if ....
   b … in case ....
   c … so that ....

21 Conditionals (3): *if you went ...*

Presentation

ⓐ Form

The second conditional is formed by using *if* + past tense and *would ('d)* + bare infinitive:

If + past tense	*would/'d* + infinitive
If I *had* his mobile number, I *'d phone* him.	

Common mistakes:

We do not use *would* in the *if* part of the sentence:

wrong: **If* trains **would be** more reliable, more people **would use** them.
right: *If* trains **were** more reliable, more people **would use** them.

The *if* clause can come in the first part of the sentence, or the second:

*If I **had** his mobile number, I**'d phone** him.*
*I**'d phone** him if I **had** his mobile number.*

ⓑ Imaginary situations

We can use the second conditional to refer to an imaginary situation now or in the future.
1 *If Anna **was** here, she**'d know** what to do.*
    (But she is not here at the moment, so she cannot help).

2 *If I **lost** my job tomorrow, I**'d move** to London to find another one.*
    (I don't think I will lose my job, but I understand the possible consequences.)

In 1 we are talking about the present, and imagining a situation that is different from reality. In 2 we are talking about a possible event in the future; however, by using the second conditional we make it clear that we do not really think it will happen.

ⓒ Variations

It is also possible to use *might* and *could* instead of *would*:

*If we had the finance, we **could** expand much more rapidly.*
*If the terms of the contract were different, we **might** accept it.*

In the *if* clause, we can use *were* instead of *was* for the verb *to be*. This is very common when we give advice using the expression *If I were you ...*

*If I **were** you, I would call the technical support helpline.*

ⓓ First or second?

If we think that a future event is reasonably likely, we use the first conditional:

*If my investments **grow** at 6% a year, they **will be** worth £20,000 in ten years.*
(This is reasonably likely and realistic.)

If we are talking about something that is unlikely or impossible, we use the second conditional:

*If the stock market **grew** by 500% over the next two years, I**'d be able** to retire.*
(But this is extremely unlikely.)

Practice

EXERCISE ❶

Form

Change the verbs in brackets using *would* + infinitive or the past tense.

A: My session with the Human Resources department didn't go too well.

B: Really? Why not?

A: Well, firstly, they said there was almost no chance of promotion in this country. There is an opportunity in the Spanish office, but that's impossible. If I ¹ accepted (accept) the job in Madrid, I ² .... (not/spend) any time with the family.

B: Couldn't you all move there?

A: No, because if we all ³ .... (move) to Spain, the children ⁴ .... (need) to change schools, and we don't want them to do that. And if we all ⁵ .... (go), Laura ⁶ .... (have) to give up her job, and I can't ask her to do that.

B: Did they have any other ideas?

A: They said there were more opportunities in the IT department, but that's not a solution either. Even if I ⁷ .... (start) next week, I ⁸ .... (not/get) a senior position for at least three years, and that is too long. So I don't really know what I'm going to do.

EXERCISE ❷

Imaginary present situations

Rewrite the following sentences with *if* and the second conditional.

1 The reason we don't use them is that they are so expensive.
   But if they weren't so expensive, we'd use them.

2 The reason I can't contact them is that I haven't got their address.
   But ....

3 The reason I work so hard is that I enjoy my job.
   But ....

4 The reason we are the market leaders is that we spend so much on R&D.
   But ....

5 The reason I can't give you an answer is that I haven't got the authority.
   But ....

EXERCISE ❸

Variations

Complete the sentences with the correct form of verbs in the box.

change	be	think	speak	~~apply~~
be	earn	be	~~get~~	produce

1 I think I might get that job in Paris if I applied for it, but I'm not interested in it.

2 If I .... you, I'd .... very carefully before investing.

3 It's a pity you've refused to talk to him. He might .... his mind if you .... to him personally.

4 It's a pity the circulation of our magazine is so low. If it .... higher, we could .... a lot more from advertising.

5 If our labour costs .... lower, we could .... cheaper goods.

First or second conditional?

Read through the following sentences. Decide whether the events are likely or imaginary, and put the verbs in brackets into the right tense.

1 If everyone contributed (contribute) 20% of their salaries to charity, there would be (be) no poverty.
2 I am confident that we .... (meet) our targets if we .... (maintain) our current level of sales.
3 If I .... (be) in your position, I .... (insist) on having more staff in the department.
4 Please have a seat. If you .... (wait) a couple of minutes, I .... (give) you a lift.
5 I'm expecting a call from Grayson's. If they .... (ring) today, please .... (let) me know at once.
6 I .... (apply) for the job if I .... (have) an MBA, but unfortunately I haven't.
7 I .... (be) back at 8.30 if the traffic .... (not/be) too bad.
8 What laws .... (you/change) if you .... (be) the Prime Minister?

Questionnaire

Read the questionnaire and for each question write a number from 1–5 to show how often you would act in this way. (1=never, 2=rarely, 3=sometimes, 4=often, 5=always). Then turn to page 201 to work out what your score means.

What is your management style?

1 If my team had to make a decision, I would encourage everyone to participate and I would try to implement their ideas and suggestions. ☐

2 If I had to teach people new tasks and procedures, I would enjoy it. ☐

3 If I was in charge of an important project, I would closely monitor the schedule to make sure it was completed in time. ☐

4 If I was faced with a very challenging task, I would really enjoy it. ☐

5 If I found a good idea in a book on training, leadership, and psychology, I would try to put it into action. ☐

6 If I had to correct an employee's mistake, I wouldn't mind upsetting them. ☐

7 If I had to manage a complex task through to completion, I would supervise every detail. ☐

8 If I was in charge of a complex task or project, I would enjoy explaining the details to my employees. ☐

9 If I had to complete a complex project, I would naturally break it up into small manageable tasks. ☐

10 I would achieve my goals, even if it meant upsetting some people. ☐

11 If I was in charge of a project, I would concentrate on building a great team. ☐

12 I would enjoy analysing problems, if I was put in charge of a very complex project. ☐

13 It would be easy for me to give employees advice on how to improve their performance or behaviour. ☐

14 If I had to carry out several complicated tasks at the same time, it would be possible for me. ☐

My Goals

Production

Answer the following questions using the second conditional.

What would you do if …

1 … you invented a new product?

   If I invented a new product, I'd patent it immediately.

2 … you lost your job?

   ....

3 … you were offered a job in Saudi Arabia for five years?

   ....

4 … your company's main competitors offered you a good job?

   ....

5 … you lost all your money and credit cards?

   ....

Write down the advice you would give in the following situations. Begin each answer with *If I were you … .*

What would you say to …

1 … an 18 year old who wanted to join your company instead of taking up a place at a well-known university?

   If I were you I'd go to university, because you could join the company at a higher level later.

2 … a colleague who had not heard about the result of an interview?

   ....

3 … a friend who asked you what kind of car he should buy?

   ....

4 … someone who was looking for a job with your company?

   ....

5 … a visitor to your town who asked which restaurants were good?

   ....

Write a short paragraph about the changes you would make in the following situation.

If I were Prime Minister, I'd raise taxes and spend more money on education. I'd reduce bureaucracy and cut defence spending. I'd abolish the monarchy, and move into the palace, which I'd make my private home.

If I were CEO of the company I work for, …

....

....

....

22 Conditionals (4): *if you had gone ...*

Presentation

a Form

Read the following information about a past action and its result:

He went to the casino. He lost all of his money.

This is what actually happened. But we can imagine a different past action and a different result:

> *if + had (not) done   would (not) + have done*

*If he **had not gone** to the casino, he **would not have lost** all his money.*

This is the 3rd conditional. In speech, these forms are often abbreviated:

*A: What **would've happened** if he **hadn't gone** to the casino?*
*B: If he **hadn't gone** to the casino, he **wouldn't've lost** all his money.*

The *if* clause can come in the first part of the sentence (as above) or the second:

*He **wouldn't have lost** all his money if he **hadn't gone** to the casino.*

b Positives and negatives

When we use the 3rd conditional we are imagining a situation that is the opposite of what happened. If what actually happened was negative, we use a positive form. If what actually happened was positive, we use a negative form:

what happened: *We (neg) **didn't put up** our prices, so we (pos) **kept** our market share.*

3rd conditional: *If we (pos) **had put up** our prices, we (neg) **wouldn't have kept** our market share.*

Common mistakes:

We do not use *would* in the *if* clause:

wrong: * *If I **would have known** you were at the office I **would have called** in.*
right: *If I **had known** you were at the office I **would have called** in.*

c Variations

We can use *could* or *might* instead of *would*:

*If we **had followed** his advice, we **could have lost** a great deal of money.* (but we didn't)
*If we **had offered** large quantity discounts, we **might have won** the order.* (but we didn't)

d Mixed conditionals

The examples in **c** are about two actions in the past. However, if we talk about a past action and its result in the present we use *if* + past perfect and *would (not)* + infinitive:

past action: *He did well on the training course.*
present result: *He is head of department now.*
mixed conditional: *If he **hadn't done** well on the training course, he **wouldn't be** head of department now.* (not: **wouldn't have been*)

Practice

EXERCISE **1**

Form

Put the verbs in brackets into the correct form. Choose either the past perfect (*had done*) or *would* + perfect infinitive (*would have done*).

1 If we **had known** (know) that the company had such huge debts, we wouldn't have invested in it.
2 We would have won that contract if we .... (make) a better offer.
3 They .... (go) out of business years ago if they hadn't invested in new technology.
4 Would sales have been higher if the price .... (be) lower?
5 If we .... (wait) a few more months, we'd have saved a great deal of money on the IT system.
6 The company .... (move) earlier if it had found suitable premises.
7 .... you .... (accept) the new job if they'd offered it to you?
8 If the flight had been delayed, I .... (stay) at the airport hotel.

EXERCISE **2**

Positives and negatives

Read the extract from a sales report and complete the sentences opposite.

SMG ··· Plasma TV screen sales news···

Electronics sales of the SMG 42 plasma TV screen held up well in the first quarter of the year; this was because our main competitor's larger 50-inch screen was delayed due to technical problems. In the second quarter, we were expecting a rise in interest rates and a fall in demand, but interest rates remained unchanged. In the third quarter, the launch of the new digital channel led to more interest in HDTV and increased sales. In the last quarter, sales went up because of the launch of the larger SGM 50 model, which received some very favourable reviews. This was a great help and meant that we just managed to reach our overall sales target for the year.

| | Quarter 1 (Jan-Mar) | Quarter 2 (Apr-June) | Quarter 3 (July-Sep) | Quarter 4 (Oct-Dec) |

1 If our main competitor *had brought out* (bring out) its 50-inch screen in the first quarter, our sales *wouldn't have held up* (hold up).
2 If they .... (not/have) technical problems, their 50-inch screen .... (come out) sooner.
3 If there .... (be) a rise in interest rates in the second quarter, demand .... (fall).
4 If the new digital TV channel .... (not/start) we .... (not/see) a rise in demand in the third quarter.
5 If we .... (not/launch) the SGM 50, sales .... (go down) in the last quarter.
6 If we .... (not/receive) such favourable reviews, we .... (not/reach) our sales target for the year.

EXERCISE ❸

Common mistakes

Read through the sentences. Put a tick (✓) next to the ones that are right, and correct the ones that are wrong.

1 ~~If I would have had~~ the chance to study another foreign language, I would have learned Russian.

If I had had ...

2 We would have moved to a bigger hall if there were any more people for the presentation.

....

3 The company would have made bigger profits if they would have been able to cut down on salaries.

....

4 If they had dealt with the complaint more quickly, they wouldn't have received such bad publicity.

....

5 If there wouldn't have been so many mistakes in the advertisement, we wouldn't have had to redo it.

....

EXERCISE ❹

Might have, could have

Match the first part of the sentences in column A with the right ending in column B.

A	B
1 If we had had the right figures,	a he might have gone into insurance.
2 Could you have worked in Paris	b they could have prevented the strike.
3 We might have lost a great deal of money	c we could have avoided a costly error.
4 If they hadn't won that order,	d if you had wanted to?
5 If he hadn't gone into banking,	e if she had been more prepared.
6 If you had left earlier,	f they might have had to close the factory.
7 Her presentation could have been better	g if we hadn't taken our lawyer's advice.
8 If they had offered a 15% pay rise,	h you might have got there on time.

EXERCISE ❺

Mixed conditionals

Rewrite the sentences using mixed conditionals.

1 We didn't order the parts at the end of June. They aren't here now.
   If we had ordered the parts at the end of June, they would be here now.
2 We felt we could trust each other. Now we are partners.

   ....

3 He lost his driving licence. Now he has to take taxis everywhere.

   ....

4 You didn't go on the course. You don't know how to operate the new equipment.

   ....

5 I went to school in France. Now I am bilingual.

   ....

Production

TASK 1

Think back to the last time you went abroad on business. Write down what you would have done if the following things had happened.

What would you have done if ...

1 ... you had lost your passport while you were abroad?
If I had lost my passport, I'd have gone to the embassy to get a replacement.

2 ... someone had stolen your credit cards and money?

....

3 ... you had needed to contact the office urgently?

....

4 ... you had fallen seriously ill?

....

5 ... you had missed your return flight?

....

TASK 2

Read the passage about the collapse of the online sports clothing retailer boo.com. Say what the company should or shouldn't have done, and explain why.

1 (advertising) *The company shouldn't have spent so much on advertising. If they hadn't spent so much they wouldn't have run out of money so quickly.*

2 (employees) ....

....

3 (financial director) ....

....

4 (complicated website) ....

....

5 (prices) ....

....

CRASH! dotcom

Boo.com was one of Europe's biggest dotcom disasters, and looking back, it's not hard to see why it all went so wrong.

In May 1999, the company had about $120 million from investors and seemed to be one of the brightest stars of the 'new economy'. The founders spent $25 million on advertising, which meant that they ran out of funds very quickly. They took on hundreds of employees, leaving the company with a huge wage bill every month. They had no competent financial director and wasted millions more on jetting round the world, staying at expensive hotels and giving large parties. The website itself was far too complicated and this made it much too slow. They sold very few clothes because their prices were much too high. In May 2000, with a weekly income of $500,000, weekly expenses of $1,500,000, and no more money in the bank, it was clear that the game was up – and the company collapsed.

23 Modal verbs (1): suggestions, advice, obligation and criticism – *shall I?*, *should*, *ought to*

Presentation

ⓐ *Shall I, shall we*

We can use *shall* + bare infinitive to make offers and suggestions:

A: *I'm a bit worried about this report.*
B: ***Shall I have** a look at it?* (offer)

A: *There's quite a lot we need to discuss.*
B: *OK. **Shall we set up** a meeting?* (suggestion)

Note that we can only use ***Shall I ... ?*** and ***Shall we ... ?*** in this way.
We cannot say **Shall he ... ?*, **Shall you ... ?*, etc.

ⓑ Other ways of making suggestions

There are a number of other phrases we use in informal English for making suggestions:

A: *Where shall we go for lunch?*
B: ***Why don't we***   *go*
   How about   *going*   *to that new fish restaurant?*
   What about   *going*
   Let's   *go*   *to that new fish restaurant.*

In the past tense, when reporting suggestions, the verb *suggest* is often followed by a *that* clause + *should* or by an *-ing* form.

*I asked Jaime the best way of getting round town and he **suggested that I should** hire a car.*
(Jaime is not involved in hiring the car.)
*I asked Jaime about meeting up one evening, and he **suggested going** to the theatre.* (Jaime is probably included in the trip to the theatre.)

ⓒ Advice and obligation

We can use *should* and *ought to* + bare infinitive (e.g., *do*), to give advice or to express obligation relating to the present or the future (see also *must* and *have to*, Unit 25):

*You **should/ought to keep** an account of all your expenses.*
(This refers to the present.)
*When you go the conference next week, you **should/ought to give** Mr Franks a ring.*
(This refers to the future trip.)

The passive is formed with *should* + *be* + past participle:

*Form BD222 **should be returned** to this office within 30 days.*

ⓓ Criticism

We can make criticisms about past actions by using *should (not)* and *ought (not) to* with *have* + past participle (perfect infinitive):

*It was a mistake to get rid of those shares. You **shouldn't have sold** them.*
*It's too late to apply for shares now. You **ought to have applied** last week.*

The passive is formed with *should* + *have been* + past participle:

*This information **should have been given** to the tax authorities two years ago.*

Practice

EXERCISE ❶

Shall I, shall we …

Re-write the sentences beginning *Shall I …?* or *Shall we …?*

1 Do you want me to email you those figures?
   Shall I email you those figures?

2 Let's set up a meeting to discuss this.
   ....

3 Would you like me to call back later?
   ....

4 Do you want me to take the boxes down to the Post Room?
   ....

5 Let's cancel this evening and meet up some other time.
   ....

6 Let's stop now and carry on again tomorrow.
   ....

7 Where do you want me to put the new computer?
   ....

EXERCISE ❷

Other ways of making suggestions

Rewrite these suggestions.

1 Shall we have lunch at Le Manoir?
   Why *don't we have lunch at Le Manoir?*

2 Why don't we wait until the next financial year?
   How ....

3 Let's organize a leaving party for Bob Simpson.
   What ....

4 How about sharing a taxi to the station?
   Let's ....

5 Let's see if we can subcontract this work.
   Why ....

6 Why don't we offer them a bigger discount?
   How ....

EXERCISE ❸

Reporting suggestions

Report these suggestions using *suggested + -ing* or *suggested that + … should*.

1 He said he wanted to go out and *suggested seeing a movie together.*
2 He said the boss was out and ....
3 He said she seemed ideal for the job, but ....
4 He said there was no point taking two cars to the conference and ....
5 He said the interview wouldn't be easy and ....

1

I'd like to go out - shall we see a movie together?

2

The boss is out. Why don't you call back at 5.30?

3

She seems ideal for the job, but you ought to check her references first.

4

There's no point taking two cars to the conference - let's go together.

5

The interview won't be easy; if I were you, I'd do some background research into the company.

Mild obligation

Fill in the blanks with the verbs from the box in the active or passive.

Memo To All Staff: Security

Following a number of recent thefts in the building, please remember the following points:

Visitors ¹*should be met* at reception by a member of staff.
They ² .... at all times. You ³ ....
anyone who is acting suspiciously to a member of the security staff.

Valuables and equipment

You ⁴ .... large amounts of cash or jewellery to the office.
Handbags and wallets ⁵ .... unattended. Any large amounts
of company cash or travellers cheques ⁶ .... in the safe.

ought/accompany	ought/not/bring	should/deposit
should/not/leave	~~should/meet~~	should/report

Criticizing

A manager has attended a new trainee's first presentation. During the presentation she made the notes below. Write down what the manager said to the trainee at the meeting where they discussed what went wrong at his presentation. Say what he *should/shouldn't have done.*

1) did not greet the audience and introduce the subject
2) try to look more relaxed and confident
3) not speaking loudly enough
4) try to stand still!
5) try to make eye contact with the audience
6) remember to repeat the main points at the end
7) did not allow time for questions at the end

1 You should have greeted the audience and introduced the subject.
2 ....
3 ....
4 ....
5 ....
6 ....
7 ....

Production

TASK 1

Make suggestions referring to your own company. Use the expressions in the box.

I think we should …	I don't think we should …
We ought to …	Why don't we …
How about …	Let's …

1 Suggest a way of improving morale among the workforce.
   I think we should increase overtime rates.

2 Suggest a way of making working hours better for secretarial staff.

   ....

3 Suggest a way of reducing staff turnover.

   ....

4 Suggest a way of cutting costs.

   ....

5 Suggest a way of improving productivity in your company.

   ....

6 Suggest a way of increasing demand for your product or service.

   ....

7 Suggest a way of increasing incentives for managers.

   ....

TASK 2

Read through the sentences about things that have gone wrong. Make criticisms using *should/shouldn't have done*.

1 Elena lost all her savings when the company she had invested all her money in went bankrupt.
   She shouldn't have put all her money into a single company.

2 Our main competitor's last product was a total failure.

   ....

3 Peter has just lost an entire morning's work on his computer.

   ....

4 The government lost the election.

   ....

5 Our profits were down sharply last year.

   ....

6 Anna completely forgot to attend an important meeting.

   ....

24 Modal verbs (2): ability, possibility and permission – *can, could, may*

Presentation

ⓐ Ability and possibility

We use *can* to talk about both ability and possibility, and it refers to the present or the future. It is followed by the bare infinitive (active or passive):

I can write shorthand. (ability)
Your computer can be customized according to your needs. (possibility)

Can has no infinitive or present perfect form – we use *be able to*:

I'd like to be able to exchange these goods, but I don't have the authority. (not: *to can …)
I haven't been able to get through to the Greek office. (not: *haven't could …)

To refer to the future, we use *will be able to*:

With broadband access, people will be able to access the Internet more quickly.

ⓑ Past ability

The past tense of *can* is *could*. When we are talking about a general ability in the past or a verb of the senses (*see, hear, feel*, etc.) we use *could* + bare infinitive. However, when we are talking about one specific action, we normally use *was able to* or *managed to*:

After a few months on the training course, I could speak Japanese quite well. (general ability)
From my hotel room I could see the sea. (verb of the senses)
Janet phoned the airline and managed to get me on the flight. (tried and succeeded)
I found an Internet café so I was able to read my email. (on a particular occasion)

However, if the sentence is negative, it is possible to use *couldn't* to talk about either a general ability or a specific action:

Even after two months, I couldn't speak Japanese at all.
Unfortunately I couldn't see the sea from the room.
Janet phoned the airline, but she couldn't get me on the flight.
There were no Internet cafés so I couldn't read my email

ⓒ Past possibility

We use *could have done* or *could have been done* (passive) to talk about something in the past which was possible, but which did not happen:

There was a fire at the warehouse last night. We could have lost all our stock.
It was foolish to leave so much money in your office. It could have been stolen.

ⓓ Requesting action and permission

We use *can*, *could*, and *will/would* to ask people to do things. We use *can*, *could*, and *may* to ask for permission. *Can* and *will* are a little more direct than *could* or *would*:

Asking for permission		Requesting action	
Can I …		Will you …	
May I …	use your phone?	Would you …	give me a hand?
Could I …		Could you …	

Practice

EXERCISE ❶

General ability

Using your dictionary if necessary, explain what the words in *italics* in the advertisements mean.

Personal Assistant
MD of leading travel firm seeks *bilingual* PA (Spanish and English). Must be *computer-literate* and *pragmatic* and will be required to run the office single-handed from time to time.

Telephone sales opportunities
Leading UK insurance group seeks enthusiastic and *persuasive* tele-sales operators. Applicants need to be *flexible* as working hours will vary.

IT Consultants
Numerate graduates wanted to train as IT consultants for banking and accountancy firms. Applicants need to be capable of *logical* analysis and of taking firm *decisive* action.

1 If you are pragmatic, you can .... find practical solutions.
2 .... make firm decisions.
3 .... make others see your viewpoint.
4 .... adapt to changing circumstances.
5 .... deal with figures.
6 .... speak two languages.
7 .... use a computer.
8 .... think clearly.

EXERCISE ❷

Can or *be able to*?

Read the following sentences. Fill in the blanks with *can, can't, be able to* or *been able to*.

1 I'm afraid that I won't be able to make that meeting on Friday.
2 We have a wide range of products, so investors .... always choose a fund that suits them.
3 I'm good at reading English but I .... understand when people speak too fast.
4 I've been trying to ring Mr Ling all day but so far I haven't .... get through.
5 We're sending Anna on a CAD course because we'd like to .... produce more brochures and leaflets in-house.

EXERCISE ❸

Past ability

Complete the sentences using either *could* or *managed to*.

1 We had a very successful meeting, and managed to get a great discount.
2 The hotel was near the beach and I .... see the sea from my balcony.
3 Although the meeting finished early, we .... cover the main points.
4 The machine was no longer in production, but we eventually .... find a spare part from a supplier in Scotland.
5 She was brought up in Paris, so by the time she was five she .... speak French perfectly.
6 He was a brilliant salesman and .... sell anything to anyone.
7 Although I was at the back of the hall, I .... hear very clearly.
8 It was very difficult to find a suitable office, but in the end we .... rent one near the Central Station.

Past possibility

Match the first part of the sentences in column A with the right endings in column B.

A	B
1 Peter could have got a job in Korea,	a and that he could have explained things more clearly.
2 He was lucky the car had air bags or	b he was lucky they only fined him £500.
3 We could have met our sales targets	c because he could have lost a great deal of money.
4 I thought the presentation was confusing	d but they decided to accept the 2.5% pay offer.
5 The unions could have gone on strike	e but unfortunately one of our main customers cancelled a major order.
6 He could have stayed at the Hilton	f but the political situation stopped us from opening an office in the capital.
7 The results last year were very bad	g but he didn't want to live abroad.
8 He could have been sent to prison for drinking and driving, so	h but he decided to get a room at the Holiday Inn instead.
9 He was lucky he sold his shares when he did,	i he could have been killed in the crash.
10 We could have done a great deal of business there	j but they could have been worse.

Polite requests

In each of the following pairs of sentences, put a tick (✓) next to the one that is more polite.

1 a Give me a beer. ....
  b Could I have a beer? ✓
2 a Caller, I'm afraid the line's busy. Will you hold? ....
  b Caller, I'm afraid the line's busy. Hold, please. ....
3 a What do you want? ....
  b What can I do for you? ....
4 a What's your name? ....
  b May I ask who is calling? ....
5 a Could I borrow your pen? ....
  b Let me have your pen. ....
6 a I'm sorry, Mr Browning's busy. Can you come back later? ....
  b I'm sorry, Mr Browning's rather busy. Could you come back later? ....
7 a What did you say? ....
  b Could you repeat that? ....
8 a May I see some identification? ....
  b Who are you? ....

Give me a beer!

Production

Complete the sentences using *can, can't,* or a form of *(not) be able to.*

1 If we send the parcel by ordinary post, it'll take a week. But if you like, ...
   we can send it with DHL.

2 I've been trying to find a solution to the problem all week, but so far ...

3 He could easily get a job as an interpreter because ...

4 If business goes well this year, we will ...

5 If you have a credit card, ...

Complete the following sentences using *could* + perfect infinitive (*could have done).*

1 In the end I decided to turn down their offer of a job, but ...

2 The machine had an electrical fault and was dangerous. You're lucky you didn't touch it, because ...

3 She left the company a month before the top job became vacant. That was unfortunate for her, because ...

4 It's a pity we placed such a large order just before they cut their prices. We ...

You are on a long distance flight to New York. Write down what you would say in the following situations.

1 You are thirsty.

2 The passenger next to you has a copy of *Newsweek*. You would like to read it.

3 You want to go to the toilet, but the passenger next to you is in the way.

4 It's lunch-time. You are a vegetarian. The stewardess has just given you the chicken.

25 Modal verbs (3): obligation and necessity – *must, have to, needn't, can't*, etc.

Presentation

a Form

The modals below can be used to express obligation. They are followed by the bare infinitive:

Obligation	No obligation	Prohibition
must	*needn't*	*mustn't*
have to	*don't have to*	*can't*
have got to	*haven't got to*	*not (be) allowed to*

b Expressing obligation, etc.

We use *must*, *have to*, and *have got to* to say that something is obligatory:

*Application forms **must** be returned by April 11th.*
*I'm afraid I'll be late tonight – **I've got to**/ I **have to** fetch Mr Shiwara from the airport.*

We use *needn't*, *don't have to*, and *haven't got to* if something isn't necessary:

*You **needn't** come in tomorrow – I can deal with the clients myself.*
*If your income is very small you **don't have to** pay tax.*

We use *mustn't*, *can't*, and *not allowed to* to say that something is forbidden:

*Passengers **mustn't** leave their bags unattended at any time.*
*I'm sorry, but you **can't/aren't allowed to** smoke in here.*

c Talking about obligations

Have (got) to, don't have to, can't, not (be) allowed to are more common when talking about obligations and prohibitions. *Must, needn't, mustn't* are more common when giving an order:

Boss to employee: *You **must** get that report to me by 5.30 at the latest. It's urgent.*
Employee to colleague: *I can't come to the meeting – **I've got to** finish that report.*

Must, *need not*, and *must not* are also more common in written language.

d Past obligation

When talking about the past, we use *had to*, *didn't have to*, and *couldn't/wasn't allowed to*:

*During my military service, we **had to** be up by 5.30. We **had to** obey orders and we **weren't allowed to** go out in the evenings. The good thing was that we **didn't have to** cook for ourselves.*

e *Didn't need to vs needn't have*

There is a difference in meaning between *didn't need to do something* (it wasn't necessary, so you didn't do it), and *needn't have done something* (you did it, but it wasn't necessary).

*Because he was from the EU, he **didn't need to** get a visa to visit Britain.*
(It wasn't necessary so he didn't get one.)

*We **needn't have rushed** to the airport as the plane was late.*
(We rushed, but this was not necessary.)

Practice

EXERCISE ❶

Form

Choose the correct word or phrase in *italics* to complete each sentence.

1 You <u>*must*</u>/*needn't* save a file before you turn the computer off, or you will lose it.
2 I'm afraid this is a non-smoking office, so you *haven't got to*/*can't* smoke in here.
3 Employees are reminded that they *mustn't*/*needn't* use the office phone to make personal calls.
4 You *needn't*/*mustn't* send that reminder to Eastwood's – they paid the invoice this morning.
5 You *don't have to*/*can't* buy or sell alcohol in Iran, Saudi Arabia, and several other countries.
6 This income tax form *must*/*needn't* be completed and returned to the Inland Revenue within 30 days.
7 You *mustn't*/*don't have to* come to the meeting if you have more important things to do.
8 This information is highly confidential, so you *mustn't*/*needn't* discuss it with anyone.
9 As you are from the EU, you *mustn't*/*don't have to* have a visa to go to France.
10 Drivers wishing to hire a car *must*/*aren't allowed to* be over 21 and have a full driving licence.

EXERCISE ❷

Talking about obligation

Read what these people say about their jobs. Fill in the blanks with *have to*, *don't have to*, or *can't*.

A

Being a pilot
is a great job in lots of ways – for a start, you
¹ don't have to work 9.00 to 5.00 in an office – but I don't think I ever wanted a job like that. As a pilot you ² .... be responsible, because a lot of people depend on you. Health is important – we have regular medicals and eye tests, because as a pilot you ³ .... be 100% fit and alert. You ⁴ .... spend weeks in the gym or anything else like that, but before any long flight you ⁵ .... make sure you get plenty of rest, and of course you ⁶ .... drink any alcohol. When you're flying, you ⁷ .... be able to concentrate really hard for long periods – this is one job where you simply ⁸ .... make mistakes.

B

Being a police officer
can mean very different things, depending on what area of the city you work in. In the suburbs, it's pretty quiet – from time to time you ¹ .... deal with car thefts or break-ins, but on the whole, it's very safe and you ² .... worry about getting attacked. But there are some areas where it's very dangerous – lots of drug crime, armed gangs – and that can be a problem for us because we ³ .... use weapons – all we have is a truncheon*. So if we ⁴ .... go and deal with a crime in an area like that, we ⁵ .... go alone because it's too dangerous. We always ⁶ .... take a partner or go in larger groups, and we ⁷ .... stay in radio contact all the time in case anything goes wrong.

*truncheon = a short, heavy stick

Telling people what to do

Write sentences using the words in brackets with *must*, *needn't*, or *mustn't*.

1 James needs these documents urgently. (fax them to him immediately)
   You must fax them to him immediately.

2 Good, we all seem to agree. (discuss the matter any further)
   ....

3 We've still got plenty of stock. (order any more yet)
   ....

4 Our health care products are selling really well. (make sure we keep our market share)
   ....

5 The CEO's been trying to get hold of you all morning. (call her right now)
   ....

6 I've got a very important meeting this afternoon. (be late)
   ....

Past obligation

Shelley Gould writes features for a leading women's magazine. Read what she says about the changes in the magazine industry that she has seen. Fill in the blanks with *had to*, *didn't have to*, or *couldn't*.

When I first started writing features for the magazine – not so very long ago – we didn't have the kind of technology everyone uses today. We ¹ **had to** type everything out on electric typewriters – or even manual ones and you ² .... work carefully because you ³ .... erase mistakes so easily – I remember I ⁴ .... use a small pot of white paint called Tippex to make corrections. Horrible stuff. In some ways, though, it was simpler because you ⁵ .... worry about computers crashing, and you ⁶ .... think too much about the layout because that was the job of the design department. The whole process was much slower – we ⁷ .... finish our features at least two weeks in advance, and we ⁸ .... just hand them over the day before like we do now. And of course there was no Internet – we ⁹ .... get any information at all just sitting in the office – if we wanted to find things out, we ¹⁰ .... go out and do the research ourselves.

Didn't need to vs *needn't have*

Fill in the blanks with *didn't need to* or *needn't have* and put the verb in brackets into the correct form.

1 We were worried we might have to cut the workforce, but we got some large orders, so we .... (make) anyone redundant.

2 We sent the manager of our Istanbul branch some important documents by air courier, but we .... (spend) so much money because he was away on holiday at the time.

3 An interpreter came with us to a meeting with some Japanese clients, but we .... (hire) her because they all spoke excellent English.

4 The negotiation in Hamburg went very well, so we .... (spend) the whole week there and we came back a day early.

Production

Write down what the following people might say in these situations using *must*, *needn't*, or *mustn't*.

1 A supervisor in a supermarket hears a check-out operator being rude to a customer. *You mustn't talk to customers like that.*

2 A clerk in a store is explaining to a customer that refunds cannot be given without a receipt.

....

3 A pension salesman is explaining that there is no obligation to pay contributions every month.

....

4 You have just heard a colleague give a terrible presentation. Give him some advice.

....

5 You notice that a colleague uses the 'save' facility on his computer every ten minutes. You know that the computer has an 'auto-save' facility.

....

6 You overhear a temporary secretary discussing travel insurance with a travel agent. Your company has a policy that covers all the employees.

....

Make notes in the columns about your current job. Then write a short paragraph about yourself using *have to*, *don't have to*, and *can't*. See the example.

obligation	no obligation	prohibition
discuss loans with clients	financial analysis	no loans over #500,000

I work as a lending officer for an American bank, and I have to discuss loans with clients and decide whether or not to authorize them. I don't have to do the financial analysis of the companies in question because we have a specialized team of analysts for that job. I can authorize loans of up to #500,000, but I can't authorize anything greater than that myself.

obligation	no obligation	prohibition

26 Modal verbs (4): speculation – *may*, *might*, *must*, *can't*

Presentation

ⓐ Speculating about the future

We can use *may*, *might*, and *could*, followed by the bare infinitive (active or passive) to speculate about the future:

*Analysts say that interest rates **may rise** before the end of the year.*
(perhaps they will rise)
*One commentator has said that the first rate rise **might come** next month.*
(perhaps it will come)
*A significant increase **could have** a dramatic effect upon business confidence.*
(perhaps it will affect it)

There is no significant difference in meaning between *may*, *might*, and *could* in this context.

(See Unit 15 for other ways of speculating about the future.)

ⓑ Speculating about the present

We use *must*, *may*, *might*, and *can't* to speculate about the present:

Shona hasn't come into the office – I'm sure that means she is ill.
*Shona hasn't come into the office – she **must be** ill.*

I'm afraid I haven't seen the file – but perhaps Khalid knows where it is.
*I'm afraid I haven't seen the file – but Khalid **may/might know** where it is.*

The bill for the meal comes to $250,000. I'm sure it isn't right.
*The bill for the meal comes to $250,000. It **can't be** right.*

If we want to talk about something happening at the moment of speaking we use a continuous form (*be doing*):

The traffic is terrible again today – I'm sure they are repairing the road again.
*The traffic is terrible today – they **must be repairing** the road again.*

ⓒ Speculating about the past

We use *may/might*, *must*, *can't/couldn't* followed by *have done, have been done*, or *have been doing* to speculate about the past:

He sold his shares at their peak, so I'm sure he made a lot of money.
*He sold his shares at their peak, so he **must have made** a lot of money.*

Mr Janssen wasn't at the meeting – perhaps he was delayed at the airport.
*Mr Janssen wasn't at the meeting – he **may/might have been delayed** at the airport.*

Herr Brasseler is on holiday in Bali – I'm sure you didn't see him this morning.
*Herr Brasseler is on holiday in Bali – you **can't/couldn't have seen** him this morning.*

There is also a continuous form (*have been doing*):

The alarm went off, I'm sure someone was trying to break in.
*The alarm went off, so someone **must have been trying** to break in.*

Practice

EXERCISE 1

Speculating about the future

Complete the newspaper article with the words in the box.

Hunt for killer bug

Scientists are planning to examine the body of a young woman who died almost 100 years ago.

They believe that the body of Phyllis Burn [1] *might harbour* the deadly virus which killed over 50 million people in the great influenza epidemic of 1918.

Experts know that the influenza virus – which can take many forms –

[2] .... again at any time; while most forms of the virus are fairly harmless, they fear that a form similar to the one in 1918 [3] .... millions of people. If they can study the 1918 virus, they [4] .... develop a vaccine against this dangerous strain. Such a vaccine [5] .... any future outbreaks of the disease, and [6] .... enormous

commercial value as well.

Some people have expressed fears about disturbing the body, pointing out that the virus [7] .... in the event of an accident. Even after 100 years, it [8] .... lethal and [9] .... a new outbreak.

~~might harbour~~	may strike	might kill
could have	might start	could escape
may be able to	could still be	could prevent

EXERCISE 2

Speculating about the present (problem-solving)

In the Despatch Department of a mail order firm selling office supplies there are three packages, but the address labels are not complete. The packages are for three different customers, Mr Green, Mr Brown, and Mr White. The packages contain paper, a personal photocopier, and a computer. The packages weigh 18kg, 20kg, and 22kg.

package:	A	B	C
name:	Mr Green		
contents:		computer	paper
weight:			18 kg

A Complete the sentences using *must, might,* or *can't.*

1 Package B .... be for Mr Brown or it .... be for Mr White. Package C .... be for Mr Green, because we know A is for him.

2 Package A .... contain the photocopier, because the computer is in B and the paper is in C.

3 Mr Brown's package .... be heavier than C, but it .... not be as heavy as A.

B Fill in the missing details in the table using the following piece of information:

Mr Green's package is not as heavy as Mr Brown's.

Speculating about the past

Write sentences using the words in brackets.

1 They say they definitely sent the shipment, but it never arrived.
  (They/must/send it/wrong address)
  They must have sent it to the wrong address.

2 You receive a memo saying that a company's phone number has changed.
  (They/must/move/new premises)

  ....

3 You have come for a 10 o'clock meeting. It is now 10.15 and no-one else is there.
  (The meeting/must/be cancelled)

  ....

4 It is 12.20. You ring a colleague but there is no reply. (He/might/go to lunch)

  ....

5 She was engaged when I rang her but I don't know who she was talking to.
  (She/might/be phoning/Sales Department)

  ....

6 The equipment was repaired last week, but it has gone wrong again.
  (It/can't/repair/properly)

  ....

Review

Rewrite each of the following sentences using *might, can't, must*, and a suitable infinitive.

1 It's possible that they will give us the discount we want.
  They *might give us the discount we want.*

2 Judging by the phone bill, I am sure she has been making long international calls.
  Judging by the phone bill, she ....

3 The factory is on a three-day week. I'm sure they aren't selling many cars.
  The factory is on a three-day week. They ....

4 It was a very bad deal. I am sure they lost a lot of money.
  It was a very bad deal. They ....

5 There's a chance he will be promoted at the end of the year.
  He ....

6 She seemed very surprised to see me, so I am sure she wasn't expecting me.
  She seemed very surprised to see me. She ....

7 He went home at 4.30, so I am sure he hasn't heard the announcement.
  He went home at 4.30, so he ....

Production

TASK 1

Speculate about possible future events based on the following information. Using *may*, *might* or *could* say what you think will happen.

1 The political situation in the Middle East is very unstable.
   The price of oil might rise.

2 The Christian Democrats are doing very well in the opinion polls.

   ....

3 The new Apple Mac laptop has had excellent reviews.

   ....

4 The government is spending much more than it is earning in taxes.

   ....

5 There have been a number of delays in the project.

   ....

TASK 2

Read the information below. Using *might*, *must*, *can't*, and a bare infinitive or *be doing*, comment on the present situations.

1 I've phoned Janine three times this morning but there is no reply.
   She must be out seeing a client.

2 Everyone in R&D is working very long hours at the moment.

   ....

3 I've got a new Rolex watch. I bought it in a market for £5.

   ....

4 Mustapha wasn't feeling well yesterday and he's not in the office today.

   ....

5 I haven't got Henry's phone number, but I know that Ann has it.

   ....

TASK 3

Read the text about the Millennium Dome in London. Using the information in the text and your own ideas, speculate about what went wrong. Use *must have*, *might (not) have*, *can't have*.

1 *It might have been built in an unsuitable location.*

2 ....

3 ....

4 ....

5 ....

6 ....

In 2000, the Millennium Dome, which was meant to be a great tourist attraction for London, was opened for one year. However, the expected numbers of visitors did not come. The organizers were constantly running out of money, and it finally closed at the end of December 2000 after making huge losses.

27 *-ing* and infinitive (1): verbs + *-ing* or infinitive

Presentation

Some verbs are followed by the *-ing* form (*I enjoy going abroad*). Others are followed by *to* + infinitive (e.g., *I want to finish this report*). There is no particular reason why some verbs take one form and some verbs take the other.

ⓐ Verbs followed by the *-ing* form

The following verbs are usually followed by the *-ing* form:

avoid	consider	enjoy	like (= enjoy)	postpone
can't help	delay	finish	look forward to*	put off
can't stand	deny	involve	mind	risk
carry on	dislike	justify	miss	suggest

*When she **finished speaking**, she asked if anyone had any questions.*
*I **look forward to seeing** you on Tuesday.*

* The word *to* in *look forward to* is a preposition. Prepositions (e.g., *in, on, at, with, from,* etc.) are followed by the *-ing* form rather than the infinitive. (For more details see Unit 29.)

ⓑ Expressions + *-ing*

The expressions below are followed by the *-ing* form:

It's a waste of time/money …   *It's no use* …
There's no point (in) …   *It's (not) worth* …

*It's **not worth arguing** with her. She never listens.*

ⓒ Verbs followed by *to* + infinitive

The following verbs are usually followed by *to* + infinitive (e.g. *to do*):

afford	demand	hope	prepare	tend
agree	deserve	learn	pretend	threaten
arrange	expect	manage	promise	train
attempt	fail	neglect	refuse	want
claim	guarantee	offer	seem	would like
decide	hesitate	plan		

*They are **threatening to take** legal action if we don't pay them this week.*

ⓓ Passive forms

The passive of the *-ing* form is made with **being** + past participle (e.g. *being done*):
*She dislikes **being told** how to run her department.*
The passive infinitive is formed by **to be** + past participle (e.g. *to be done*):
*He expects **to be promoted** soon.*

Practice

EXERCISE ❶

Verbs + -ing form

Read the email. Complete the sentences using the verbs in the box in the -ing form.

do	get	give	go	hear
set	~~take~~	write	use	

To: Michael

Subject: Web-based publishing project

Dear Michael

I'm just writing to ask if you would be interested in [1] taking part in a new web-based publishing project that we are planning.

It's probably not worth [2] going .... into all the details at the moment, so I'll give you a quick overview. The basic proposal involves [3] .... up a website to give business students a web-based learning programme. We are considering [4] .... all sorts of different types of media – text, audio, and video, because we know that learners generally enjoy [5] .... a variety of different tasks. Our IT specialists have just finished [6] .... the special programs that we will need, so we're almost ready to start. Luis suggested [7] .... in touch with you to see if you'd be interested, and I thought that you'd be great for the project too. Would you mind [8] .... me a ring some time in the week? Or just send me an email if that's easier.

I look forward to [9] .... from you.

Best wishes

Christina

EXERCISE ❷

Verbs + infinitive

Read the reply to the email above. Complete the sentences, using the verbs in the box in the infinitive form.

be	change	do	finish	go
~~hear~~	meet	take	teach	

To: Christina

Subject: Web-based publishing project

Dear Christina

Many thanks for your message – it was great to hear from you and I'd like very much [1] to hear more about the new project and what you are planning [2] ....

First of all let me fill you in with details of my schedule. I've agreed [3] .... some students on a short English course at the Lake Enterprise Training Centre – I'm starting next Monday, but it's only a short course and I expect [4] .... on the 25th. I was planning [5] .... on holiday the following week, but I can easily arrange [6] .... a break some other time.

How about meeting up on Monday 28th, say at 9.30 or maybe 10 o'clock as the traffic tends [7] .... a bit better later on? If you can't manage [8] .... me that Monday and want [9] .... it to some other day, just let me know.

All the best

Michael

Review: *-ing* form or infinitive?

Complete the following letter. Put the verbs in brackets into either the *-ing* form or the infinitive with *to*.

Vinos Velasquez
Calle
Obregón 15
28020 Madrid

A. Sandbach
Top Up Wines
High Wycombe
Bucks.
UK

Dear Mr Sandbach

Thank you for your letter of 12 June in which you stated that, following the visit of your chief buyer Mr Lindfield, you are considering ¹ placing (place) an order for our Sauvignon Blanc table wine.

We can arrange ² to _____ (supply) you with an initial order of 1,000 cases, and I enclose our current trade price list, which I believe you will find very competitive. If you decide ³ _____ (go) ahead with the order, we will agree ⁴ _____ (give) you the 14% discount you mentioned and details are enclosed. Please note that we guarantee ⁵ _____ (deliver) firm orders within four weeks.

You mentioned also that you wanted ⁶ _____ (market) the wine under your own brand name, which will involve ⁷ _____ (change) the labels. I would suggest ⁸ _____ (get) the labels printed here because it is probably not worth ⁹ _____ (have) them printed in the UK and then ¹⁰ _____ (send) them here. I have contacted our personal printer for a quotation and I hope ¹¹ _____ (be able to) send you a firm price shortly.

Please do not hesitate ¹² _____ (contact) me if you have any further queries. I look forward ¹³ _____ (hear) from you soon.

Yours sincerely

A. Velasquez

Alfonso Velasquez
Managing Director

Complete the sentences with the verbs in brackets, using the passive *-ing* form or the passive infinitive.

1 Our profits are up this year, so I expect to be given (give) a pay rise.
2 You'd better come back later. Mr Schmidt dislikes being interrupted (interrupt) when he's in a meeting.
3 You deserve _____ (pay) more because you do a lot of overtime.
4 When I am giving a presentation, I don't mind _____ (ask) questions.
5 Most of our sales team in Spain tend _____ (recruit) locally.
6 The company avoided _____ (take over) by splitting up into several different groups.
7 She hopes _____ (send) to our Paris office when it opens next year.
8 He took the telephone off the hook because he didn't want _____ (disturb).

Production

TASK 1

As part of their work, people often have to do the following things:

travel to work in the rush hour   take work home   attend meetings
deal with difficult customers   stay late   travel abroad
speak English on the phone   ask for more money   take clients out

A **Choose four of these things and say how much you like or dislike them using the verbs in the box.**

really enjoy	like	don't mind	dislike	can't stand

1   I don't mind staying late.
2   ....
3   ....
4   ....

B **Now say what other things you like and dislike doing at work.**

1   ....
2   ....
3   ....
4   ....

TASK 2

Continue the sentences using the verbs in brackets together with a verb in the infinitive.

1   We were very unhappy with the service they had provided, so …
   (refuse) we refused to pay them.

2   The company is taking on a lot of new staff and …
   (plan) ....

3   He was angry about the way the company had treated him and even …
   (threaten) ....

4   Maria was getting tired of her job so …
   (decide) ....

TASK 3

Complete these sentences about yourself, using an *-ing* form or infinitive.

1   I enjoy my work, but I wouldn't mind having a bit more responsibility.
2   When I was 16, I decided ....
3   If I moved to another town, I would miss ....
4   At the moment I can't afford ....
5   I am really looking forward to ....
6   In a few years time, I hope ....
7   At the moment I'm considering ....

28 -*ing* and infinitive (2): verbs and objects

Presentation

a Verb + object + infinitive

There are a number of verbs that can take a direct object and *to* + infinitive. Common examples are:

advise	*allow*	*ask*	*enable*	*encourage*	*force*
invite	*order*	*persuade*	*remind*	*tell*	*warn*

*I have **told him to ring** back later.*
*The company **persuaded the Venture Capitalists to provide** additional investment.*

b Reporting what people say

Many of these verbs can be used to report what other people say (see also Units 31–32):

'Could you ring me on Monday?' she asked me.
*She **asked me to ring** on Monday.*

The verb *warn* is usually used with *not to do*:

He said, 'Don't leave the car unlocked'.
*He **warned me not to leave** the car unlocked.*

c *Make* and *let*

The verbs *make* and *let* are followed by an object and the bare infinitive (e.g. *go, work*):

We use *make* to talk about something we have to do (but don't want to do):

*The World Bank **made the government cut** benefits as a condition of the loan.*

We use *let* when we talk about being given permission for something:

*Some employers will **let their staff watch** the World Cup during working hours.*

The verb *help* can be followed by an infinitive with or without *to*:

*He says he will **help me (to) get** a recording contract.*

d Verbs of perception

The verbs *see, watch, notice, hear, listen to* and *feel* (called 'verbs of perception' or 'verbs of the senses') are followed by a bare infinitive or by an *-ing* form (present participle). If we want to say that we heard or saw the whole action from beginning to end, we usually use the bare infinitive:

*I **saw him walk** out of the room.*
(He walked out of the room. I saw him.)

If we want to say that we only saw or heard part of the action, we use the *-ing* form (present participle):

*I **saw you walking** in Hyde Park this morning.*
(I saw you this morning. You were walking in Hyde Park but I didn't watch you all the time you were there.)

Practice

EXERCISE **1**

Verb + object +infinitive

The words in the following sentences are in the wrong order. Rewrite them in the correct order.

1 The law allows on to open supermarkets Sundays.
   The law allows supermarkets to open on Sundays.
2 They finance bank persuaded project the the to.

3 The court pay company compensation ordered the to.

4 The fall cut demand forced in us production to.

5 They at conference have invited me speak the to.

EXERCISE **2**

Reporting what people say

Rewrite the sentences using the verbs in brackets + object + *to* + infinitive.

1 'Don't forget to post that letter!'
2 'Go on, apply for the job.'
3 'If I were you, I'd make a formal complaint.'
4 'Would you finish the report as soon as possible, please?'
5 'You can leave early if you like.'
6 'Don't rush into a decision.'

1 (remind) *He reminded me to post the letter.*
2 (encourage)
3 (advise)
4 (ask)
5 (allow)
6 (warn)

EXERCISE **3**

Make* and *let

Rewrite the sentences beginning with *They made us ...* or *They let us ...*

1 We had to work extremely hard on the training course.
   They made us work extremely hard on the training course.
2 We were allowed to go out at the weekends.

3 We had to give a presentation every morning.

4 We had to speak English all the time.

5 There was a TV we could watch.

Review: verb + object + infinitive and *make/let*

Read the article below. Fill in the blanks, using the words in the box, and making any changes that are necessary.

ask / put	enable / increase	force / breathe in
encourage / bring in	invite / talk	let / smoke
not make / have	~~not allow / smoke~~	persuade / ban

No smoke without fire
• • • • • • • • • • • • • • •

An old fashioned pub in the quiet town of Shrewsbury is at the front of a controversial new revolution that is threatening to spread across the country. Of the 60,000 pubs in the country, the Three Fishes is one of only four that ¹ do not allow the customers to smoke.

The landlady, Avril Wardrop, is all in favour of the idea. The tourists love it, and even regulars like the fact that the landlady ² .... them .... a drink or meal in a smoke-filled room. What is more, it is good for business – the ban on smoking has ³ .... her .... turnover by 30% in the past two years.

The changes at the Three Fishes would be welcomed by Stanton Glantz, Professor of Medicine at the University of California. He is the tobacco companies' public

enemy number one because he has ⁴ .... California and other US states .... smoking in all bars and restaurants.

Glantz is in Britain because the Department of Health has ⁵ .... him .... to ministers and officials about the dangers of passive smoking. He is shocked by the levels of passive smoking that he can see around him, and feels that non-smokers should do more to ⁶ .... the government to .... stricter laws. 'I feel like I'm in a time warp here – it's like we were in California in 1985.' Many offices may now be no-smoking zones but apart from that, people have no legal protection from passive smoking. According to the law, taxi drivers cannot ⁷ .... their passengers .... out their cigarettes, and the law actually ⁸ .... childminders .... in the presence of children if they have the parents' permission. Even hospitals are not required to be smoke free.

Glantz believes passionately in free choice for smokers and non-smokers. 'Smokers have a right to smoke. It's stupid, but I'm fat and that's stupid.' Everyone is allowed to be stupid, but smokers do not have the right ⁹ .... other people .... their smoke. It's as simple as that.

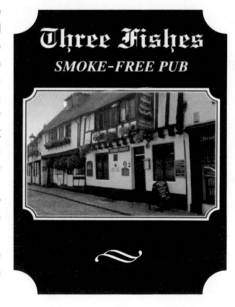

Three Fishes
SMOKE-FREE PUB

Verbs of perception

Rewrite these sentences starting with the verb in brackets.

1 He was talking to someone on the phone. I heard him. (hear)
   I heard him talking to someone on the phone.

2 Something was burning. I could smell it. (smell)
   ....

3 She left. I didn't see her. (see)
   ....

4 He gave a talk on 'Quality Control'. I heard it all. (hear)
   ....

5 Some robots were assembling cars. The visitors watched them. (watch)
   ....

Production

TASK 1

Complete these sentences using (*not*) *to* + infinitive.

1 We made record profits last year, and this will enable us …

....

2 My parents encouraged me …

....

3 The government should train more young people …

....

4 The conference organizers have invited me …

....

5 Before I went to New York, a colleague warned me …

....

TASK 2

Write a short paragraph using *make* and *let*. See the example.

Someone is being sent to Japan for an intensive training course. A friend has already been on this course, and is telling him what it will be like.

'They'll probably make you work fairly hard, but I expect they'll let you have the weekends free. They'll make you learn a little Japanese, of course, but it's not very difficult. And you'd better learn some songs too because they'll definitely take you out to a Karaoke bar and make you sing!'

A colleague of yours is going to a health spa for a week. You went there last year. Tell him or her what life there will be like.

....

....

....

....

TASK 3

Say what advice you would give in these situations.

1 Your accountants have made a number of mistakes, and you have to pay the tax authorities a large fine.

I would ask them ....

and I would tell ....

2 The 16-year-old daughter of a friend comes to you to ask for advice about what career she should take up.

I would encourage her ....

and I would advise ....

29 -*ing* and infinitive (3): changes in meaning

Presentation

a Verb + -*ing* or infinitive?

Some verbs can be followed by either the -*ing* form or the infinitive, and the meaning of the verb changes. Here are some common examples:

*I **remember booking** the tickets.*
(I booked them and I can remember where I was at the time.)
*I **remembered to book** the tickets.*
(I remembered that I needed to book the tickets, and then I booked them.)

*I **will never forget meeting** Nelson Mandela.*
(I met him, and he impressed me.)
*I **won't forget to pick you up** from work.*
(I have made a note of it, and I will definitely come and collect you).

*We **have stopped using** Spencers as our accountants.*
(We used to deal with them, but we don't deal with them any more.)
*At 12.00 we **stopped to have a break**.*
(We stopped driving down the motorway in order to have a break.)

*I **regret saying** that I was not interested in the job.*
(I said I was not interested in the work and I now think that was a bad mistake.)
*I **regret to say** that you have not got the job.*
(I'm sorry to say this, but we have given the job to someone else).

*If the computer crashes, **try turning everything off** and starting again.*
(Do this and see what happens.)
*This year we **are trying to increase** our turnover by 20%.*
(We are making an effort to do this.)

*Our website **needs redesigning**.*
(The website needs to be redesigned – passive meaning)
*We **need to attract** more visitors.*
(It is necessary to do this.)

b *Like* and *would like*

Like (enjoy), is followed by the -*ing* form. *Would ('d) like* (want to), is followed by the infinitive:

*I **like meeting** new people.* (I enjoy this.)
*I**'d like to live** in a big city.* (It sounds like a nice idea.)

We can also use *prefer* and *would prefer* in the same way:

*I **prefer travelling** by train to driving.* (I enjoy this more.)
*'Shall I get you a sandwich or **would you prefer to have** a salad?* (What do you want?)

c *To* + -*ing* or infinitive?

The word *to* can be part of the infinitive (*I want to see you*). However, in the following examples, *to* is a preposition, so it is followed by the -*ing* form:

look forward to	*respond to*	*object to*	*to be/get used to*
in addition to	*a response to*	*be accustomed to*	*a reaction to*

Practice

-ing or infinitive?

Match the beginning of the sentences in column A with the right endings in column B.

A

1 I'm sure we've paid that invoice. I remember
2 Did you remember
3 I've given my PA a list of jobs that need
4 There are plenty of hotel rooms available, so you don't need
5 He lost several hours' work. He switched off the computer but he had forgotten
6 I don't mind giving talks now, but I'll never forget
7 He wasn't at the office when I phoned, so I think I'll try
8 For a long time, the company tried

B

a to save the file.
b ringing him on his home number. He might be there.
c to give Peter my message?
d to book one in advance.
e signing the cheque and sending it to them.
f giving my first presentation. It was a disaster.
g to enter the Japanese market, but it was extremely difficult.
h doing before the sales conference starts.

Verb + -ing or infinitive?

Fill in the blanks with the verbs in brackets, using the -ing form or to + infinitive.

1 There's nothing wrong with the photocopier. It just needs servicing. (service)
2 We need .... (look) at this proposal very carefully before we make a decision.
3 I'll make a note in my diary so that I will remember .... (send) you the information you need.
4 I'm not sure if I have met Mr Martino, but I remember .... (hear) his name.
5 I will never forget .... (walk) into the office on my first day at work.
6 Could you take this file to Mrs Armstrong? I meant to let her have it this morning, but I forgot .... (give) it to her.
7 He found it very difficult to get work because he was unemployed, and soon regretted .... (resign) from his previous job.
8 We have appointed another candidate to the post, so I regret .... (say) that we will not be able to offer you the job.
9 As a company, we always try .... (provide) our customers with the best service possible.

Like and would like

Put the verbs in brackets into the -ing form or the infinitive.

1 Our Director is very sociable. He likes going (go) out and meeting (meet) new people.
2 Ken is busy tomorrow, so we'd like .... (arrange) the meeting for Monday.
3 I prefer .... (work) at home to .... (commute) to the office.
4 I'd like .... (have) a word with you about next week's meeting.
5 I like .... (work) with my new boss because he encourages me.
6 Could you let me know when you would like me .... (come) and see you?

EXERCISE 4

To + -ing or infinitive?

Read the following article about the use of the metric system. Put the verbs in brackets into the *-ing* form or the infinitive.

An expensive bunch of bananas

On 1 January 2001, an EU directive ordering shops to sell goods in grams and kilograms instead of pounds and ounces* came into force in the United Kingdom.

It was not long before traders began to object to
1 **implementing** (implement) the new regulations. In many places, shops continued to
2 .... (sell) goods in pounds and ounces. Trading Standards Officers were not amused, and their response to 3 .... (see) the law being deliberately disobeyed was to take action.

In a Sunderland market, a fruit seller called Steve Thoburn carried on selling fruit in pounds and ounces because his customers were not used to
4 .... (deal) in kilos and grams. Undercover officers decided to 5 ....
(move) in, were offered a pound of bananas, and Thoburn was quickly arrested.

The newspapers' reaction to
6 .... (hear) of the arrest of Mr Thoburn was to turn him overnight into a national celebrity. In addition to 7 .... (write) articles in praise of the 'metric martyr', they agreed to
8 .... (offer) him financial support. In the end, however, Mr Thoburn was found guilty. He failed to
9 .... (win) his appeal, and faced huge costs.

A government spokesman said he was pleased that the law was now clear, and spoke up in support of the change. He feels that the metric system is much

simpler. In his view, people will soon get used to 10 ....
(deal) in grams and kilos and will wonder what the fuss was all about. As for Mr Thoburn, things have turned out quite well. He is a local hero, and the publicity has led to a huge increase in business. He has bought an additional shop and can now look forward to
11 .... (sell) thousands of bananas for years to come.

* 1 ounce = approx 30 grammes
16 ounces = 1 pound

Production

TASK 1

Complete these sentences with a verb in the *-ing* form or the infinitive.

1 I know for sure that we placed an order with them. I remember ...
sending them the form myself.

2 The meeting had gone on for two hours already, so we stopped ...

....

3 I'll never forget ...

....

4 I'm a very organized person. I like ...

....

5 I have quite a lot of responsibilities at work. In addition to ...

....

6 I am really looking forward to ...

....

7 A lot of business people in this country object to ...

....

TASK 2

A Say which of the following you like or prefer doing, and why.

1 have holidays abroad/in your own country
I prefer having holidays abroad because the weather is much better.

2 start work early/stay late

....

3 work alone/with other people

....

4 eat lunch out/at my desk

....

B Say which of the following you would prefer, and why.

1 be rich or be famous
I'd prefer to be rich because if I were famous, I wouldn't be free.

2 have a larger house or a bigger car

....

3 work for a man or a woman

....

4 have a more demanding job or more time for yourself

....

30 *-ing* and infinitive (4): other uses

Presentation

ⓐ Infinitive of purpose

The infinitive (e.g., *to work, to stay*) can be used to explain why we do something:

*Mr Lee has just phoned **to say** he'll be late for the meeting.*

Common mistakes:

We do not use *for* + infinitive to explain why we do something.

wrong: **Mrs Larsen was posted to Athens **for to set up** the new branch*
right: *Mrs Larsen was posted to Athens **to set up** the new branch.*

ⓑ Infinitives after question words

We use the infinitive after question words (except *why*). We often use the infinitive in this way after verbs of thinking and knowing, teaching, etc. to talk about things we can do or should do:

*We'll **teach** you **how to manage** your time more effectively.*
*We'll **show** you **what to do** when negotiations start getting difficult.*
*I can't **think what to do** about increasing our visibility.*
*Could you **explain how to transfer** calls to my mobile?*

ⓒ *-ing* form as the subject

We can use the *-ing* form of the verb (the gerund) as the subject of a sentence:

***Developing** new and effective anti-AIDS drugs requires years of research and a great deal of investment.*

ⓓ *-ing* form after prepositions

We use the *-ing* form (the gerund) after a preposition (in, *on, at, to, by, from, over*, etc.). We do not use the infinitive. Here are some examples of how we can use the following prepositions:

We can use *before* and *after* to talk about when something happened:

***Before founding** Southwest Airlines, Herb Kelleher worked as a lawyer.*
***After being** in business for just two years, Southwest made its first profit in 1973.*

We can use *by* to explain how something happened:

*Southwest grew rapidly **by offering** passengers great value for money.*

We can use *without* to talk about something that doesn't happen:

*Southwest passengers can fly **without booking** a ticket through a travel agent.*

We can use *instead of* to talk about something that happens in the place of another action:

***Instead of offering** passengers expensive cabin service, Southwest concentrates on low fares.*

(For adjective + preposition combinations, noun + preposition combinations, and verb + preposition combinations, see Units 42, 43, and 44.)

Practice

EXERCISE ❶

Infinitive of purpose

Complete the sentences, using the verbs in the box.

attract	demand	~~go~~	increase
inform	miss	prevent	reduce

1 I need a day off next week to go to an interview.
2 He decided to take a later train .... the morning rush hour.
3 I am writing .... you of our change of address.
4 It is likely that the union will go on strike .... a pay rise.
5 The company had to move to cheaper offices .... its overheads.
6 We will have to employ more factory workers .... production.
7 We have cut the price of our products by 10% .... more customers.
8 The government may soon raise interest rates .... inflation growing.

EXERCISE ❷

Infinitives after question words

Complete the text using a suitable question word and infinitive from the box.

~~what/do~~	what/look out for
what financial institutions/approach	where/manufacture
how/identify	how/write

```
                                    jobs@execnet.com

  Back  Forward  Reload  Home  Search  Guide  Images  Print  Security  Stop

  Location:   http://www.execnet.com
```

Templars College

TRAINING COURSES FOR ENTREPRENEURS AND INVENTORS

Innovations and inventions can look promising, but ideas alone are never enough to guarantee commercial success. The aim of the Templars College seminars is to guide inventors and entrepreneurs through the complex world of finance, patent applications and production.

Course features:

Patents – you will learn ¹ what to do if you want to protect your idea with a patent.

Funding – one of the key areas for a successful product is adequate backing; you will learn ² .... a good business plan that you can submit to investors, and we will tell you ³ .... for funding. Banks, private investors and venture capitalists operate on different lines and we will warn you about ⁴ .... before signing a contract.

Production – If your idea is further down the line, we can give advice on ⁵ .... suitable partners and producers, as well as ⁶ .... the product.

Course formats:

Intensive course	1 day	$800.00	Non-residential
Extended courses	3 days	$1,400.00	Residential

```
  64% of 21K (at 1.4K/sec, 5 secs remaining)
```

EXERCISE ③

-ing form as the subject

Match the beginnings of the sentences in column A with the right endings in column B.

A	B
1 Giving employees shares	a is difficult without local contacts.
2 Flying Business Class	b can make overseas trips less stressful.
3 Taking over other businesses	c can help to increase motivation.
4 Becoming a fully-qualified doctor	d is one of the government's priorities.
5 Breaking into the Japanese market	e takes about seven years.
6 Getting unemployment down	f is one way of increasing market share.

EXERCISE ④

-ing form after prepositions

Rewrite the following sentences, using the *-ing* form of the verb in *italics* and the preposition in brackets.

1 He left the office. He did not *speak* to his boss. (without)
   He left the office without speaking to his boss.

2 She *left* university. Then she got a job with Microsoft. (after)
   ....

3 We won't *offer* them a discount. We'll give them better credit terms. (instead of)
   ....

4 We managed to expand. We didn't *increase* our debts. (without)
   ....

5 He worked in industry for many years. Then he *joined* the government. (before)
   ....

6 The company *made* 700 workers redundant. That is how it became more profitable. (by)
   ....

EXERCISE ⑤

Review

Put the verbs in brackets into the infinitive or *-ing* form.

The chocolate revolution

After ¹ reaching (reach) Europe with Columbus in 1502, chocolate rapidly became popular as a drink that people took ² .... (improve) their health. ³ .... (eat) solid chocolate, however, was unpopular; it was dark and bitter, and manufacturers did not know how ⁴ .... (mix) it with milk or cream ⁵ .... (make) it taste better.

The discovery of milk chocolate was made in 1876 by Daniel Peter in Switzerland. After ⁶ .... (try) unsuccessfully for eight years to mix milk and dark chocolate, Peter began working with his neighbour, the chemist Henri Nestlé. Nestlé had developed a new product ⁷ .... (feed) babies; in the process, he had discovered how ⁸ .... (make) condensed milk, which Peter tried instead of ⁹ .... (use) ordinary milk. The result was an instant success, and the two men joined forces ¹⁰ .... (manufacture) milk chocolate for a grateful world.

Production

Continue the following sentences. Give people's reasons for doing these things.

1 I've written to the bank …
   to ask them for some more information about their charges.

2 The managers changed the layout of the department store …

....

3 Our Sales Director has gone to New York …

....

4 Next month I need a few days off …

....

5 I'll phone up the travel agent this afternoon …

....

Brian Pelcinski is the agent for a number of people in the entertainment industry. Read the following interview with him.

Reporter: [1] Which part of your job do you find the most difficult?

Brian: Dealing with financial forecasts. It's a nightmare because I hate figures.

Reporter: [2] Which part of your job would other people find the most difficult?

Brian: Dealing with the emotional problems of my clients. They can be very unreasonable.

Reporter: [3] Which part of your job gives you the most satisfaction?

Brian: Finding a new talent and seeing him or her become a star.

Reporter: [4] Which part of your job is the most glamorous and exciting?

Brian: Being invited to film premieres and concerts, and knowing so many people.

Reporter: [5] Which part of your job are you not very good at?

Brian: Remembering appointments. But that's why I have a PA to do it for me.

Answer the same interview questions about the activities you do at work. Begin each answer with the *-ing* form of a verb, as in Brian's answers above.

1 ....
2 ....
3 ....
4 ....
5 ....

Write sentences about important dates in your career history. Begin each sentence with the *after + -ing* form or *before + -ing* form.

....

....

....

31 Reported speech (1): statements, thoughts, commands, requests

Presentation

a Introduction

There are three ways to report what someone said. We can:

1 repeat the exact words using inverted commas (' '):
   The Prime Minister said: 'Unemployment is falling.'
2 use a reporting verb in the present tense and keep the same tense as the original words:
   The Prime Minister says that unemployment is falling.
3 use a reporting verb in the past and change the tense:
   The Prime Minister said that unemployment was falling.

b Tense changes

Tenses change in reported speech when we use a reporting verb in the past tense:

Actual words	Reported speech
'I work for IBM.'	*He said (that) he worked for IBM.*
'I am working for IBM.'	*He said (that) he was working for IBM.*
'I worked for IBM.'	*He said (that) he had worked for IBM.*
'I was working for IBM.'	*He said (that) he had been working for IBM.*
'I have worked for IBM.'	*He said (that) he had worked for IBM.*
'I will work for IBM.'	*He said (that) he would work for IBM.*
'I may/can work for IBM.'	*He said (that) he might/could work for IBM.*

We do not change the past perfect, or *might/could/should/would/ought to*.

We don't have to use the word *that* after the reporting verb. So we could also say:

He said he worked for IBM.

c Reporting thought

We use the same tense changes when we are reporting what people think or know (e.g. after *I didn't realize, I knew, I thought, I had no idea*, etc.):

I didn't realize you were Canadian. I thought you were American.

d Reporting commands and requests

We report commands and requests using *tell* or *ask* and the infinitive:

'Come in.'	*He told me to come in.*
'Don't take the train.'	*He told me not to take the train.*
'Please join me for lunch.'	*He asked me to join him for lunch.*
'Please don't smoke.'	*He asked me not to smoke.*

e Other changes

It is sometimes necessary to change other words:

'I saw him here yesterday.'	*She said she had seen him there the previous day.*
'I'll send him this information.'	*She said she would send him the/that information.*
'I'll drop in tomorrow.'	*She said she would drop in the following day.*

Practice

Tense changes

Look at the picture story of a customer who came to a car showroom in an old car. Look at some of the things the customer and the salesman said. Then complete the passage using the verbs in the correct tense.

A man and an elderly lady arrived at a car dealership in a battered old car; the man told the salesman that he [1] *was thinking* about buying a new car. The salesman pointed out the new S500, which [2] .... very good value, and said the man [3] .... it for a test drive. The customer said that he [4] .... any identification, but said that his grandmother [5] .... The salesman said that [6] .... fine and handed him the keys. Two hours later, the man had not returned and the salesman remarked to the old lady that her grandson [7] .... a long time. The old lady looked very surprised and told him that the man [8] .... her grandson. She explained that he [9] .... to drive her to the shops but that she [10] .... never .... him before.

Reporting thought

Match the comments in column A with a response from column B.

A
1 I'm just off to play golf.
2 Celine is working in London today.
3 These PCs are made in Taiwan.
4 Juan is moving to his new job next week.

5 I'll need an interpreter.
6 Shin is away on leave.
7 My boss needs more time to do the report.
8 We had to pay extra for phone calls.

B
a I thought you spoke Japanese.
b I thought he'd already been on holiday.
c Oh. I thought they were free.
d That's odd! I thought I saw her here this morning.
e I didn't realize you played.
f I had no idea he was leaving.
g I thought they were American.
h I thought she had finished it.

Reporting commands and requests

Report the requests or commands using *He asked me …* or *He told me …*

1 'Please come to dinner at 8.00.' He asked me to come to dinner at 8.00.
2 'Send the letter immediately.' ....
3 'Please don't mention the plans to anyone.' ....
4 'Please return the form as soon as possible.' ....
5 'Don't put any calls through to my office.' ....

Other changes

Read the situations, and underline the correct words in *italics*.

1 At 10.00 this morning, Julia says to you, 'Dr Bangermann is arriving this afternoon.' At 10.30 the same morning you say to your boss, 'Julia said that Dr Bangermann was arriving *this afternoon/that afternoon*.'
2 The sales manager says to you, 'I'll show the visitors round the factory tomorrow.' Three weeks later, you say to your boss, 'He said he would show the visitors round the factory *the following day/tomorrow*.'
3 A client calls from his office and says, 'I'd like to hold the meeting here'. Later you speak to your boss in your own office and say, 'He said he'd like to hold the meeting *here/there*.'
4 A customer rings to say, 'We sent the cheque yesterday'. A week later you say to your boss, 'When I spoke to him, he said that he had sent the cheque *yesterday/the previous day*.'
5 A client rings you at your office and says, 'I'll meet you there tomorrow'. The same day at your office you say to your boss, 'He said he would meet me *here/there* tomorrow.'

Review

Look at these famous quotations and re-write them using reported speech.

1 'Radio has no future.'
   William Thomson, English scientist, 1899
2 'Everything that can be invented has been invented.'
   Charles H Duell, Office of Patents, 1899
3 'I think there's a world market for about five computers.'
   Thomas J Watson, chairman of the board of IBM.
4 'Only the little people pay taxes.'
   Leona Helmsley
5 'The secret of success is to rise early, work hard, and strike oil.'
   J Paul Getty
6 '640k ought to be enough for anybody.'
   Bill Gates
7 'You can have any colour you like, as long as it's black.'
   Henry Ford, speaking about the Model T car

1 In 1899, William Thomson said that radio had no future.
2 ....
3 ....
4 ....
5 ....
6 ....
7 ....

Production

TASK 1

A headhunter took you out to dinner last night. Now a colleague is asking you about what you said. Answer his questions using reported speech.

1 'What personal details did you give him about yourself?'
I told him I was married and that I lived in London.

2 'What did you tell him about the company?'

....

3 'What did you say your responsibilities were?'

....

4 'What did you tell him about the salary you would need?'

....

5 'What did he tell you about the new company?'

....

6 'What did he tell you about the new job?'

....

7 'So in the end what did you say to him?'

....

TASK 2

Respond with surprise to the following comments.

1 A They are discontinuing this model at the end of the year.
 B *Really? I thought it was selling well.*

2 A It's my 40th birthday next week.
 B Really? I had no idea ....

3 A You will have to wait about three months for delivery.
 B Really? I didn't realize ....

4 A I've just seen Mr Takashi in Reception.
 B Really? I thought ....

5 A The bill for dinner came to £145 each.
 B Really? I had no idea ....

TASK 3

Complete the sentences using *ask* or *tell* + infinitive.

1 They were late paying the bill, so I *phoned and told them to pay at once.*

2 I was too busy to see Jane, so I ....

3 I could see that he had had too much to drink, so I ....

4 Peter said he was going to the bank, so I ....

5 The machine they sold us was faulty, so I ....

6 I wanted the mechanic to tell me how much the repairs would cost, so ....

....

32 Reported speech (2): questions and reporting verbs

Presentation

ⓐ *Wh-* questions

Some questions begin with a question word (*who, where, which, why, when, what, how, how much*, etc.). Look at the way we report these questions:

'When will the shipment arrive?' they asked me.
They asked me when the shipment would arrive.

Common mistakes:
When we report a question, the word order changes from verb + subject to subject + verb:

'Where is the file?' he asked me.
wrong: **He asked me where was the file.*
right: *He asked me where the file was.*

Note that the tense changes are the same as with reported speech (see Unit 31) and we do not use a question mark.

ⓑ *Yes/no* questions

When we report *yes/no* questions, we use *if* or *whether* and the tense changes explained in Unit 31:

direct question: *'Are you planning to stay late?'*
reported question: *She asked me if I was planning to stay late.*
direct question: *'Do you know anyone in Marketing?'*
reported question: *He asked me whether I knew anyone in Marketing.*

ⓒ Embedded questions

When we begin a sentence with one of the following phrases, we need to use the same word order as for reporting questions. We do not need to change the tense if the introductory phrase is in the present tense:

'I wonder...	*where Henk is.'*	(not: **where is Henk.*)
'I'm not sure ...	*if it is a good investment.'*	(not: **is it a good investment.*)
'Could you tell me ...	*what my bank balance is?'*	(not: **what is my bank balance?*)
'Do you know ...	*when the plane leaves?'*	(not: **when does the plane leave?*)

ⓓ Reporting verbs

We often use other verbs instead of *say, tell*, etc. to report what someone says.
The verbs *warn, order, advise, encourage, remind, persuade* are followed by an object + infinitive:

'I think you ought to look for another job.' – *He advised me to look for another job.*

The verbs *offer, refuse, promise* are followed by an infinitive:

'We will not accept less that 5.5%.' – *They refused to accept less than 5.5%*

The verbs *admit, deny, apologize for* are followed by the *-ing* form:

'Sorry to keep you waiting.' – *He apologized for keeping me waiting.*

Practice

EXERCISE ❶

Reporting questions

After announcing very bad figures for the year, the CEO of TSL Engineering faced questions from shareholders and investors. Look at the questions and then report them in the correct way.

1 Why has the company done so badly?

2 How many people are going to lose their jobs?

3 Where can you cut costs?

4 How much money has the company lost?

5 When will the company return to profit?

6 Who is responsible for these figures?

7 What dividend will the company pay?

8 When are you going to resign?

1 They asked him why the company had done so badly.

2 ....

3 ....

4 ....

5 ....

6 ....

7 ....

8 ....

EXERCISE ❷

Yes/no questions

A colleague of yours came back from a business trip, and you asked her the following questions. Rewrite the questions using reported speech.

1 'Did you have a good trip?'
   I asked her if she had had a good trip.

2 'Have they signed the contract?'

   ....

3 'Will you need to go back again?'

   ....

4 'Was the hotel any good?'

   ....

5 'Did you manage to have any time off?'

   ....

6 'Are you feeling tired?'

   ....

7 'Did you have any problems?'

   ....

8 'Did they like the idea of a joint venture?'

   ....

Embedded questions

Rewrite the following sentences. Use the introductory phrases and either a question word or *if*.

1 Can you use cash cards in Myanmar?
I wonder if you can use cash cards in Myanmar.

2 When will the plane get in? Do you know?
Do you know when the plane will get in?

3 How are the negotiations going, I wonder?
I wonder ....

4 Is Peter coming to the meeting? Do you know?
Do you know ....

5 When is the talk going to start? Could you tell me?
Could you tell me ....

6 Should I take the job? I'm not sure.
I'm not sure ....

7 Where is their head office? I don't know.
I don't know ....

8 Will they accept our offer, I wonder?
I wonder ....

9 Have they sent us an order form? Could you find out?
Could you find out ....

10 How did they get this information, I wonder?
I wonder ....

Reporting verbs

Re-write these sentences using the reporting verbs and structures in brackets.

1 'I'll report you to the police.' (threaten to do something)
He threatened to report me to the police.

2 'Go on, give a talk at the conference.' (encourage someone to do something)
He ....

3 'No, I will not give you a pay rise.' (refuse to do something)
He ....

4 'I didn't leave the office unlocked – it wasn't me.' (deny doing something)
He ....

5 'Don't leave your hotel after dark – it's dangerous.' (warn someone not to do something)
He ....

6 'I'm sorry I missed the meeting.' (apologize for doing something)
He ....

7 'I think you should get an agent.' (advise someone to do something)
He ....

Production

A colleague has overheard you say the following things on the phone. Explain who you were talking to and what they asked you.

1 'Yes, the 15th would be fine.'
   That was Mr Jackson. He asked me if he could change the date of our next meeting to the 15th, and I said it would be fine.

2 'No, I am afraid that 15% is the maximum.'

   ....

   ....

3 'I will be there first thing on Wednesday.'

   ....

   ....

4 'Yes, I am sure we have paid it. I remember writing the cheque myself.'

   ....

   ....

5 '$16,000'.

   ....

   ....

Complete the sentence with a suitable embedded question.

1 The office is very different without Ahmed. I wonder *how he is getting on in his new job.*

2 No, I'm afraid I don't know .... I am a stranger here myself.

3 I'll just have a look at the new price list. I'm not sure ....

4 I need to go to New York next Wednesday. Could you tell me ....

5 I can't understand this letter. Do you know ....

Complete the sentences using the verbs in brackets.

1 She was offered a very good job, so …
   (advise) *I advised her to accept it.*

2 He said that the guarantee was out of date, and …
   (refuse) ....

3 They said that they couldn't bring the price down any more, but …
   (offer) ....

4 The bank realized that they were in the wrong, and they …
   (apologize) ....

33 Relative clauses (1): *who, that, which, whose, whom*

Presentation

ⓐ People and things

We can use a relative clause beginning with **who**, **that** or **which** to describe and define a person or thing. To refer to people, we use **who** or **that**. To refer to things, we use **which** or **that**:

people:	*The architect **who/that** drew these designs trained in New York.*
	(The clause *who/that drew these designs* helps to identify the architect.)
things:	*The mistakes **which/that** the company made were very basic.*
	(The clause *which/that the company made* identifies the mistakes.)

ⓑ Subject and object relative clauses

Look at the way these two underlying sentences can be combined into one sentence using a subject relative pronoun:

I share an office with a colleague. She dislikes everybody.
*I share an office with a colleague **who** dislikes everybody.*

In sentences like this, where the relative pronoun **who**, **which**, or **that** is followed by a verb, we must keep the relative pronoun.

Look at the way these two underlying sentences can be combined into one using an object relative pronoun:

I share an office with a colleague. Everybody dislikes her.
*I share an office with a colleague **who/that** everybody dislikes.*

In sentences like this, where the relative **who**, **which**, or **that** is followed by a noun or pronoun + verb, we very often leave it out. So we can say:

I share an office with a colleague everybody dislikes.

In object relative clauses, it is possible to use **whom** to refer to people. However, this is only found in formal language, and rarely used in speech.

Formal:	*The man **whom** they arrested was charged with fraud.*
Spoken:	*The man (**that**) they arrested was charged with fraud.*

ⓒ Whose

The relative pronoun **whose** is used to show possession:

Yesterday I met someone. His brother works in your department.
*Yesterday I met someone **whose** brother works in your department.*

ⓓ To whom, from which, etc.

It is possible, particularly in formal or written language, to put words like **to**, **from**, **about**, **on**, etc. in front of **whom**, **which**, and **whose** (but not: ***who** or **that**):

*The sales assistant **to whom** I complained was most unhelpful.*

However, it is much more common to put words like **to**, **from**, **about**, **on**, etc. at the end of the relative clause:

*The sales assistant I complained **to** was most unhelpful.*

Practice

EXERCISE ❶   **People and things**

Complete the sentences in this job advertisement with *who* or *which*.

EUROPEAN SALES MANAGER
Barcelona
€130,000 *plus car*

Our client manufactures and markets sports clothing and equipment ¹ **which** is sold to leading department stores in Europe and the USA. We currently have a vacancy in our Spanish headquarters for a Sales Manager ² .... will be in overall control of a sales force ³ .... consists of 15 representatives.

We are looking for someone ⁴ .... has a proven track record of success in retailing and ⁵ .... will be able to motivate the existing team. This is a position ⁶ .... requires flair and enthusiasm and preference will be given to applicants ⁷ .... have experience in the retail clothing sector. We are offering an excellent package ⁸ .... includes free health insurance, generous pension contributions and full relocation expenses.

So if you are someone ⁹ .... wants to get ahead in an organisation ¹⁰ .... is expanding fast, send your CV to:

***DKN* Europe Recruitment Consultants**
87 Freeman Road Sheffield SN2 3BA

DKN
EUROPE

EXERCISE ❷   **Subject and object relative pronouns**

Re-write these sentences using the relative pronoun *that*.

1 We've appointed a new non-executive director. Everybody knows him.
   We've appointed a new non-executive director *that everybody knows.*
2 We've appointed a new non-executive chairman. He knows everybody.
   We've appointed a new non-executive director ....
3 You interviewed a man. What did you think of him?
   What did you think of the man ....
4 A man interviewed you. What did you think of him?
   What did you think of the man ....
5 Mandy's got a new boss. She doesn't like him.
   Mandy's got a new boss ....
6 I've got a new company car. It runs on electricity.
   I've got a new company car ....

In which of the above sentences can you leave out the word *that*?

Whose

Finish each sentence using one of the pieces of information in the box. Join the two parts with *whose*.

> Her department was doing well.
> Their car had broken down.
> Its key competitors are Sony and Sanyo.
> ~~Their CVs were very good.~~
> His/her mother tongue must be English.
> Its headquarters are in Helsinki.

1 We drew up a shortlist of candidates whose CVs were very good
2 We are looking for a secretary ....
3 Nokia is a large Finnish company ....
4 I gave a lift to a couple of colleagues ....
5 Casio is a Japanese electronics company ....
6 They promoted one of the managers ....

Relative clauses in formal language

Complete the sentences with the phrases in the box.

to which	~~from which~~	in which
to whom	with whom	by whom

1 The enclosed tax form must be returned to the office from which it originated.
2 On starting a telephone call, record the name of the person .... you are talking.
3 The hotel has a large hall .... presentations and exhibitions can be held.
4 Expense claims should provide names of the clients .... you have had lunch.
5 Postage prices depend on the country .... a package is being sent.
6 The enclosed memorandum gives information about the managers .... loans over $40,000 may be authorised.

Relative clauses in informal language

Rewrite the sentences without relative pronouns, putting the prepositions at the end of the relative clause.

1 I was talking to a man. He is the head of Al Jazeerah.
   The man I was talking to is the head of Al Jazeerah.
2 You were looking for an invoice. Jan has found it.
   Jan has found the ....
3 I deal with customers. Most of them are very pleasant.
   Most of the ....
4 We wanted to stay in a hotel. It was fully booked.
   The hotel ....
5 She works for a company. It has a very good reputation.
   The company ....
6 We went to a restaurant. It wasn't very good.
   The restaurant ....

Production

Find the name of a large industrial corporation by completing the puzzle. The clues are below.

1	i	n	v	o	i	c	e	

(crossword grid)

1. i n v o i c e
2.
3. s a l a r y
4.
5. s u b s i d i a r y
6.
7. c a t a l o g u e
8.
9. c o l l e a g u e
10.

Clues

2 A legal document that gives details of an agreement between two or more people.
4 A building or company in which people keep their money.
6 A person whose job it is to give legal advice.
8 A list of things that are discussed at a meeting.
10 A machine that allows you to talk to people who are in a different place.

Now write clues for the words that you were given, using relative clauses.

1 An invoice is ....

3 A salary is ....

5 A subsidiary is ....

7 A catalogue is ....

9 A colleague is ....

Complete the following sentences about yourself and your work, using relative clauses.

1 I work for a company that manufactures components for aircraft

2 I have a boss ....

3 I am in a department ....

4 In my work, I deal with people ....

5 I sometimes have to do things ....

6 I prefer to work with people ....

7 I dislike working with people ....

8 In my spare time, I like to do things ....

34 Relative clauses (2): *where, with, what* and non-defining clauses

Presentation

ⓐ *Where*

The relative pronoun *where* is used to refer to places. It means *in which*.

The room in which we held the meeting was very cold.
The room where we held the meeting was very cold.

Where is not used if there is a preposition at the end of the clause:

wrong: **The room **where** we held the meeting **in** was very cold.*
right: *The room **which/that/Ø** we held the meeting **in** was very cold.*

ⓑ Use of *with*

When we want to describe what someone or something has, we can use a relative clause or *with* + a noun. So we can say:

*I've got a new laptop **that has** an excellent screen.*
or
*I've got a new laptop **with** an excellent screen.*

ⓒ Use of *what*

We can use the relative pronoun *what* to replace *the thing(s) that …* . So we can say:

*I'm afraid we haven't got **the things that** you want in stock.*
or
*I'm afraid we haven't got **what** you want in stock.*

ⓓ Non-defining relative clauses

Some relative clauses define what you are talking about. Some relative clauses simply add extra information. Look at the difference between the two types:

defining relative clause:

*The colleague **who I was telling you about** is planning to retire next year.*

(This indicates which colleague I'm talking about.)

non-defining relative clause:

*My mother, **who runs her own business**, is planning to retire next year.*

(The speaker does not need to define 'my mother', and the fact that she runs her own business is just an extra piece of information.)

In non-defining relative clauses we:

a) must use commas at the beginning and end of the clause
b) must use a relative pronoun (but not the word *that*)

wrong: **Intel's latest chip **which was launched last week** is very fast.*
           (no commas)
wrong: **Intel's latest chip, **that was launched last week**, is very fast.*
           (use of *that*)
right: *Intel's latest chip, **which was launched last week**, is very fast.*

Practice

EXERCISE ❶

Defining relative clauses and *where*

Rewrite the following sentences using *where*.

1 I've got the details of the hotel. You'll be staying there.
   I've got the details of the hotel where you'll be staying.

2 Would you like to visit the factory that we make the cars in?
   ....

3 I recently went back to the town. I used to work there.
   ....

4 Ivrea is the town in which Olivetti has its headquarters.
   ....

5 This is the building. They filmed the Pepsi advert here.
   ....

EXERCISE ❷

Defining relative clauses and *with* or *that*

Complete the sentences using *with* or *that* and the phrases in the box.

has a better view	a DVD drive	a bit more experience
has a lot of mistakes	a matching tie	~~has all the latest information~~
~~a $5,000 credit limit~~	a sense of humour	

1 I've got a new credit card *with a $5,000 credit limit.*
2 I'll send you a brochure *that has all the latest information.*
3 Have you got a laptop ....
4 I'm afraid we're looking for someone ....
5 I'd prefer a room ....
6 We've received an invoice ....
7 I've bought him a Gucci shirt ....
8 I wish I had a boss ....

EXERCISE ❸

Defining relative clauses and *what*

Rewrite these sentences using *what*.

1 He was selling something. I wasn't interested in it.
   I wasn't interested in what he was selling.
2 You asked me to do something. I've done it.
   I've done ....
3 You want a computer to do some things. This computer can do them.
   This computer ....
4 You need something. We can deliver it tomorrow.
   We can ....
5 I'm sorry, you said something. I didn't hear it.
   I'm sorry, I didn't ....

Non-defining relative clauses

Join the following sentences together using non-defining relative clauses and the relative pronoun in brackets.

1 The new air traffic control system is a disaster.
   It cost a great deal of money. (which)
   The new air traffic control system, which cost a great deal of money, is a disaster.

2 The Oriental Hotel is said to be the best in the world.
   Many famous people have stayed in it. (where)

   ....

   ....

3 BMW's new Mini has been a great commercial success.
   It is built at Cowley in England. (which)

   ....

   ....

4 Exxon Mobil is building a $3.5bn pipeline in Chad.
   It is the world's second largest corporation. (which)

   ....

   ....

5 Their new range of cosmetics will be launched next month.
   They've spent €10 million on it. (on which)

   ....

   ....

6 Mr Warburg would like to meet you next week.
   I have discussed your proposal with him. (with whom)

   ....

   ....

Review

Correct the mistakes in the following sentences.

1 Yesterday I spoke to your director, ~~that~~ seemed to be very pleasant.
   Yesterday I spoke to your director, who seemed to be very pleasant.

2 The room where we held the meeting in was a little too small.

   ....

3 Brazil which had high inflation in the 1990s is now the leading economic power in South America.

   ....

4 The negotiators finally reached a formula on what everyone could agree.

   ....

5 I found it difficult to hear that the speaker was talking about.

   ....

6 Tim Lang only joined the company six months ago is going to be promoted.

   ....

7 BMW its headquarters are in Germany produces the new Mini in England.

   ....

8 I suggest we have a meeting in Romsey Street, which we rent a few offices.

   ....

Production

Read the text below and then look through the list of extra information. Add these clauses to the text in the spaces provided, using relative clauses.

1 The East India Company grew opium in India.
2 They were concerned about the growing number of addicts.
3 Canton was at the centre of the opium trade.
4 The traders had powerful allies in London.
5 Their weapons were all old and outdated
6 The war ended in 1842.
7 The treaty was signed the following year.
8 The war broke out in 1856.
9 The British were assisted by the French.
10 The treaty was signed in 1858.

In the 1830s the use of opium was becoming more and more widespread in China. The British East India Company, ¹ which grew opium in India, regularly sailed to Canton to sell the drug. The Chinese authorities, ² .... , wanted to stop the opium trade.

In 1839 Lin Tse-hsu was appointed Imperial Commissioner at Canton, ³ .... One of his first acts was to seize and destroy thousands of chests of opium belonging to the East India Company and other British traders. The traders, ⁴ .... , persuaded the British government to go to war to protect 'free trade'. Heavily armed warships were sent to Canton and the Chinese, ⁵ .... , stood almost no chance. The First Opium War, ⁶ .... , resulted in the complete defeat of China. Under the Treaty of Nanking, ⁷ .... , the Chinese agreed to pay a large fine, to give Hong Kong to the British and to open up five more ports for trade.

The Second Opium War ⁸ .... , ended with a second defeat for China. This time the British, ⁹ .... , gained control of more Chinese ports. Under the terms of the Treaty of Tientsin, ¹⁰ .... , the opium trade became completely legal, with disastrous consequences for Chinese society for the rest of the century.

Think of yourself, colleagues and members of your family. Describe something that each of them might like, adding information about special features it has or what it can do.

1 I'd like a digital camera with a zoom lens.
2 ....
3 ....
4 ....
5 ....
6 ....

35 Countable and uncountable nouns

Presentation

ⓐ Countable nouns

Countable nouns are things like people, animals, plants (*a boss, a dog*), objects (*a desk, a modem*), or units of measurement (*a metre, a Euro*).

ⓑ Uncountable nouns

Uncountable nouns are things like substances, materials, and commodities (*coal, cotton, coffee*), abstract ideas (*progress*), and languages (*Arabic*). These are things that we cannot count – we do not talk about *'three informations'*, *'six monies'*, etc.

When we use abstract nouns in general, we do not use *the*.

wrong: * ***The happiness*** *is hard to measure.*
right: ***Happiness*** *is hard to measure.*

Some other uncountable nouns which sometimes cause difficulty are:

advice	*equipment*	*luggage*	*progress*	*travel*
accommodation	*furniture*	*machinery*	*research*	*trouble*
advertising	*hardware*	*money*	*room (= space)*	*weather*
baggage	*information*	*news*	*software*	*work*
cash	*insurance*	*permission*	*traffic*	

ⓒ Singular or plural?

Countable nouns can be singular or plural. Uncountable nouns are singular:

*The **letter** (countable, singular) is on your desk and the **two faxes** (countable, plural) are here. This **junk mail** (uncountable, singular) is very annoying.*

ⓓ Determiners

We use different determiners for countable and uncountable nouns.

Countable	Uncountable
*I've got **a** book for you.*	*I've got **some** information for you.*
*I haven't got **many** books for you.*	*I haven't got **much** information for you.*
*I've got **a few** books for you.*	*I've got **a little** information for you.*

wrong: *He gave me **an** advice.*
right: *He gave me **some** advice.*

ⓔ Parts of a mass

We refer to parts of a mass with words of measurement, e.g. ***a cup*** *of coffee,* ***a kilo*** *of sugar.*

We often use these measurements when talking about price:

*At the moment oil is about $25 **a barrel**.*

Practice

EXERCISE ❶

Countable or uncountable?

In the following pairs of words, one is countable and the other is uncountable. Write *some* or *a* before each word.

1	*a*	book	*some*	literature
2	....	report	....	news
3	....	desk	....	furniture
4	....	accommodation	....	hotel
5	....	chance	....	luck
6	....	water	....	litre
7	....	equipment	....	machine
8	....	dollar	....	money
9	....	cheque	....	cash
10	....	letter	....	correspondence

EXERCISE ❷

Singular or plural?

Fill in the blanks with *is* or *are*.

1 The software you ordered .... here.
2 What .... the weather in Spain like at this time of year?
3 There .... a lot of cars in the car park this morning.
4 The agenda for tomorrow's meeting .... on your desk.
5 The reports that I have just received from Tokyo .... not very good.
6 Your Japanese visitors have gone to the hotel, but their luggage .... still at the office.
7 The traffic on the M40 .... very bad this morning.
8 Travel .... one of our major expenses.

EXERCISE ❸

Determiners

Read the mini-dialogue. Choose the correct option from the words in *italics*.

David: Could you give me ¹ *an/some* advice about finding ² *an/some* apartment?
Petra: Sure – this means you've had ³ *a/some* good news, does it?
David: Yes, I got ⁴ *the/some* job – I'm going to be doing ⁵ *an/some* advertising for a PR agency.
Petra: That's great – when are you going to start?
David: The beginning of next month, so I haven't got ⁶ *much/many* time.
Petra: Well, I know ⁷ *a few/a little* people who might be able to help you, but it really depends on how ⁸ *much/many* money you want to spend and where you want to be.
David: Somewhere small and central, not too expensive – preferably near ⁹ *a/some* metro station. I just need somewhere with a bedroom and kitchen, ¹⁰ *a little/few* furniture – there's only me, so I don't need ¹¹ *much/many* room.
Petra: OK, I'll see what I can do – and of course you're welcome to come and stay with me for a few weeks until you find ¹² *a/some* suitable accommodation of your own.
David: That would be great – thanks very much.

EXERCISE **4**

Parts of a mass

Use a word from box A and a word from box B to describe the items below.

1	2	3	4	5	6	7

a litre of water	....	....	....	....	....	....

A

a litre	a pint	a kilo
a tonne	a barrel	a glass
a sheet		

B

paper	oil	wine
coal	beer	sugar
water		

EXERCISE **5**

Prices and quantities

Complete the following items of news with the words from the box.

a packet	a tube	a barrel
a pint	a litre	a bottle

A recent report on the prices of everyday items in the EU states shows big variations between countries. In France, for example, Evian mineral water costs less than €1 [1] a bottle, but in Finland it costs four times as much. Sweden comes out overall as the most expensive place to live, whereas Spain is the cheapest. Different tax and VAT rates explain some of the differences – in the UK, cigarettes cost almost €8 [2] .... , but most of that is tax. Similarly, beer in an English pub will cost €3 [3] .... , whereas in Madrid it will be substantially less. Spain is also the place to buy bargain toothpaste. Colgate is €1 [4] .... compared to nearly double that in the UK. Motoring costs vary a great deal as well. Although the world price of oil, currently $25 [5] .... , is the same for everyone, drivers in Greece only pay €0.84 [6] .... compared to drivers in the Netherlands, where it costs €1.21.

Production

TASK 1

Fill in the blanks with an uncountable noun. Use one word only.

1 A: Would you like to try the salmon? The trout is good as well.
   B: No thanks, I don't really like *fish*.

2 A: Would you like wine, or a beer, or a gin and tonic, or something?
   B: No thank you. I'll have mineral water. I don't drink ....

3 A: Could I have a talk with you about the arrangements for next week?
   B: I'm sorry, could we talk later? I haven't got .... at the moment.

4 A: It's been raining here for two weeks.
   B: Oh dear. When we were on holiday we had marvellous ....

5 A: So your wife handles the accounts, does she?
   B: Yes, it's because I'm no good with ....

6 A: ¿Me podría decir dónde hay un cajero automático?
   B: I'm sorry, I don't speak ....

7 A: What will you have? Chicken, a steak, or a hamburger?
   B: Actually, I'm a vegetarian. I don't eat ....

8 A: Did they say why you didn't get the job?
   B: Yes. They said I hadn't got enough .... yet for a managerial position.

TASK 2

Fortune cookies are traditional Chinese biscuits that contain a little piece of paper with a short philosophical message. You have been asked to write some of these messages.

Money: Money can be both freedom and a prison.

Time: ....

Meetings: ....

Work: ....

Men: ....

Women: ....

Experience: ....

Productivity: ....

MONEY CAN BE BOTH FREEDOM
AND A PRISON

36 Articles: *a/an, the* or Ø (no article)

Presentation

ⓐ *A* vs *an*

We use *a* before consonant sounds, and *an* before vowel sounds:
consonant sounds: *a director, a code, a question, a Euro, a unit*
vowel sounds: *an appraisal, an hour, an interview, an office, an MBA*

ⓑ Uses of *a, an*

We use *a* or *an* before unspecified singular countable nouns:
'Could you let me have a receipt?'
We use *a* or *an* to talk about jobs, (but not areas of business):
Michel is an accountant and his wife Amélie is in Ø computers.
We use *a* or *an* to talk about frequency:
We have in-company appraisals twice a year.

ⓒ Uses of *the*

We use *the* with a specific noun we have mentioned before:
We have bought a Mac and a PC. The Mac cost $2500 and the PC cost $2100.
We use *the* when we add information that defines something:
Have you read the report I gave you last week?
We use *the* when it is clear what we are referring to because there is only one:
Please come this way. The President will see you now.
We use *the* with superlatives:
Coca-Cola is the most valuable brand name in the world.
We use *the* with adjectives to refer to a group:
The rich do not do enough to help the poor.
We use *the* to refer to rivers, mountains, seas, and names of countries that include a noun like *republic, kingdom, union*, etc.:
The Aral Sea in the former Soviet Union is very polluted.

ⓓ No article (Ø)

We use no article (Ø) to generalize about uncountable or plural nouns:
Money is the root of all evil. (i.e., money in general, or all money)
We do not use an article to refer to companies, cities, roads, lakes or single islands:
I work for Merrill Lynch in New York, and I have an apartment on 14ᵗʰ Street. I also have a vacation home near Lake Tahoe and another in Hawaii.

Practice

EXERCISE 1

A vs an

Complete the dialogue. Fill in the blanks with *a* or *an*.

A: I had [1] an appraisal with the Personnel Manager the other day, and …

B: Oh really? How did it go?

A: Fine. We were talking about qualifications and career development, and she suggested I should consider doing [2] .... course in Business Administration.

B: That's not [3] .... bad idea. You've already got [4] .... university degree, haven't you?

A: Yes, and I'm doing [5] .... evening course in accounting, but that only takes up about [6] .... hour a week.

B: That sounds like [7] .... absolute waste of time to me. What you need to do is [8] .... MBA at [9] .... institution like Insead, so that you end up with [10] .... decent qualification.

EXERCISE 2

Uses of *the*

In each pair, fill in one blank with *a* and the other with *the*.

1 A: You don't know where .... key to the filing cabinet is, do you?

   B: No, but there's .... key on Jane's desk – why don't you try that one?

2 A: I phoned you last week to make .... complaint about late deliveries.

   B: Yes Sir, I remember, and I can assure you that .... complaint is being dealt with.

3 A: Do you suppose Coca-Cola is .... most famous brand name in the world?

   B: Maybe – but McDonalds is .... famous brand name too.

4 A: Does Mrs Rodin come from .... United States?

   B: No, she's from .... small town in Canada.

5 A: I need to talk to .... technician about this computer.

   B: Well, ... Head of the IT Department is right here – I'll send him up.

EXERCISE 3

A, the, Ø (no article)

Read the following newspaper extract. Fill in the blanks with *a* or *the* or Ø (no article).

Rome hosts the World Food Summit

At [1] the World Food Summit in [2] .... Rome, leaders from all over [3] .... world met to discuss plans to deliver [4] .... food to [5] .... hungry. During the morning, [6] .... stream of limousines and police outriders escorted [7] .... leaders from their luxury hotels on the Via Veneto, and brought them to [8] .... FAO headquarters, near [9] .... Colosseum.

At [10] .... summit, [11] .... Secretary General of [12] .... United Nations said that [13] .... hope needed to be given to [14] .... starving, and called for improvements in [15] .... technology, [16] .... healthcare, and [17] .... infrastructure projects. Other delegates discussed the crisis in [18] .... Somalia and Zimbabwe, but there was a strong sense that [19] .... West, and [20] .... United States in particular, should be doing more to help countries in [21] .... Africa and elsewhere.

The vs Ø (no article)

Read the information about world hunger. Complete the sentences with *the* or Ø (no article).

THE HUNGRY PLANET

MONGOLIA

Mongolia is still suffering from the effects of [20] .... worst winter in 30 years. Several hundred thousand animals died during [21] .... winter and farmers' livelihoods are threatened.

NORTH KOREA

North Korea is currently facing food shortages and severe shortages of [17] .... fuel and [18] .... fertiliser. Only international deliveries of [19] .... food have allowed the regime to escape mass starvation.

HAITI

Haiti is [1] the poorest country in [2] .... northern hemisphere. Because of [3] .... corruption and civil unrest, about 80% of [4] .... population lives in [5] .... poverty.

TAJIKISTAN

This is [12] .... least developed republic of [13] .... former Soviet Union. It now depends heavily on [14] .... aid from [15] .... Russia and [16] .... Uzbekistan.

ZIMBABWE

Political problems in [6] .... Zimbabwe have led to a collapse in commercial farming, and millions of people are in need of [7] .... aid. This year's harvest is expected to be [8] .... worst on record.

SOMALIA

Somalia is [9] .... poorest country in the world. Although [10] .... most recent harvest was good, hundreds of thousands of people are threatened by droughts and [11] .... political instability.

Production

A politician is discussing what his party intends to do if they win the next election. Using your own ideas, make sentences about the groups in the box.

| ~~the elderly~~ | the poor | the rich | the unemployed | the sick |

1 We will make sure that the elderly have a better quality of life and have access to the best medical facilities.

2 ....

3 ....

4 ....

5 ....

Read the notes about these two organizations. Write a short paragraph about each one.

1 ....

....

....

....

2 ....

....

....

....

MÉDECINS SANS FRONTIÈRES
ARTSEN ZONDER GRENZEN

Médecins Sans Frontières
MSF = international aid organization

works in over 80 countries

emergency medical assistance training - local personnel

uses media to raise awareness - countries in crisis

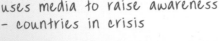

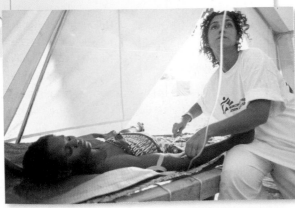

WFP

World Food Programme branch of UN; based in Rome

provides emergency food aid e.g. after Mozambique floods

supports long-term economic and social development

funded by governments (largest donors in 2000 = United States, Japan, European Union)

37 *Some* and *any*

Presentation

ⓐ *A/an, some, any*

We use *a* or *an* with singular countable nouns. We use *some* and *any* with plural countable nouns and with uncountable nouns:

single countable:	*I've got a report for you.*
plural countable:	*I've got some reports for you.*
uncountable:	*I've got some advice for you.*

ⓑ *Some* **or** *any*

We normally use *some* in positive statements; we use *any* in questions and negative statements.

'Are there any extra brochures for the trade fair?'
'No, there aren't any brochures, but we have printed some leaflets.'

However, we often use *some* in questions if the question is an offer or request, or if we expect the answer to be 'yes':

Would you like me to send you some catalogues?
Could I take some copies with me?

ⓒ *Something, anything*

We can use *something/anything, someone/anyone, somewhere/anywhere* in a similar way:

Someone has used my computer, and now I cannot find anything anywhere!

ⓓ **Free choice**

We can give people permission to do things using *anything, anywhere*, etc.:

With our lightweight laptop and its in-built super-fast modem to connect to the Internet, you can work anywhere you like and send anything to anyone, any time you want.

ⓔ *How much* **and** *how many*

We use *How many, not ... many, only ... a few* with plural countable nouns:

'How many people did you meet?'
'I didn't meet many people. I only met a few people.'

We use *How much, not ... much, only ... a little* with uncountable nouns:

'How much money did we save last month?'
'We didn't save much money. We only saved a little money.'

In positive answers, we use *a lot of* with both countable and uncountable nouns:

I talked to a lot of people at the conference. (This is more common than *many people*.)
People waste a lot of time at meetings. (This is more common than *much time*.)

Practice

EXERCISE 1

A/an, some, any

Underline the correct option from the words in *italics*.

1 I'd like *an/some* advice about the government's latest tax proposals.
2 I've just received *a/some* very nice gift from one of my suppliers.
3 Shall we carry on working, or would you like to go out for *a/some* meal?
4 Do you have *an/any* information about conference facilities in Monaco?
5 I just have to go to the bank to get *a/some* money.
6 Henk wants you to phone him. He says he has *a/some* good news for you.
7 Did you meet *an/any* interesting people at the trade fair?
8 The engineers are having *a/some* problems with the new engine.

EXERCISE 2

Some or *any*?

A manager is getting the results of some 'upward feedback', and is hearing what his staff think about him. Complete the dialogue with *some* or *any*.

Manager: So what did they say? Were there [1]............................ serious problems?
Consultant: Well, we interviewed all the people who work for you, and there are [2]............................ aspects of your management style that are very good.
Manager: Did they make [3]............................ complaints? I'd like to start with them first.
Consultant: As you like. There are some people who work for you who feel that you don't listen very much. They say that you don't spend [4]............................ time talking to them and that you seem very busy.
Manager: I am. Were there [5]............................ other criticisms?
Consultant: Yes, but I would like to suggest [6]............................ ways of dealing with this particular point before we carry on. I think there should be [7]............................ fixed times when staff can come and see you. If they don't have [8]............................ opportunities to discuss their problems, they will feel nervous about coming to talk to you. The other thing that they mentioned is that you don't give them [9]............................ responsibility, and that they don't make [10]............................ decisions themselves. Now, this is a common problem, and I think it's something you should think about.
Manager: Excellent. Now, I hope that's all because I'm a bit late for an important meeting.

EXERCISE 3

Some or *any*?

Read the following sentences. Put a tick [✓] by the ones that are right, and correct the ones that are wrong.

1 Could you send me some information about your latest range of furniture? ✓
2 Did you make any progress in the meeting? ....
3 I've got any letters for you to sign. ....
4 Shall I send you some samples of our latest fabrics? ....
5 We haven't had some major orders for several weeks. ....
6 Would you like me to get you some money from the bank? ....
7 I'm having any problems with this new software. ....
8 Are there any seats left on the BA flight to Tokyo next Tuesday? ....

Something, anything, etc.

Fill in the blanks with the words from the box.

someone	anyone	something
anything	somewhere	anywhere

1 Did anyone ring when I was out?
2 We've got to find that letter! It must be here _____ !
3 We returned the machines because there was _____ wrong with them.
4 By the way, _____ called in to see you when you were away last week.
5 These plans are secret. You mustn't discuss them with _____ .
6 We are trying to cut down on hotel bills, so now our executives can't stay _____ that costs more than $100 a night.
7 Yes, a meeting next Thursday would be fine. I'm not doing _____ .

Free choice

Fill in the blanks with *anyone, anywhere* or *anything.*

1 This is not confidential. You can discuss it with _____ you like.
2 If you hire a car, you will be able to go _____ you want.
3 I am now responsible for recruitment, so I can hire _____ I like.
4 George Soros' Quantum Fund has so much money that the company can buy almost _____ it wants.
5 You have to attend the course from 8.00 a.m. to 5.00 p.m., but in the evening you can do _____ you like.
6 Most of the hotels are empty, so you can stay _____ you like.

Much, many, etc.

Two colleagues are discussing the opening of a new office in Madrid. Fill in the blanks with the words from the box.

much	many	a lot of	a little	a few

A: How are things in Madrid?
B: We're nearly ready. We didn't have [1] much trouble finding a suitable office. There seem to be [2] _____ empty places at the moment.
A: How [3] _____ work will you need to do on the building?
B: Nothing really. We only need to do [4] _____ painting and decorating, and it'll be fine.
A: How [5] _____ people are going to be working there?
B: About twenty. We've filled most of the jobs, so it'll only take [6] _____ weeks to find the other people we need. We haven't appointed a sales manager yet, but there has been [7] _____ interest in the job, so we'll get someone soon.
A: How [8] _____ time do you think you'll spend there?
B: At the beginning, I'll have to spend [9] _____ time over there, so I've rented an apartment. But I'm hoping that it will only go on for [10] _____ months, and then the office will be able to look after itself.

Production

TASK 1

Answer the following questions, using the words in brackets.

1 Why do we need to stop at the garage?
(any) We haven't got any petrol left.

2 Why did you see a lawyer?
(some) ....

3 Are you sure they have moved offices?
(somewhere) ....

4 Did you tell the staff about the redundancies we are planning?
(anything) ....

TASK 2

Reply to the questions using *anyone/anywhere/anything you like*.

1 What is the company policy about hotels?
You can stay anywhere you like.

2 Is this information confidential?

....

3 Are any of these seats reserved?

....

4 What sort of information can you store on a CD-ROM?

....

TASK 3

Write short paragraphs answering the questions. Use the words in the box.

not much	a lot of	a little	a few	not many

1 Did you lose a lot of stock in the break-in?
No. Luckily the burglars didn't have much time, because the alarm went off. They took a lot of cheap pieces of jewellery, and they took a little money as well.

2 I'm sorry to hear your trip wasn't successful. What went wrong?

....

....

....

3 Tell me about your training course in England. Did it go well?

....

....

....

'I'm sorry to hear your trip wasn't successful. What went wrong?'

38 Adjectives and adverbs

Presentation

a Form of adverbs

Most adverbs can be formed by adding *-ly*, *-y*, *-ally*, or *-ily*, depending on the spelling of the adjective or noun on which they are based:

expensive/expensively   *full/fully*
dramatic/dramatically   *day/daily*

Some adverbs and adjectives have the same form. Common examples of these are:

daily	early	fast	hard
late	monthly	quarterly	weekly

Some words ending in *-ly* are adjectives and have no corresponding adverbs. Common examples are *friendly, elderly, lonely, silly, costly.*

b Adjectives vs adverbs

Adjectives describe nouns. Adverbs describe verbs.

adjective: *We've had a **dramatic** increase in our orders.*
           (Gives more information about the noun *increase*.)
adverb: *Our orders have increased **dramatically**.*
           (Gives more information about the verb *have increased*.)

c Adverbs + adjectives

Adverbs can also describe adjectives, past participles, and other adverbs:

adverb + adjective: *She is **extremely** intelligent.*
adverb + past participle: *She's **well** paid.*
adverb + adverb: *She does her job **absolutely** brilliantly.*

d Verbs and adjectives

Some verbs are qualified by adjectives rather than adverbs. Most of these are verbs of appearance or verbs of the senses:

appear	be	become	feel	get
look	seem	smell	taste	sound

*You **look exhausted**. Why don't you take the rest of the day off? (not:* look exhaustedly)*
*He **sounded very angry** on the phone. (not: *sounded angrily)*

e *Good* and *well*

Good is an adjective. *Well* is an irregular adverb.

*Mr Hajimoto is a **good** golfer.* (adjective + noun)
*Mr Hajimoto plays golf **well**.* (verb + adverb)

The word *well* can also be an adjective meaning *in good health*:

*She's gone to see the doctor because she isn't **well**.*

Practice

EXERCISE ❶

Form of adverbs

Fill in the blanks with words from the box. Make any necessary changes to the adjectives to form adverbs.

heavy	late	patient	public
punctual	quarter	~~safe~~	silent

1 When you get to New York, give me a ring to let me know you've arrived safely.
2 The Economic Review is published .... , and comes out in March, June, September, and December.
3 Trains in Japan arrive so .... that you can set your watch by them.
4 The train to the airport arrived .... , and as a result I very nearly missed the plane.
5 Most stockbrokers will buy and sell shares in ....-quoted companies.
6 Before privatization, many nationalized industries were .... subsidized by the government.
7 He was not in a hurry, so he waited .... until the client was ready to see him.
8 The new motor is very quiet, and at most speeds it operates almost ....

EXERCISE ❷

Adjectives vs adverbs

Look at the graph showing trends in the share price of a telecoms company. Rewrite the sentences using verbs and adverbs.

1 There was a sudden fall in the shares in March.
   In March the shares fell suddenly.
2 There was a brief recovery in April.
   In April they ....
3 In June there was a dramatic collapse.
   In June they ....
4 There was a considerable fall in July.
   In July they ....
5 There was only a slight fall in August.
   In August they only ....
6 There was a steady improvement in September and October.
   In September and October they ....
7 There was a gradual improvement from mid-November.
   From mid-November, they ....

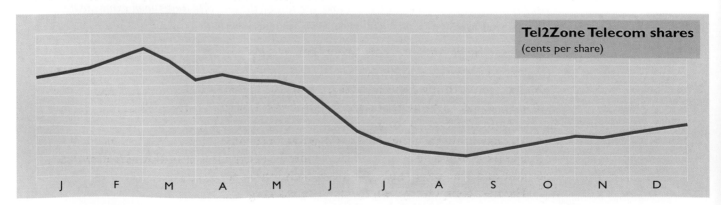

Tel2Zone Telecom shares
(cents per share)

J F M A M J J A S O N D

EXERCISE ❸ **Adverbs + participles, adjectives, adverbs**

Choose a word from box A and one from box B to complete the sentences.

A

surprisingly	~~well~~
badly	totally
commercially	terribly

B

~~qualified~~	viable
quickly	good
designed	illegal

1 He has a PhD and an MBA so he's well qualified.
2 The results at the end of the year were .... ; certainly much better than we had thought.
3 The bank decided that the project was not .... , so they refused to given them a loan
4 Insider dealing is .... If they catch you, you could go to prison.
5 The engine on the XR86 was very .... , and the car soon gained a reputation for unreliability.
6 He spoke .... , so I couldn't really understand what he was saying.

EXERCISE ❹ **Adjective or adverb?**

Read the newspaper review of a new product available in supermarkets. Choose either an adjective or an adverb from the words in *italics*.

TOKYO KITCHEN'S latest offering for lovers of Japanese food is an
¹ *attractive/attractively* packaged selection of sushi. The sushi rice was
² *excellent/excellently* – unlike some other brands, where the rice is too
³ *soft/softly*. The ⁴ *raw/rawly* salmon tasted ⁵ *fresh/freshly*, and the only problem was the octopus which was a little ⁶ *tough/toughly*. All in all a
⁷ *nice/nicely* presented pack and very ⁸ *competitive/competitively* priced. To accompany the dish, try Yamasa Sushi Soya Sauce which is made
⁹ *special/specially* in Japan and which is now ¹⁰ *wide/widely* available at major supermarkets and delicatessens.

Presentation: 9/10
Flavour: 7/10 Value: 9/10
Overall Rating: 8/10

EXERCISE ❺ ***Good* and *well***

Complete the sentences with either *well* or *good*.

1 Did you have a good flight?
2 I've been learning English for three years, so I speak it quite ....
3 He's on sick leave at the moment, but it won't be long before he's .... enough to return to work.
4 The magazine gave their latest fridge-freezers a very .... review.
5 I think it would be a .... idea to discuss this at next week's meeting.
6 Jane and I are old friends. We know each other very ....
7 The new computer system seems to be working ....

Production

TASK 1

Read this email from a retailer to a manufacturer of air conditioners. Choose either the adjective or the adverb in *italics*.

To: Jamil@airnet.com

Subject: Air conditioning

Dear Mr Jamil

I am writing with reference to a ¹ *recent/recently* shipment of 16 M-113 air conditioning units which we received on Tuesday 18 May from your Istanbul factory.

Unfortunately three of the units are not working ² *proper/properly*. One of them may have been broken in transit as the packing case was ³ *bad/badly* dented, and I suggest you take this matter up with your insurers. The other two looked ⁴ *fine/finely*, but when we tested them, they sounded very ⁵ *noisy/noisily* and the cooling systems seemed very ⁶ *ineffective/ineffectively*. I am therefore arranging for the three units to be returned to you ⁷ *immediate/immediately*. I would be ⁸ *grateful/gratefully* if you could send us three new units as soon as possible as the ⁹ *warm/warmly* weather is approaching and we are expecting a ¹⁰ *strong/strongly* demand for air conditioners in the next few weeks.

I look forward to hearing from you.

Fatima Hussein
Manager

TASK 2

Write short sentences connected to the words in brackets about a product or service you received that was unsatisfactory. In each sentence, underline the adjective or adverb that you use.

1 (a repair) I had to take my car back to the garage because the power steering wasn't working <u>properly</u>.

2 (a financial service – bank, etc.) ....

3 (a product you bought) ....

4 (food or drink) ....

5 (a problem on holiday) ....

6 (transport) ....

TASK 3

Write a short extract from a sales letter to a potential customer describing one of the products or services you offer.

I would like to tell you about ....

....

....

....

....

39 Comparison (1): comparing adjectives

Presentation

a **Short adjectives**

To make comparisons, adjectives with one syllable add *-er* and *-est*:

	Comparative	Superlative
old	older	the oldest

*Renault is **large**. Honda is **larger** than Renault. GM is **the largest** car maker in the world.*

If the adjective ends in a short vowel and a single consonant, then we double the consonant when adding *-er* or *-est*. However, if the consonant is *w* or *y*, it is not doubled.

big	bigger	biggest

Adjectives ending in *-y* (e.g. *friendly, wealthy, easy*) and some two-syllable adjectives (e.g. *clever, quiet, narrow*) follow this pattern:

friendly/friendlier/friendliest   *clever/cleverer/cleverest*

Two important exceptions are *good* and *bad*:

good	better	the best
bad	worse	the worst

b **Longer adjectives**

With most other adjectives of two or more syllables, we use *more/less than* and *the most/the least*:

	Comparative	Superlative
modern	more/less modern than	the most modern
profitable	more/less profitable than	the most profitable

*Unilever is **profitable**. Siemens is **more profitable than** Unilever. Daimler Chrysler is **the most profitable** company in Europe.*

c **As ... as, etc.**

We can also make comparisons using *as ... as,* or negative comparisons using *not as ... as ...* In this case the adjective does not change:

*American Airlines is nearly **as large as** United Airlines. Air France is **not as big as** Lufthansa.*

d **Present perfect and superlatives**

The present perfect + *ever* is often used with superlatives:

*That was one of the most interesting talks I **have ever been to**.*

e **Ranking**

The superlative can be used with *second, third,* etc. to rank items:

*Philip Morris is **the largest** tobacco company in the USA.*
*BAT is **the second largest** tobacco company in the USA.*

Practice

EXERCISE 1

Form

Complete the table showing the adjectives and their comparative and superlative forms.

valuable	more valuable than	the most valuable
....	....	the most expensive
good	....	....
....	wealthier than	....
....	....	the biggest
narrow	....	....
....	cheaper than	....
....	....	the worst
profitable	....	....
....	longer than	....
....	....	the most interesting

EXERCISE 2

Comparatives

Fill in the blanks by putting the adjectives in brackets into the correct form.

video g a m e s

Console Wars

The video games industry, which is getting
1 .... (large) and 2 ....
(competitive) day by day, is currently in the middle of a vicious three-way battle between Sony, Nintendo and Microsoft.

A round of massive price cuts took place recently – Sony's PlayStation, which was $100 3 ....
(expensive) than Nintendo's GameCube, came down by 33%; Nintendo replied by making the GameCube $50 4 .... (cheap), and Microsoft had to bring down the price of the Xbox to remain as 5 .... (competitive) as Sony.

All the companies are losing money on the consoles, but are getting it back on the games, which typically cost $50 each. The PlayStation is 6 .... (popular) than its 7 ....
(new) rivals because it has a 8 .... (good) range of games than either of them, but they are working hard to extend their choice.

Games are big business, and according to Goldman Sachs, may soon become 9 .... (important) than the film industry. One of the most important changes is demographic, and the products are not just aimed at kids and teenagers. A generation that grew up with games has simply kept on playing. As they have grown 10 .... (old) they have also become 11 .... (wealthy), making gaming an even 12 .... (lucrative) market than before.

Superlatives

Read the information about Poland, Norway, and Mexico . Using superlatives, write sentences comparing them.

	NUMBER OF McDONALDS RESTAURANTS	LIFE EXPECTANCY (YEARS)	GROSS DOMESTIC PRODUCT PER CAPITA (US$)	UNEMPLOYMENT (%)
Poland	181	73.66	9,900	18.2
Norway	55	78.94	31,100	3.6
Mexico	205	72.03	9,300	2.2

1 (number of McDonalds restaurants/great) Mexico has the greatest number of McDonalds restaurants.
2 (number of McDonalds restaurants/small) Norway has the smallest number of McDonalds restaurants.
3 (life expectancy/long) ....
4 (life expectancy/short) ....
5 (GDP per capita/high) ....
6 (GDP per capita/low) ....
7 (unemployment rate/good) ....
8 (unemployment rate/bad) ....

Present perfect and superlatives

Rewrite the sentences using the present perfect and a superlative.

1 I have never been to such a long meeting.
   That was the longest meeting I have ever been to.
2 I have never heard such a boring presentation.
   That was ....
3 I have never dealt with such difficult customers.
   They are ....
4 We have never produced a product as good as this.
   This is ....
5 I have never used a program as simple as this.
   This is ....

Ranking

Read the information and write sentences using the words in brackets.

1 India has a thriving computer sector. After the US, it was ...
   (no.2/large/exporter of software/last year) the second largest exporter of software last year.
2 Korean financial institutions have undergone a revolution recently. The Kookmin bank was ...
   (no.2 profitable company/Korea/last year)...
3 According to the Sunday Times, Larry Ellison of Oracle has bucked the trend in tech stocks. He is ...
   (no.3 wealthy/person/world)..
4 According to the United Nations, AIDS is still spreading rapidly. Statistics show that it is now ...
   (no.4 /big/killer/in the world)..

Production

TASK 1

Write sentences comparing the following items.

1 the company I work for/the last company I worked for
(big) The company I work for now is bigger than the last company I worked for.
(small) It is not as small as the last company I worked for.

2 the job I do now/my last job
(hard) ....
(easy) ....

3 inflation this year/it was last year
(high) ....
(low) ....

4 our company/our main competitor
(large) ....
(small) ....

TASK 2

Complete the sentences using the present perfect and a superlative adjective.

1 (good meal/have) The best meal I've ever had was in France.
2 (interesting course/go on) ....
3 (good computer/use) ....
4 (nice country/visit) ....
5 (expensive hotel/stay in) ....
6 (fast car/drive) ....
7 (reasonable boss/work for) ....
8 (bad job/have) ....

TASK 3

Write a short paragraph comparing one of your products or services with a product or service of one of your competitors. See the example.

I work for Darlingtons, a law firm that specializes in commercial property, and our main competitors are Kenworth & Brown. We are not as large as they are, but we have the best taxation department in the City. Because we are smaller, we offer our clients a better service, and our charges are significantly lower.

....
....
....
....
....

40 Comparison (2): comparing adverbs and nouns

Presentation

ⓐ Pattern 1: short adverbs

Most adverbs of one syllable, and the adverb *early*, add *-er* and *-est*. These adverbs are usually the ones that have the same form as the adjective:

early	*earlier*	*the earliest*
fast	*faster*	*the fastest*

*He drives **faster** than I do.*

The most important irregular short adverbs are *well* and *badly*:

well	*better*	*the best*
badly	*worse*	*the worst*

*Last year the UK economy performed slightly **better** than its main European partners.*

ⓑ Pattern 2: longer adverbs

Adverbs with two or more syllables are compared using *more/less than* and *the most/the least*:

efficiently	*more/less efficiently than*	*the most/least efficiently*
fluently	*more/less fluently than*	*the most/least fluently*

*It is important that we cut costs and that we start to produce coal **more efficiently**.*

ⓒ Adverbs and participles

We often need adverbs when we are comparing present participles (e.g. *growing*) and past participles (e.g. *defined*, *chosen*):

*China has one of the **fastest growing** economies in the world.*
*We have presented the staff with a set of **clearly defined** proposals.*
*The brochure was illustrated with some **well chosen** photos of the production process.*

ⓓ Comparing nouns

We can compare quantities and amounts by using *more, less, fewer, not as much as, not as many as*, etc. The correct word depends on whether the noun in question is countable or uncountable (see Unit 35):

countable (*more, fewer, many*):

*We need to employ **more** people in our department than in yours.*
*There will be **fewer** opportunities for growth next year.*
*There weren't **as many** opportunities in that market **as** we'd hoped.*

uncountable (*more, less, much*):

*He's got **more** experience than the other applicants.*
*He spends **less** time with his family than he would like.*
*We didn't make **as much** progress at the talks **as** we had hoped.*

Practice

EXERCISE ❶

Short and long adverbs

Complete the text by changing the adjectives in the brackets into adverbs of comparison.

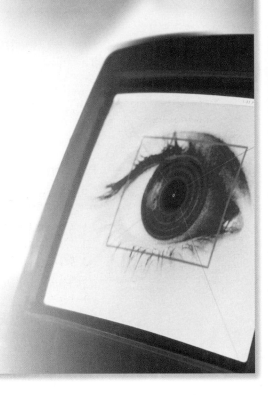

V i s E x p r e s s 6

NEW only $185

V i s E x p r e s s 6 the latest version of our award-winning image-editing software, comes with a great range of improvements to make it the best photo-processing package available.

The new tools allow you to work **more efficiently** ¹ (efficient) and .... ² (fast) than before, and changes to the file management program mean that you can archive your files .... ³ (reliable) and

retrieve them .... ⁴ (quick) than in previous versions.

New or inexperienced users will love the brand new, friendly drag and-drop interface which allows anyone to get productive even .... ⁵ (rapid) than before, and the re-designed Help menu comes with wizards and tutorials that explain complex procedures .... ⁶ (good) and .... ⁷ (clear) than any other image-editing program on the market.

EXERCISE ❷

Adverbs and participles

Rewrite the sentences using superlatives and present or past participles.

1 In the earthquake, few areas were affected as badly as southern California.
   In the earthquake, southern California was one of **the worst affected** areas.
2 Few drugs on the market have been tested as extensively as this.
   This is one of .... drugs on the market.
3 None of our products is selling as well as this.
   This is our .... product.
4 Few departments in the company are managed as efficiently as this one.
   This is one of .... departments in the company.
5 Few countries in the world are developing as rapidly as Taiwan.
   Taiwan is one of .... countries in the world.
6 Few buildings in London are guarded as heavily as the Bank of England.
   The Bank of England is one of .... buildings in London.

EXERCISE ❸

Comparing countable/uncountable nouns

Look at the information about the three Telecoms companies and complete the exercises below.

mm0₂

Moody's credit rating:	Baa2
Moody's outlook:	Stable
Value lost:	£4.85bn
Major shareholders:	
Merrill Lynch	4.43%
Legal & General	2.89%
CGNU	2.88%
Customers	17.25m

VODAFONE

Moody's credit rating:	A2
Moody's outlook:	Stable
Value lost:	£72bn
Major shareholders:	
Legal & General	2.79%
Barclays Global investors	2.37%
Standard Life	2.22%
Customers	101m

ORANGE

Moody's credit rating:	Baa3
Moody's outlook:	
Negative	
Value lost:	£17.3bn
Major shareholders:	
France Telecom	84.16%
Customers	39.3m

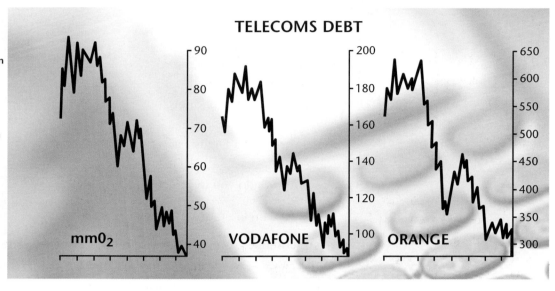

TELECOMS DEBT

mm0₂   VODAFONE   ORANGE

A Complete the sentences using the words in the box.

the most	the fewest	as many … as	more … than

1 Of the three major shareholders in mmO², Merrill Lynch has **the most** shares.
2 Of the three major shareholders in mmO², CGNU owns .... shares.
3 In mmO², Legal and General owns .... shares .... CGNU.
4 Of the three companies, Vodafone has .... customers.
5 mmO² does not have .... customers .... Orange.

B Complete the sentences using the words in the box.

more … than	as much … as	the least	the most	less … than

1 Orange has lost .... value .... mmO².
2 Orange has lost .... value .... Vodafone.
3 mmO² has not lost .... value .... Vodafone.
4 mmO² has lost .... value.
5 The Moody's outlook suggests that of the three companies, Orange is in .... trouble.

EXERCISE ❹

Review: comparing countable/uncountable nouns

Complete the sentences with *more, less, much, many* or *fewer*.

1 Eurotunnel had to spend .... money than it had expected to deal with the unforeseen problem of illegal immigrants.
2 Because of ATMs, banks don't have as .... branches as they used to.
3 They made 2,000 staff redundant, so now they employ .... people than they did last year.
4 Now that I'm in management, I don't spend as .... time at home as I would like.
5 Thanks to the new ring road, there is much .... traffic in the town centre.

Production

TASK 1

Write sentences comparing your life now with your life five years ago. Use a comparative adverb (e.g., *more easily*, or *not as ... as*).

1 How early do you get up now?
I get up earlier than I used to.

2 How regularly do you go abroad now?

.... I used to.

3 How hard do you work now?

.... I used to.

4 How late do you stay at work now?

.... I used to.

5 How well do you speak English now?

.... I used to.

6 How far from work do you live now?

.... I used to.

TASK 2

Complete the sentences using an adverb of your choice in the superlative.

1 Of the three of us, I would say that I probably drive *the fastest.*

2 Of all the people in the Sales Department, I think Peter works ....

3 We all go abroad quite often, but Gerard goes ....

4 Of all the shares I have, the ones I have in ICI have performed ....

5 Of all the companies we looked at, DHL deliver mail ....

6 I did not like any of their reps at all, but I thought Enrique behaved

....

TASK 3

Answer the questions comparing the present with five years ago. Use *more than, less than, fewer than, not as much as,* or *not as many as* in your answers.

1 Do you do a lot of work at the weekends?
I don't do as much as I used to.

2 Do you have a lot of free time?

....

3 Do you go to a lot of dinners?

....

4 Do you go on many training courses?

....

5 Do you get a lot of sleep?

....

6 Do you buy a lot of books?

....

41 Degree: *too, not enough, so, such*

Presentation

ⓐ *Too* and *not ... enough*

We use *too* and *not enough* to talk about the problems of either excess or insufficiency. *Too* and *not enough* can be used with adjectives, adverbs, verbs and nouns. Notice that we use *too* before adjectives and adverbs; *enough* comes after adjectives and adverbs.

	Describing problems with *too*	Describing problems with *not enough*
adjectives:	My office is **too small**. I will have to move.	My office **isn't big enough**. I will have to move.
adverbs:	You're talking **too quietly**. They can't hear you at the back.	You aren't talking **loudly enough**. They can't hear you at the back.
verbs:	You work **too much**. You ought to have a break some time.	You **don't relax enough**. You ought to have a break some time.
countables:	There are **too many people** looking for work, so unemployment is rising.	There **aren't enough jobs**, so unemployment is rising.
uncountables:	We are spending **too much money**. We need to be more careful.	We **aren't saving enough money**. We need to be more careful.

ⓑ *Too/enough* (+ *for*)

Too and *not ... enough* can be followed by an infinitive or *for someone/something* + infinitive. We do not use a pronoun at the end of the sentence:

The seminar was too complicated. I couldn't understand it.
The seminar was **too complicated (for me) to understand**. (not: *... to understand it.)

ⓒ *So* and *such*

So and *such* can be used to add emphasis. *So* is used with adjectives and adverbs, and *such (a)* is used with a noun or adjective + noun:

so before adjectives	She is **so reliable**.
so before adverbs	She works **so hard**.
such a with singular countables	I've got **such a bad headache**.
such with plural countable nouns	He gives **such good talks**.
such with uncountable nouns	He gives me **such good advice**.

So much and *so many* are used to emphasize the quantity of something. We use *so much* with uncountable nouns and *so many* with countables.

I can't see how we have spent **so much money**.
The government has introduced **so many new taxes**.

ⓓ *So* and *such (a)* + *that*

So and *such* + *that* can be used to express result.

It was **such a bad manual that** I couldn't understand it.
The manual was **so bad that** I couldn't understand it.
The manual was written **so badly that** I couldn't understand it.

Practice

EXERCISE **1**

Form

Complete the sentences with *too* or *enough*. Leave one gap blank.

1 We need new premises. This building isn't .... big *enough.*
2 We've changed our insurers because the premiums were .... high
   ....
3 He's not a very good manager. He doesn't communicate his ideas .... clearly
   ....
4 You'd better email them the information or it will arrive .... late
   ....
5 I must have an assistant because I've got .... much work ....
6 We haven't got .... money .... to buy any more equipment.

EXERCISE **2**

Too and _enough_

A group of executives is on a team-building course on a remote island in Scotland.
Re-write each of the sentences using the words in brackets.

1 Our tents aren't big enough.
   (small) Our tents are too small.
2 We have too little food.
   (enough) ....
3 We have brought too few warm clothes.
   (enough) ....
4 They make us walk 20 miles a day.
   (far) ....
5 We're having arguments all the time.
   (too many) ....
6 We're disagreeing all the time.
   (much) ....
7 The weather is too bad for this kind of exercise.
   (enough) ....
8 The instructors hardly ever help us.
   (often/enough) ....
9 We're only sleeping for three hours a night.
   (enough) ....
10 We're carrying an unnecessary amount of equipment.
   (much) ....

Too/enough + infinitive

Combine the following sentences using *too* or *enough*.

1 The exhibition was too far away. We couldn't attend it.
  The exhibition was too far away for us to attend.
2 Your products are too expensive. We can't stock them.

  ....

3 This contract is too complicated. I can't understand it.

  ....

4 My fax wasn't clear enough. He couldn't read it.

  ....

5 Your quotation wasn't low enough. We couldn't accept it.

  ....

6 The project was too risky. They couldn't go ahead with it.

  ....

So and *such*

Fill in the blanks with *so* or *such*. Then match the descriptions to the things in the box.

1 A film   : *so* entertaining; *such* marvellous acting; *so* well-directed
2 .... : .... good graphics; .... fast; .... user-friendly
3 .... : .... a good idea; .... clever; .... useful
4 .... : .... tasty; .... nicely-presented; .... good value
5 .... : .... light; .... modern; decorated .... beautifully
6 .... : .... good food; .... style; .... friendly staff
7 .... : .... illogical; .... useful; .... easy to learn
8 .... : .... fair; .... a support; .... conscientious

an office	an invention	a language	a colleague
a film	software	a meal in a restaurant	a hotel

So/such + *that*

Match the sentences in column A with the results in column B. Then re-write them as one sentence, using *so* and *such*.

A

1 The meeting went on for a long time.

2 The company was in a very bad financial state.
3 Frankfurt was very busy during the book fair.
4 They treat their employees very well.
5 My laptop is very unreliable.
6 The new drug was very successful.
7 He had a very good CV.

B

a The factory couldn't meet the demand for it.
b Nobody ever wants to leave.
c We decided to interview him.
d They called in the receivers.
e I missed the train home.
f We couldn't get a hotel room.
g I don't like to use it.

1 The meeting went on for such a long time that I missed the train home.
2 ....
3 ....
4 ....
5 ....
6 ....
7 ....

Production

TASK 1

Reply to these questions using your own ideas and *too* and *enough*.

1 Why are you thinking about moving jobs?

I've been here too long.

2 Why don't you think we should give him the job?

....

3 Why can't we use your office for the meeting?

....

4 Why don't you get on with your boss?

....

5 Why can't you finish the job by Friday?

....

6 Why didn't you go on the course?

....

TASK 2

Re-write the following sentences in two ways, using *too* and *not enough*.

1 Emerging markets are too volatile. You shouldn't invest in them.

a (too/volatile) Emerging markets are too volatile to invest in.

b (enough/stable) Emerging markets aren't stable enough to invest in.

2 Their forecasts are always very inaccurate. We never use them.

a (too/inaccurate) ....

b (enough/accurate) ....

3 Our tax laws are very complicated. Most people can't understand them.

a (too/complicated) ....

b (enough/simple) ....

4 Rents in the city are very high. We can't have an office there.

a (too/high) ....

b (enough/low) ....

5 The town is very small. We don't have a branch there.

a (too/small) ....

b (enough/big) ....

TASK 3

Add extra comments to these sentences, using *so* or *such*.

1 I'm surprised he is the Managing Director. He seems so young.

2 I've got to get to bed early tonight. ....

3 I really thought you were English. ....

4 I'm amazed that she has resigned. ....

5 How can she complain about her salary? ....

6 I always go to his talks. ....

42 Adjective + preposition combinations

Presentation

ⓐ Adjectives + prepositions

Many adjectives are followed by a particular preposition. Here is a list of common adjectives and the prepositions that normally follow them:

accustomed to	*enthusiastic about*	*related to*
afraid of	*excited about*	*rich in*
answerable to	*famous for*	*satisfied with*
attached to	*guilty of*	*serious about*
aware of	*interested in*	*similar to*
capable of	*opposed to*	*suitable for*
dependent on	*pleased with*	*suspicious of*
different to	*popular with*	*used to (= accustomed to)*
doubtful about	*proud of*	*worried about*

ⓑ Form

These adjectives and prepositions may be followed by a noun or noun phrase:

*The sales department were very **excited about** the new model.*

When followed by a verb, the *-ing* form must be used:

*I would be **interested in** looking into your proposals in some more detail.*

ⓒ Adjective + choice of preposition

Some adjectives can be followed by either of two or more prepositions. Look at these common examples and at the differences in meaning:

*annoyed **about** something*	*He was annoyed **about** the mistakes in the brochure.*
*annoyed **with** someone*	*They were annoyed **with** us for the late delivery.*
*good/bad **at** something*	*I'm very bad **at** chemistry.*
*good/bad **for** something*	*A rise in interest rates would not be good **for** industry.*
*good/bad **with** something*	*She's studying to be a vet because she's good **with** animals.*
*responsible **to** someone*	*The Sales Manager is responsible **to** the Marketing Director.*
*responsible **for** something*	*In my job, I am responsible **for** checking the accounts.*
*sorry **about** something*	*I am sorry **about** the way my department has performed this year – it has been a difficult time.*
*sorry **for** doing something*	*I am so sorry **for** keeping you waiting.*
*(feel) sorry **for** someone*	*I feel very sorry **for** Mr Hasan. He has been made redundant.*

Practice

EXERCISE ❶

Adjectives + prepositions

Complete the sentences with a suitable preposition or adjective. Then complete the puzzle to find the missing words.

1 The Curico Valley in Chile is famous *for* its fine wines.
2 If you are serious .... going ahead with this, let's have a meeting.
3 These new mobile phones are very popular .... our younger customers.
4 The DVL767 digital camcorder is .... to the DV3000 in many ways, but it is slightly cheaper.
5 The salesman did not want to sell me the most expensive model he had because he said it would not really be .... for me.
6 Wage demands are .... to inflation in a number of important ways.
7 The Finance Director said he was strongly .... to awarding everyone a 5% pay rise, and explained that the company could not afford it.
8 South Africa is .... in natural resources like diamonds and gold.
9 I have to travel by car or boat because I am .... of flying.
10 He has very little experience. I don't think he would be .... of running such a large project.
11 He was found .... of fraud and was sent to prison for three years.
12 I would be very .... in discussing the idea of a joint venture.

```
1              f  o  r
2
3
4
5
6
7
8
9
10
11
12
```

EXERCISE ❷

Form

Fill in the blanks with the verbs from the box, using the *-ing* form.

~~buy~~	hire	manufacture	move	run	take

1 I am interested in *buying* a new computer. Could you tell me a little about the different models you have?
2 Some of the staff are not very enthusiastic about .... to our new offices.
3 My boss is not afraid of .... risks.
4 Most politicians know nothing about business, and wouldn't be capable of .... a small business.
5 Our Personnel Manager is responsible for .... new staff.
6 Ferrari is famous for .... sports cars.

EXERCISE **3**

Adjectives + choice of preposition

Complete the newspaper article with the adjectives and prepositions in the box.

annoyed with	bad for	~~good at~~	good with
responsible for	responsible to	sorry about	

As another accounting scandal breaks in the USA, there have been calls for changes in the regulation of audits. It is clear that the current system is not very [1] *good at* detecting fraud. It seems it is all too easy for someone who is [2] .... figures to create a completely misleading impression, as the black hole of $4 billion in Worldcom's accounts shows. The Securities and Exchange Commission, which is [3] .... overseeing audits, has proposed a number of changes, and others have suggested making the

Chief Financial Officers of all Fortune 500 companies personally [4] .... shareholders for the accuracy of the accounts.

Many institutional investors are [5] .... the SEC for failing to act sooner. As one analyst explained 'It is no good apologizing and saying you are [6] .... these failings after they happen. We need to stop them before they happen, because another scandal like this would be really [7] .... investor confidence'.

EXERCISE **4**

Review

Complete this letter from a conference centre to a potential customer, using the words in the box.

accustomed	aware	capable	famous	interested
popular	proud	~~responsible~~	rich	

HOTEL
SELANGOR

Jalan Ampang Baru,
P.O. Box 21493,
Jakarta
INDONESIA
Tel: (62-21) 9086541,
Fax: (62-21) 9086522
Internet: www.hotelselangor.com
Email: welcome@hotelselangor.com

Miss L. Wu
P.O. Box 36293
Sai Kung
Hong Kong

Dear Miss Wu,
I am delighted to hear that you may choose the Hotel Selangor as the venue for your next conference in Indonesia, and I am writing to introduce myself as the person [1] *responsible* for liasing with potential conference organisers.

We are [2] .... of the high levels of service we offer and are [3] .... to organizing large conferences. As you will see from the enclosed brochure, we are [4] .... of providing facilities ranging from a small meeting room to a large banqueting hall for over 1,200 people.

The hotel has an excellent range of facilities including an Olympic swimming pool, tennis courts, and a seven-hectare garden, and you may be [5] .... of the fact that the area is [6] .... in cultural interest. In addition, our seven restaurants are [7] .... for their excellent cuisine, and I am enclosing samples of the menus that have been [8] .... with conference delegates in the past.

Please let me know whether you would be [9] .... in taking the matter further, and I will be happy to discuss any further requirements you have.

I look forward to hearing from you.

Yours sincerely

Abdullah

Nooraini Bt Abdullah
(Conference Manager)

Production

Rewrite the sentences, using the words in brackets.

1 A lot of executives like the BMW 5 series.
   (popular) The BMW 5 series is popular with executives.

2 I don't think she can do the work.
   (capable) ....

3 Everyone knows Bordeaux because of its fine wines.
   (famous) ....

4 Mr Renaldinio is the person who hires new staff.
   (responsible) ....

5 The Industrial Society thinks that higher taxes are a bad idea.
   (opposed) ....

6 Would you like to arrange a meeting?
   (interested) ....

Answer the following questions, using the words in *italics*.

1 What are you *responsible for* in your job?
   In my job, I'm responsible for researching new allergy drugs.

2 Who are you *answerable to*?
   ....

3 What are you *good at*?
   ....

4 What other jobs in the company would you be *capable of* doing?
   ....

5 What sort of salary would you be *satisfied with*?
   ....

Using a word from box A, and a word from box B, write sentences about yourself.

A		B	
~~capable~~	afraid	to	in
interested	proud	~~of~~	of
different	similar	of	to

1 I think I'd be capable of doing what my boss does.

2 ....

3 ....

4 ....

5 ....

6 ....

43 Noun + preposition combinations

Presentation

a Nouns + prepositions

Here is a list of common nouns and the prepositions that normally follow them:

access *to*	cost *of*	invitation *to*	reply *to*
advantage *of*	demand *for*	lack *of*	request *for*
advice *on*	difference *between*	matter *with*	rise *in/of*
alternative *to*	example *of*	need *for*	solution *to*
application *for*	experience *of/in*	opinion *of*	tax *on*
benefit *of*	fall *in/of*	order *for*	trouble *with*
cause *of*	increase/decrease *in/of*	price *of*	
cheque *for*	interest *in*	reason *for*	

b Nouns followed by a choice of prepositions

Words referring to increases and decreases can be followed by *in* or *of*. *In* refers to the thing that has risen or fallen; *of* refers to a quantity or amount:

*There has been a large fall **in** exports over the last few months.*
*There has been a fall **of** 9.7%.*

c Prepositions + nouns

Here is a list of some common preposition and noun combinations:

at a good price	*by post*	*in person*	*on sale*
at a profit/loss	*by return*	*in stock*	*on the whole*
at cost price	*for lunch*	*in the end*	*on time*
at short notice	*for sale*	*in writing*	*out of date*
at your convenience	*in a hurry*	*on application*	*out of order*
by airmail/email	*in advance*	*on business*	*out of stock*
by car/bus,	*in bulk*	*on foot*	*to my mind*
by cheque/credit card	*in charge of*	*on hold*	*under pressure*
by hand	*in debt*	*on holiday*	*with reference to*
by law	*in general*	*on loan*	
by mistake	*in my opinion*	*on order*	

Look at the following examples:

*Because of the traffic, I often come to work **on foot**.*
*I'll confirm that **in writing**.*
*What department are you **in charge of**?*

Practice

EXERCISE ❶

Noun + preposition

Complete the sentences using a noun from box A and a preposition from box B.

A

difference	solution
request	~~invitation~~
experience	reply
trouble	advantage
cheque	price

B

of	to
of	for
of	for
~~to~~	between
to	with

1 Thank you very much for your *invitation to* the launch party.
2 At the moment the bank is considering our .... a larger overdraft, and it will let us have a decision next week.
3 In my opinion, the main .... having a credit card is that you can pay for things over the phone.
4 Have we received a .... that letter we sent them last week?
5 Yes, they've paid us. We received a .... $18,000 a few days ago.
6 I don't think he would be suitable for the job in Tokyo. He has had very little .... working overseas.
7 In the long term, inflation is linked to the .... raw materials.
8 Is there any .... these two modems? They look the same to me.
9 We had a lot of .... one of our customers who wouldn't pay us, so we took legal advice.
10 Let me know if you can think of a .... the problem.

EXERCISE ❷

Noun + choice of prepositions

Read the newspaper extract. Fill in the blanks with *in* or *of*.

No change in Eurozone rates

■ **The European Central Bank** has left interest rates unchanged despite worries over the German economy. The last time there was a fall [1] .... interest rates was on 10 May, when the bank announced a cut [2] .... 0.25%, bringing the key interest rate for the Eurozone countries to 4.5%. The decision came hours after official figures showed a surprising increase [3] .... unemployment in Germany. Analysts had been forecasting a rise [4] .... 5,500 but the official figures reported an increase [5] .... 18,000, taking the total to just under four million. The ECB is also facing the problem of a sharp increase [6] .... Eurozone inflation. The increase [7] .... 0.3% has pushed the annual rate to 2.9%, compared with a target of 2%.

Preposition + noun combinations

In the following telephone conversations, fill in the blanks with the missing prepositions.

A   A: Hello, Finance.

    B: Good morning. I'm calling ¹*with* reference to a cheque I've just had from you. I'm afraid you have put the wrong year on it ²................................ mistake. The bank have just returned it because it is ³................................ of date.

    A: I'm so sorry. It must be because it's January. If you send it back we'll issue a new one ⁴................................ return.

B   A: Hello, can you put me through to the Marketing Department, please?

    B: Yes, of course … I'm afraid the line's busy, I'll have to put you ¹................................ hold for a moment.

    A: OK …

    C: Hello, Marketing.

    A: Could I speak to the person who is ²................................ charge of booking advertising space, please?

    C: I'm afraid she's away ³................................ business at the moment. Can I help you?

    A: Well, we are currently offering some attractive discounts for next month's issue of *Face* magazine.

    C: Well, ⁴................................ the whole we don't book advertising space ⁵................................ such short notice, but if you'd like to give us details of your rates ⁶................................ writing, we'll look at them and let you know.

Review

Complete the following extract with the missing prepositions.

If you're looking for an alternative ¹................................ *the traditional high street bank, then Internet banking may be a solution.*

PROS: The main advantage ²................................ Internet banks is that they have lower charges because they have no need ³................................ buildings or a branch network. ⁴................................ the whole, they also offer slightly better rates for savers. After getting set up, a further benefit ⁵................................ Internet banks is that you can have access ⁶................................ you money 24 hours a day and can make payments or transfer funds ⁷................................ your convenience.

CONS: Some customers worry about the potential lack ⁸................................ security of dealing with money online, but the banks have worked hard to find solutions ⁹................................ security problems. Internet banks do not offer the facilities to meet a bank manager ¹⁰................................ person, and paying in cheques still has to be done ¹¹................................ post. Some banks also suffer from a lack ¹²................................ cash machines.

Production

TASK 1

Complete the following sentences using your own ideas.

1 I don't have much experience *of dealing with difficult customers.*
2 I don't think there is much difference ....
3 Do you think immigration is responsible for the rise ....
4 It will be difficult to find a solution ....
5 During the winter months, the demand ....

TASK 2

Rewrite the following sentences in a different way, using one of the phrases from page 175, section C, *Prepositions + nouns*.

1 This machine doesn't work.   This machine is *out of order.*
2 Quick! I can't wait.   I'm ....
3 We lost money when we sold the car. We sold the car ....
4 I usually drive to work.   I usually go to work ....
5 The train didn't arrive late.   The train arrived ....
6 My house is on the market.   My house is ....
7 He owes money.   He is ....
8 We expect delivery of the goods soon. The goods are ....

TASK 3

Look through this extract from the Oxford Wordpower Dictionary, which gives a number of different idioms using the word *hand*. Then fill in the blanks with the correct expression.

1 I have a problem *on my hands*, and I'd like your advice about what to do.
2 At first, some of the strikers on the picket line threw stones at the police; then more joined in and soon the demonstration got

....
3 We don't use machines at all; everything is made ....
4 When you arrive at your holiday villa, one of our representatives will be

.... to help you with any problems you may have.
5 I can't stop the court case from going ahead. Everything is now .... of my lawyer, and I can't discuss it with you.
6 On the one hand, a job in England would be a good career move for me.

...., I would miss the people I know here in Milan.

IDIOMS (close/near) at hand (*formal*) near in space or time: *Help is close at hand.*
be an old hand (at sth) → OLD
by hand **1** done by a person and not by machine: *I had to do all the sewing by hand.*

(at) first hand (used about information that you have received) from sb who was closely involved: *Did you get this information first hand?* ••► Look at second-hand.

in your hands in your possession, control or care: *The matter is in the hands of a solicitor.*

off your hands not your responsibility any more
on hand available to help or to be used: *There is always an adult on hand to help when the children are playing outside.*
on your hands being your responsibility: *We seem to have a problem on our hands.*
on the one hand...on the other (hand) used for showing opposite points of view: *On the one hand, of course, cars are very useful. On the other hand, they cause a huge amount of pollution.*
(get/be) out of hand not under control: *Violence at football matches is getting out of hand.* ••► opposite in hand
out of your hands not in your control; not your responsibility: *I can't help you, I'm afraid. The matter is out of my hands.*

178   Noun + preposition combinations

Verb + preposition combinations

Presentation

ⓐ Verb + preposition

Here is a list of common verbs and the prepositions that normally follow them:

account *for*	complain *about*	look *at*	talk *to*
agree *on*	comply *with*	look *for*	think *about* (= consider)
agree *with*	consist *of*	pay *for*	think *of* (= have an opinion of)
apply *for*	depend *on*	rely *on*	wait *for*
belong *to*	hear *about*	take care *of*	write *to*
complain *to*	hear *from*		

I complained to the manager about the poor service we had received.
Whether or not the project succeeds will depend on a number of factors.
I liked the last candidate. What did you think of her, Bernard?

ⓑ Verb + object + preposition

The following verbs can be followed by an object and a preposition:

ask *someone for*	divide *something into*	provide *someone with*
blame *someone for*	insure *something against*	spend *something on*
borrow *something from*	invest *something in*	supply *someone with*
congratulate *someone on*	protect *someone from*	thank *someone for*

I rang to congratulate Hasan on getting the promotion.
I would be grateful if you would provide me with a reference.
We currently spend over $20m a year on R&D.

ⓒ Verb + no preposition

These verbs are not usually followed by a preposition:

phone	*meet*	*enter*	*tell*	*discuss*

I'll phone the Director in the morning. (not: *phone to the Director)
Do you need a visa to enter Ecuador? (not: *enter into Ecuador)

Note: We can say *have a meeting with someone*, and in American English it is also possible to say *meet with someone*.

Practice

Verb + preposition

Complete the letter with the correct prepositions.

Medieta Juguetes
Avenida Revolución 1910
Guadalajara
Jalisco
Mexico

KinderFarben

Gartenstrasse 25
D-97259
Greussenheim
Deutschland

Dear Ms Medieta

RE: KinderFarben Painting Packs

Many thanks you for your email about the KinderFarben range of children's paints.

Here are the answers to the points you mentioned:

- All KinderFarben paints fully comply ¹ **with** EU food and safety standards. The paints are non-toxic and washable.

- Each pack in the JuniorArtist range consists ² .... a paintbox with eight colours, a paintbrush and a leaflet in Spanish.

- Average delivery time to Mexico for orders over 5,000 is fourteen days. We do not rely ³ .... rail transport, so would be unaffected by the current strike. We can also take care ⁴ .... insurance and any other documentation.

- The discounts we offer depend ⁵ .... the size of orders – I would be happy to talk ⁶ .... you about this.

- Goods should be paid for in euros. We offer flexible credit terms, so I am sure we could agree ⁷ .... suitable terms.

Please contact me if you have any further questions. I look forward to hearing ⁸ .... you.

Martin Ballack

Martin Ballack
Sales Manager

Verb + preposition

Complete the sentences with a verb from box A and a preposition from box B.

A	
~~agree~~	think
hear	wait
look	write

B	
about	to
at	~~with~~
for	of

1 Mr Langer thinks we should go ahead with this proposal, but I'm afraid that I don't *agree with* him.
2 Did you .... what happened in the meeting? Miss Johanssen resigned.
3 Please .... me at the above address or phone me on 082 756 4537.
4 How long do you think we will have to .... a reply to our proposal?
5 I am not sure about these changes. What do you .... them?
6 If you .... the small print at the bottom of the insurance form, you will see that we are not covered for accidental damage.

EXERCISE **3**

Verb + object + preposition

Complete the sentences with a suitable verb. Then complete the puzzle to find the name of a famous French company. (All the verbs are in section ⓑ of the grammar notes on page 179.)

1 Who do you *blame* for the current rail strike? Do you think the management or the unions are responsible? (5 letters)
2 I have asked my former employer to .... me with a reference. (7 letters)
3 We have had a very good year, and in particular, I would like to .... Gupta on the excellent results he has achieved in R&D. (12 letters)
4 I phoned Bernard to .... him for all his help. (5 letters)
5 Many companies will not .... your premises against flooding, if you live in certain areas of the country, because the risk is too high. (6 letters)
6 When you write back, I think you ought to check how many units they will be able to .... us with each month. (6 letters)
7 A property developer bought the building and decided to .... it into six separate apartments. (6 letters)
8 The government is planning to .... about £30 billion on social security payments and unemployment benefit. (5 letters)

EXERCISE **4**

Verb + preposition or no preposition?

Complete the following sentences with a preposition if it is necessary. If it is not necessary, leave a blank (✗).

1 Well-qualified graduates with some work experience find it fairly easy to enter ✗ the job market but people who leave school with no qualifications find it very hard.
2 When you see the tax inspector, you will have to account .... all the money you have received over the past six years.
3 If they won't help you, you should complain .... their Head Office.
4 If you need information about Senegal, phone .... the Embassy.
5 We have offered Helen a job in New York, but she says she needs a few days to think .... it.
6 I'm looking .... that letter from Marlino's – have you seen it?
7 Yesterday the Prime Minster met .... the Secretary General of the United Nations in Geneva.
8 The next item on the agenda is promotion, and I would like to discuss .... the plans we have for next year.

Verb + preposition combinations   181

Production

TASK 1

Answer the following questions, using the words in brackets.

What would you do if …

1 … you were not satisfied with the service in a restaurant?
(complain) I'd complain to the head waiter.

2 … you had a serious personal problem?
(talk) ....

3 … you wanted a copy of a company's annual report?
(write) ....

4 … you were offered a job in a different city?
(think) ....

5 … you were asked to sign a contract that you couldn't understand?
(rely)
....

TASK 2

Using the words in the box, report what the following people said.

~~blame~~	congratulate	provide	thank	ask

1 She said to me, 'You caused the accident! It's all your fault!'
She blamed me for the accident.

2 He said to me, 'Here is the information you wanted.'
....

3 She said to me, 'Thanks a lot. You've been very helpful.'
....

4 He said to me, 'What's your opinion of the new Marketing Assistant?'
....

5 They said to us, 'Brilliant! Well done! You solved the problem!'
....

TASK 3

Give advice on the following problems using the words in brackets.

1 'I have a great business idea, but I have no money.'
(borrow … from) You ought to borrow what you need from the bank.

2 'I have inherited $50,000 from my aunt who died last month.'
(invest … in) You ought to ....

3 'What should I do with my £500 clothing allowance?'
(spend … on) You ought to ....

4 'Do you think it is safe to keep this valuable painting in my office?'
(insure … against) Yes, but you ought to ....

45 Phrasal verbs

Presentation

(a) Meaning changes

Sometimes verbs are followed by a word like *in, off, at,* etc. and this can change the meaning of the verb. Compare:

1 *He looked at the photograph.*
2 *I'm looking after my colleague's clients while she's away. (I'm taking care of them.)*

In 1, the word *at* is a normal preposition and does not change the meaning of the verb *look*. In 2, the word *after* gives the verb *look* a different meaning. Verbs like this are called phrasal verbs, and they are very common in informal English. *Look after* is one example.

(b) Separable phrasal verbs

Sometimes it is possible to separate the two parts of a phrasal verb. If the object is a noun, we can put it in two places:

We had to put the meeting off. We had to put off the meeting.
(We had to delay the meeting.)

If the object is a pronoun (i.e. *me, you, him, her, it,* etc.), it must come after the verb:
*We had to put it off. (not: *put off it)*

Here is a list of common separable phrasal verbs and approximate meanings:

back ... up (support)	*give ... up (stop doing)*	*put ... off (delay)*
clear ... up (tidy)	*hold ... up (delay)*	*put ... through (connect)*
close ... down (shut)	*keep ... down (maintain low price)*	*ring ... up (phone)*
cut ... off (disconnect)	*look ... up (find in a list)*	*take ... over (get control of)*
fill ... in (complete a form)	*make ... up (invent)*	*throw ... away (dispose of)*
find ... out (discover information)		

(c) Inseparable phrasal verbs

Some two-part phrasal verbs and all three-part phrasal verbs are inseparable. Many inseparable verbs do not have objects:

*We ran out of petrol on the motorway. (not: *ran petrol out of)*
You must call on me next time you're in the States.

Here is a list of common inseparable phrasal verbs :

back out of (withdraw)	*cut down on (reduce)*	*look after (take care of)*
break down (stop working)	*do without (manage without)*	*look into (investigate)*
call on (visit)	*get on with (like someone)*	*run into (meet by chance)*
carry on (continue)	*get over (recover from)*	*run out of (have none left)*
come across (appear to others)	*go through (read carefully)*	*take up (occupy)*
come down (fall in price)	*hold on (wait a moment)*	*turn up (arrive)*
check in (register)		

Practice

EXERCISE 1

Meaning changes

In the following sentences, decide whether the verb keeps its ordinary meaning (OM) or whether it is a phrasal verb (PV).

1 What shall we *give* Amanda *for* a leaving present?   OM
2 His doctor said he was drinking too much and should *give* it *up*. PV
3 I was talking to her on the phone, but we were suddenly *cut off*. ....
4 The other day I *cut* my finger *with* a knife, but it's not serious. ....
5 I'll *take* your letter *to* the Post Office if you like. ....
6 Hanson PLC *took* the company *over* last year. ....
7 Sorry we're late. We were *held up* by roadworks on the Ring Road. ....
8 He *held* his hand *up* because he wanted to ask a question. ....

EXERCISE 2

Separable phrasal verbs

Look at the pictures and re-write each of the following sentences in two ways. In a, change the word order, and in b, use a pronoun.

1 I think we need to clear the office up.
   a I think we need to clear up the office.
   b I think we need to clear it up.

2 You should never throw receipts away.
   a ....
   b ....

3 They've closed the factory down.
   a ....
   b ....

4 We've managed to keep inflation down.
   a ....
   b ....

EXERCISE 3

Common separable phrasal verbs

In the following dialogue, fill in the blanks with a phrasal verb from the box that means the same as the words in brackets.

cut ... off	pick ... up	put ... off	put ... through

A: Could you (connect me) [1] .... to extension 234 again?
B: Certainly. OK, you're through now.
C: Sorry about that. They (disconnected us) [2] .... for some reason.
A: I know. Anyway, I can't make the meeting on the 18th, as I'll still be in Germany, so could we (postpone it) [3] .... until the 24th?
C: Yes, I can't see any problem there.
A: Good, can I have a word with Hugo? He's coming over and I need to know when he wants me to (collect him) [4] .... from the airport.

Inseparable phrasal verbs

Complete the following email, using the phrasal verbs from the box which mean the same as the words in brackets.

~~break down~~	do without	look into	run out of	take up
call on	check in	hold on	look after	turn up

From: Brian@crisp.com

To: Amanda@crisp.com

Subject: 1 service lift   2 Mr Takashi

- The service lift in the warehouse has (stopped working) [1] broken down again. Could you please get the Otis engineer to (investigate) [2] .... what has gone wrong and to fix it ASAP? This is urgent, because we really can't (manage if we don't have) [3] .... it. We're having to move everything upstairs by hand, and this is (occupying) [4] .... a lot of time and pretty soon everyone is going to (have no more) [5] .... patience.

- We are expecting Mr Takashi from Japan some time this afternoon. I have rung the hotel, but he hasn't (registered) [6] .... there yet, so he may just (arrive unexpectedly) [7] .... at the office. If he does, could you (take care of) [8] .... him and ask him to (wait) [9] .... until I get back? I have to (visit) [10] .... a client at about 2.30, but I should be back by 3.15.

Thanks,
Brian

Review

In the following sentences, choose the best option from the words a–d.

1 The latest iMacs are expensive, but if you wait, prices will .... down.
   a back   b run   c turn   d come

2 I agree, and if they criticize you at the meeting, I will back you ....
   a up   b down   c in   d out

3 By the way, I .... into Siti in York, and she sends you her regards.
   a looked   b turned   c came   d ran

4 Could you ring British Airways and find .... if there are any seats on the flight to Rome?
   a up   b in   c over   d out

5 Work is always so much better if you have a boss you .... on with.
   a get   b carry   c take   d hold

Production

TASK 1

There are a large number of phrasal verbs in English, and it is helpful to keep a note of the ones that you meet. Here is one suggestion about how you can record them.

Write the verb on the left-hand page, and write sample sentences on the right-hand page, showing the phrasal verbs in context. As you meet more phrasal verbs with the same stem, add them to the left-hand page and put examples on the right-hand page.

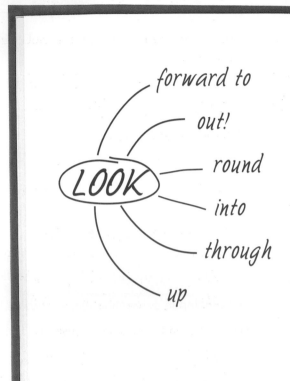

I look forward to meeting you next week.

Look out! That car is on the wrong side of the road.

In the afternoon, the delegation from Korea want to see the offices and look round the factory.

Leave this problem with me. I'll look into the matter and find out what went wrong.

I need a few minutes to look through my notes before the presentation.

If you don't know his address, I'll look it up in a book.

Now complete the following sentences using a phrasal verb with *look*.

1 Could I have the afternoon off? I'd like to look round a house that we're thinking of buying.

2 I've forgotten the code for the DX16 exhaust pipe. Could you look it .... in the price list?

3 At the moment the accident investigators are looking .... the cause of the crash.

4 I am really looking .... to going away on holiday next week.

5 You'd better look .... – the boss is coming and he is in a bad mood.

6 Could you look .... this letter quickly and see if there is anything you would like to add to it?

TASK 2

Use your dictionary to make a list of phrasal verbs with *come*, *take* and *get*.

Write an example sentence for each one.

Appendix 1 – Spelling rules

1 Verbs

With most verbs, we add -s to the verb in the 3rd person, and make no other changes:

I/you/we/they run	*he/she/it runs*

With verbs that end in -o, -ch, -ss, -sh, and -x, we add -es:

I/you/we/they go	*he/she/it goes*
I/you/we/they teach	*he/she/it teaches*
I/you/we/they miss	*he/she/it misses*
I/you/we/they rush	*he/she/it rushes*
I/you/we/they fix	*he/she/it fixes*

With verbs that end in a consonant + *y*, we remove the -*y* and add -*ies*:

I/you/we/they try	*he/she/it tries*

2 Nouns

Most nouns just add -s to make the plural form:

pen	*pens*

Nouns ending in -*ch*, -*ss*, -*sh*, and -*x* add -*es* in the plural:

match	*matches*
class	*classes*
dish	*dishes*
box	*boxes*

Nouns ending in a consonant + *y* drop the -*y* and add -*ies*:

party	*parties*

Nouns ending in a vowel + *y* add -*s*:

day	*days*

3 -*ing* form

With most verbs, we add -*ing* to the verb and make no other changes:

build	*building*
try	*trying*

With one-syllable verbs that have a short vowel sound, and end in a consonant, we double the consonant and add -*ing*:

sit	*sitting*
run	*running*

If the vowel sound is long, we do not double the consonant:

read	*reading*
speak	*speaking*

If the verb ends in a silent -*e*, we delete the -*e* and add -*ing*:

take	*taking*
drive	*driving*

4 Past tense, regular verbs

With most regular verbs, we add -*ed* to form the past tense:

look	*looked*
stay	*stayed*

If the verb ends in a silent -*e*, we just add -*d*:

like	*liked*
behave	*behaved*

If the verb ends in a consonant + *y*, we remove the -*y* and add -*ied*:

try	*tried*
deny	*denied*

If the verb has a short vowel sound and ends in a consonant, we double the consonant:

stop	*stopped*
ban	*banned*

Appendix 2 – Irregular verbs

Verb	Past tense	Past participle
arise	arose	arisen
be	was, were	been
beat	beat	beaten
become	became	become
begin	began	begun
bend	bent	bent
bet	bet	bet
bind	bound	bound
bite	bit	bitten
bleed	bled	bled
blow	blew	blown
break	broke	broken
bring	brought	brought
broadcast	broadcast	broadcast
build	built	built
burn	burnt	burnt
	burned	burned
burst	burst	burst
buy	bought	bought
catch	caught	caught
choose	chose	chosen
come	came	come
cost	cost	cost
creep	crept	crept
cut	cut	cut
deal	dealt	dealt
dig	dug	dug
do	did	done
draw	drew	drawn
dream	dreamt	dreamt
	dreamed	dreamed
drink	drank	drunk
drive	drove	driven
eat	ate	eaten

Verb	Past tense	Past participle
fall	fell	fallen
feed	fed	fed
feel	felt	felt
fight	fought	fought
find	found	found
fly	flew	flown
forbid	forbade	forbidden
forget	forgot	forgotten
forgive	forgave	forgiven
freeze	froze	frozen
get	got	got
give	gave	given
go	went	gone
grind	ground	ground
grow	grew	grown
hang	hung	hung
have	had	had
hear	heard	heard
hide	hid	hidden
hit	hit	hit
hold	held	held
hurt	hurt	hurt
keep	kept	kept
know	knew	known
lay	laid	laid
lead	led	led
lean	leant	leant
leap	leapt	leapt
learn	learnt	learnt
	learned	learned
leave	left	left
lend	lent	lent
let	let	let
lie	lay	lain

Verb	Past tense	Past participle
light	lit	lit
lose	lost	lost
make	made	made
mean	meant	meant
meet	met	met
pay	paid	paid
put	put	put
read	read	read
ride	rode	ridden
ring	rang	rung
rise	rose	risen
run	ran	run
say	said	said
see	saw	seen
seek	sought	sought
sell	sold	sold
send	sent	sent
set	set	set
shake	shook	shaken
shine	shone	shone
show	showed	shown
shrink	shrank	shrunk
shut	shut	shut
sing	sang	sung
sink	sank	sunk
sit	sat	sat
sleep	slept	slept
slide	slid	slid
smell	smelt	smelt
	smelled	smelled
speak	spoke	spoken
speed	sped	sped
	speeded	speeded
spell	spelt	spelt
	spelled	spelled
spend	spent	spent

Verb	Past tense	Past participle
spill	spilt	spilt
	spilled	spilled
spin	spun	spun
split	split	split
spoil	spoilt	spoilt
	spoiled	spoiled
spread	spread	spread
spring	sprang	sprung
stand	stood	stood
steal	stole	stolen
stick	stuck	stuck
sting	stung	stung
strike	struck	struck
swear	swore	sworn
sweep	swept	swept
swim	swam	swum
swing	swung	swung
take	took	taken
teach	taught	taught
tear	tore	torn
tell	told	told
think	thought	thought
throw	threw	thrown
understand	understood	understood
wake	woke	woken
wear	wore	worn
win	won	won
wind	wound	wound
write	wrote	written

Verbs from these tables are also irregular when they have a prefix, e.g. *mistake – mistook – mistaken, withstand – withstood – withstood.*

Answer key

1   Present simple

Practice

EXERCISE 1

2 come
3 do you do
4 work
5 do you live
6 don't live
7 spend
8 go
9 comes
10 Do you travel
11 visit

EXERCISE 2

2 meets
3 allow
4 provide
5 do not function
6 offers
7 works
8 grows
9 looks
10 does not seem
11 invests
12 helps

EXERCISE 3

2 doesn't work
3 works
4 does she come
5 comes
6 doesn't stay
7 starts
8 goes

EXERCISE 4

2 use
3 stands
4 combines
5 passes
6 splits
7 burns
8 turns
9 does not cause
10 means
11 takes
12 believe

EXERCISE 5

2 gets
3 goes
4 doesn't get
5 leaves
6 reaches
7 doesn't leave
8 stops
9 arrives

Production

TASK 1

2 A stockbroker buys and sells
3 An architect designs
4 Venture capitalists invest
5 Auditors check
6 Management consultants advise
7 A journalist writes
8 Personnel officers arrange

TASK 2 (Sample answer only)

I work for a large software development company. We employ over 500 programmers, and we specialize in developing software for large manufacturing companies. Our headquarters are in Bristol, but we have regional offices all over the country.

TASK 3 (Sample answers only)

1 I come to work by car.
2 It usually takes me about an hour.
3 I open my emails, answer phone calls and go to meetings.
4 I usually have a sandwich.
5 I usually leave the office to visit clients.
6 I usually finish between 5 and 6.
7 I visit friends or go to my house in the country.

2   Present continuous

Practice

EXERCISE 1

2 are having
3 are you doing
4 is expecting
5 isn't working
6 Are you calling
7 am phoning

EXERCISE 2

2 f
3 a
4 h
5 e
6 d
7 g
8 c

EXERCISE 3

2 am attending
3 are you staying
4 is affecting
5 aren't spending
6 aren't getting
7 aren't buying
8 isn't doing
9 is managing
10 are looking

EXERCISE 4

2 is declining
3 are taking
4 are cutting
5 is transforming
6 is improving
7 are starting
8 are holding
9 are not travelling

Production

TASK 1 (Sample answers only)

2 The printer isn't working.
3 Bob's having a meeting with Jane.
4 She's having a coffee with Linda.
5 Someone's coming.

TASK 2 (Sample answers only)

2 I'm running the R&D department.
3 We're giving all our staff language lessons.
4 I'm doing a part-time course in accounting.
5 I'm trying to find a bigger house nearer the office.

TASK 3 (Sample answers only)

2 The trains aren't running at all reliably at the moment. They're carrying out a lot of track repairs, so everything is taking much longer.

3 We're very understaffed at the moment. I'm doing George's job because he's away doing a course, and our secretary is having a holiday in Malta.

4 The situation in the Middle East is getting more and more dangerous every day.

TASK 4 (Sample answers only)

2 … cars are getting much safer thanks to air bags and better designs.

3 Cars are becoming much more fuel efficient.

4 Most cars are becoming more reliable and manufacturers are offering longer guarantees.

5 Electric cars are beginning to appear in the showrooms but are still expensive.

6 Pollution is still getting worse in big cities.

3 Present simple vs present continuous

Practice

EXERCISE 1

2 Do the farmers bring	7 passes
3 we always collect	8 operates
4 deliver	9 isn't working
5 do you have	10 are changing
6 test	

EXERCISE 2

2 design	6 are setting up
3 look	7 is having
4 get	8 require
5 spend	

EXERCISE 3

2 aren't sending	6 varies
3 am dealing	7 am learning
4 leads	8 come
5 aren't doing	

EXERCISE 4

2 go	7 is beginning
3 put	8 are starting
4 run	9 are attacking
5 takes	10 is losing
6 seems	

EXERCISE 5

2 are carrying, want	5 am trying, means
3 are trying, sounds	6 am applying, depends
4 Do you know, is doing	7 tastes, is becoming

Production

TASK 1 (Sample answers only)

2 I speak French and I'm learning Arabic.

3 I normally like my work but I'm not enjoying it at the moment.

4 I want to be a management consultant, so I'm doing an MBA at Insead.

5 I usually work from 9 to 5 but I'm staying late this week because I've got a lot to do.

6 My boss travels a lot and at the moment she's visiting Australia.

7 We have several subsidiaries in Europe and at the moment we're setting up another one in Brussels.

8 We normally export a lot to Greece but we aren't getting many orders at the moment.

TASK 2 (Sample answers only)

2 Who are you writing to?

3 What does Ken's father do?

4 How do you normally come to work?

5 How often does your Sales Director go abroad?

6 Is business going well?

7 So you know each other already, do you?

8 Are you taking anyone on?

4 Past simple

Practice

EXERCISE 1

2 Did (you) study	5 Did (you) visit
3 didn't accept	6 placed
4 complained	7 did (you) hire

EXERCISE 2

A	B
1 did	2 did business
2 made	3 made a profit
3 go	4 went abroad
4 wrote	5 wrote a report
5 have	6 had problems
6 paid	7 paid by credit card
7 sell	8 sold out/ran out

EXERCISE 3

2 got	12 gave
3 introduced	13 developed
4 set	14 opened
5 made	15 grew
6 sold	16 kept
7 carried	17 went
8 married	18 trained
9 had	19 brought
10 founded	20 took
11 came	

EXERCISE 4

2 When did she marry Joseph Lauter?
  on
3 When did they have their first child?
  in
4 When did she set up the company?
  at
5 When did she get her first big break?
  in
6 When did Leonard take over as CEO?
  in

Production

TASK 1 (Sample answers only)

2 They moved to much larger offices.
3 They installed some modern equipment.
4 They renovated the workspace.
5 They sold the subsidiaries off at a small loss.
6 They expanded the sales and marketing department.
7 They advertised nationally and internationally.
8 They brought in new lines.
9 They set up a web site.
10 They computerised all accounting procedures.

TASK 2 (Sample answer only)

I left school when I was 18 and joined a supermarket. I stayed with them for two years, and then I was promoted. I went on a management training course, and in 2002 I became the assistant manager of one of the new stores in Bath.

 Present perfect (1)

Practice

EXERCISE 1

2 have fallen
3 Have you written
4 have spent
5 have shut
6 have drawn
7 haven't spoken
8 Have you found
9 has just got
10 have you met

EXERCISE 2

2 The Euro has fallen against the Dollar.
3 They have redecorated the office.
4 We have re-located to Korea.

EXERCISE 3

3 announced – last week
4 gave – last week
5 have welcomed – no information
6 has stated – no information
7 carried – yesterday
8 has suffered – no information
9 has fallen – no information
10 has already agreed – no information

EXERCISE 4

2 have just read
3 have just given
4 have just bought
5 has just arrived
6 have just spoken
7 has just announced

EXERCISE 5

2 has been
3 have been
4 has gone
5 have (not) been

Production

TASK 1 (Sample answers only)

2 she has run out of them.
3 she has just had a baby.
4 we have already reached our sales targets.
5 it has introduced a lot of new taxes on business.
6 they have had floods and hurricanes.
7 the market has fallen by 40%.

TASK 2 (Sample answers only)

2 It has been changed into a big open plan area. Everyone has lost their own space, and it feels very strange.
3 It has spent millions on a new network linking the HQ with all the other outlets in this country and abroad.

TASK 3 (Sample answers only)

2 He has just phoned to say he is ill.
3 I have left it on your desk.
4 They have secured a large contract with the US government.
5 has just opened.
6 I have rung her three times but there's no reply.
7 I've just had one.

 Present perfect (2): *ever, never, already, yet*

Practice

EXERCISE 1

2 Have you ever been to Japan before?
3 Have you ever learned a foreign language?
4 Have you ever organized a conference like this?
5 Have you ever worked for a Japanese company?
6 Have you ever eaten sushi?

EXERCISE 2

2 A: Have you ever been
  B: had
  A: did you go
  B: went
3 A: Have you ever been
  B: went
  A: was it
  B: thought, was
4 A: Have you ever visited
  B: have never visited, have been
  A: did you do
  B: gave

EXERCISE 3

2 have already done
3 have not found any major problems yet
4 have already fixed
5 Have you checked
6 have already altered
7 haven't ordered them yet
8 haven't worked it out yet
9 haven't finished work yet

EXERCISE 4

2 have already reached
3 have gone
4 has managed
5 have had
6 have grown
7 have opened

EXERCISE 5

2 b	6 c
3 e	7 d
4 g	8 a
5 f	

Production

TASK 1 (Sample answers only)

2 I have never invested in the stock market.
3 I have never been to Peru
4 I have never read any.
5 it has never gone wrong.
6 They have never had a strike.

TASK 2 (Sample answer only)

2 I have already written a business plan, and I have raised the finance that I will need. I have already leased a new production site but I haven't recruited any staff.

TASK 3 (Sample answers only)

2 ... we have had over half a million hits.
3 ... it has made 2,000 people redundant.
4 ... haven't had any calls at all.

 7 ## Present perfect (3): *for* and *since*

Practice

EXERCISE 1

2 right	6 wrong – she has had
3 wrong – I have known	7 wrong – has been
4 wrong – have you been	8 right
5 right	

EXERCISE 2

2 since	6 since
3 for	7 since
4 since	8 for
5 for	

EXERCISE 3

2 A: How long have you had a website for investors?
   B: We have had a website for investors for three months.
3 A: How long has the property been on the market?
   B: It has been on the market for six months.
4 A: How long have you had an office in Spain?
   B: We have had an office there since 2000.
5 A: How long has Jason been in the States?
   B: He has been there since the 18th.

EXERCISE 4

2 The company hasn't made a profit for three years.
3 I haven't had a pay rise for two years.
4 We haven't looked at their proposal since July.
5 We haven't raised our prices in real terms since 2002.
6 We haven't played golf together for three months.
7 There hasn't been a fall in unemployment here since 2001.
8 I haven't been on a sales trip abroad since January.

EXERCISE 5

2 have become	8 have joined
3 has spread	9 has built
4 has helped	10 have added
5 have made	11 has transformed
6 has spent	12 has driven
7 has announced	

1 *One, three* and *four*.
2 *Since 1997, in the last year or two*, and *over the last few decades*.
3 *Back in 2001*.

Production

TASK 1

1 b I have known Mr Christiansen since 1998.
2 a Dyson built a factory in Malaysia in 2002.
   b Dyson has had a factory in Malaysia since 2002.
3 a Austria, Finland and Sweden joined the European Union in 1995.
   b Austria, Finland and Sweden have been members of the European Union since 1995.

TASK 2 (Sample answers only)

2 I haven't looked at them for some time.
3 I haven't heard any news for some time.
4 we haven't had any orders from them for several months.
5 I haven't spoken it since I left Tokyo.

TASK 3 (Sample answer only)

Over the last two or three years, the travel business has changed a great deal. We are doing more and more of our business on line, and we have closed down a lot of our High Street outlets. Short city breaks have become much more popular, and there has been a drop in the traditional two-week summer package deals.

8 Present perfect (4): continuous and simple

Practice

EXERCISE 1

2 have been exporting
3 has been falling
4 have not been investing
5 have not been flying
6 have been trying
7 have been making
8 have you been using

EXERCISE 2

2 Q: How long have you been selling children's books?
   A: We have been selling children's books since 1997.
3 Q: How long have you been producing books for schools?
   A: We have been producing books for schools since 1999.
4 Q: How long have you been making educational software?
   A: We have been making educational software for three years.
5 Q: How long have you been working with InterSat TV?
   A: We have been working with InterSat TV for two years.
6 Q: How long have you been running the online book club?
   A: We have been running the online book club for six months.

EXERCISE 3

3 has been looking
4 Have you been waiting
5 has increased
6 have made
7 have been looking
8 have been visiting

EXERCISE 4

2 I haven't had a meeting with them for two weeks.
3 My computer hasn't been working properly recently.
4 They haven't given their workers a pay rise for three years.

EXERCISE 5

2 f
3 b
4 a
5 c
6 e

Production

TASK 1 (Sample answers only)

2 I've been doing a lot of overtime and I've been bringing in a lot of new business.
3 I've been listening to English programmes on the radio and I've been studying grammar.
4 I've been setting up a new outlet in Paris so I've been going there two or three times a week, and I've also been interviewing new staff.

TASK 2 (Sample answers only)

2 I haven't been getting enough sleep.
3 Ink – I've been trying to mend the photocopier.
4 I've been playing a lot recently.
5 I think she's been going to interviews.
6 I've been having problems with my boss.
7 I've been taking clients out.

9 Past simple, present perfect and present perfect continuous

Practice

EXERCISE 1

2 was
3 made
4 has joined
5 has agreed
6 has performed
7 has been
8 announced
9 issued
10 have recovered

EXERCISE 2

2 have just had
3 have you booked
4 have already ordered
5 rang
6 have never needed
7 have been to
8 have never had
9 went

EXERCISE 3

2 heard
3 sold
4 known
5 been writing

EXERCISE 4

2 have been
3 arrived
4 went
5 met
6 saw
7 left
8 have been
9 has been
10 have never had
11 has been growing
12 have been buying
13 had
14 worked
15 came
16 has been acting
17 haven't given
18 have just had
19 heard
20 went

Production

TASK 1 (Sample answer only)
We're developing a new range of cruelty-free cosmetics which we hope to launch before Christmas. We have set up a factory in Poland and we have already started production. We have chosen an advertising agency but they haven't finalized all the details of the campaign yet.

TASK 2 (Sample answer only)
I have been in computers for five years now. I did a degree in computing at MIT, and then I joined Microsoft as a programmer. I moved to IBM three years ago and worked as a systems analyst for 18 months. For the last year and a half I have been working the Business Support division.

TASK 3

2 I have had two interviews.
   I have been looking for a new job.
3 he has fired three people.
   he has been making a lot of changes.
4 it has already sold over 250,000 units.
   we have been selling over 50,000 units a week.

10 Past continuous

Practice

EXERCISE 1
2 was calling
3 was discussing
4 was having
5 were organizing
6 were you doing
7 wasn't working
8 were having

EXERCISE 2
2 knocked
3 made
4 was working
5 was carrying
6 left
7 were testing
8 realized

EXERCISE 3
2 a the fire alarm went off, we were having a meeting.
  b the fire alarm went off, we left the building.
3 a they took our company over, we were losing a lot of money.
  b they took our company over, they made a lot of people redundant.
4 a Mr Takashi arrived, I was having lunch in the canteen.
  b Mr Takashi arrived, my secretary went to meet him.
5 a Herr Striebel arrived at the airport, the chauffeur was waiting.
  b Herr Striebel arrived at the airport, he came straight to the office.

EXERCISE 4
2 met, was going
3 was giving, interrupted
4 was finalizing, rang
5 noticed, were looking
6 happened, was cleaning
7 dropped, was bringing
8 approached, was working

Production

TASK 1 (Sample answers only)
2 a Peter was talking to the receptionist.
  b I opened my emails.
3 a the trainee was cleaning the machine.
  b we had to close the factory down.
4 a they were losing €300,000 a week.
  b they made everyone redundant.

TASK 2 (Sample answers only)
2 because he wasn't making any progress in the company.
3 because she was doing a lot of travelling.
4 because they were bringing in a lot of business.
5 because the air conditioning wasn't working.

TASK 3 (Sample answer only)
I was once stopped by the police because I was driving too fast and I wasn't wearing my seat belt. When I heard the siren and saw the light, I pulled over and stopped. I got out and said I was sorry and explained that I was tired because I had been in hospital all night and my wife had just had a baby. He congratulated me and told me to drive a bit more carefully.

11 Past perfect

Practice

EXERCISE 1
2 had closed
3 had turned
4 had disappeared
5 had not changed
6 had opened
7 had grown
8 hadn't cut

EXERCISE 2
2 so I phoned the police.
  because someone had broken in.
3 because we had won a major contract.
  so we opened a bottle of champagne.
4 because they had not reached an agreement.
  so they got out their diaries.
5 so I called Directory Enquiries.
  because they had moved to new premises.
6 so she went straight home from the airport.
  because there had been a security alert in Tokyo.

EXERCISE 3
2 he hadn't had enough experience.
3 a fax had just arrived for her.
4 I hadn't finished work.
5 I had never been to Russia.
6 we had just closed a major deal.

EXERCISE 4
2 they had been marketing the auto-injectors in the USA for five years.
3 Dr Pierce had been running it for four years.
4 Dr Warner had been the Medical Director for three years.
5 they had been manufacturing cholesterol test kits for two years.
6 they had been operating a production unit in Spain for a year.

Production

TASK 1 (Sample answers only)
2 it had not been paid for several months.
3 it had broken the law.
4 he had arrived early and had taken a taxi.
5 she had already sold most of her investments.

TASK 2 (Sample answer only)

2 They had appointed a new team of designers and were busy expanding the range of products. They had fired the old CEO and appointed a new one who had previously been with one of their competitors.

TASK 3 (Sample answer only)

2 someone had been supplying their competitors with details of their plans.

3 she hadn't been doing well at work.

4 had been phoning his friend in Australia.

5 had been waiting for over nine hours.

12 The future (1): *will*

Practice

EXERCISE 1

2 f 5 e
3 a 6 d
4 c

EXERCISE 2

2 Unemployment will fall slowly.
3 Inflation will rise slowly.
4 Consumer prices will remain stable.
5 Interest rates will fall sharply.

EXERCISE 3

2 will be, takes
3 will phone, arrives
4 will show, leave
5 will fall, opens
6 moves, will lose
7 will give, come
8 is, will feel
9 will fall, put
10 will tidy, gets

EXERCISE 4

2 I won't be late again.
3 The finance group 3i will loan us $18m for the project.
4 The company will offer a 5% pay rise in return for a no-strike deal.
5 I won't discuss this information with anyone.
6 They won't increase our discount.
7 The company will pay my re-location expenses.
8 The cash machine won't take my card.
9 I'll give you a hand with those boxes.

Production

TASK 1 (Sample answers only)

2 Then I'll have a bottle of La Lagune '67.
3 OK I'll call back later.
4 All right, I'll go with them.
5 Really? I'll give her a ring.

TASK 2 (Sample answers only)

2 The Internet and e-commerce will become increasingly important for businesses that are established. Most people will have broadband connections at home and a lot of people will work using video-conferencing.

3 The workplace will be very different, as very few people will have full time jobs. Most tasks will be done by machines and computers, and people will have a great deal of leisure time.

4 I will get married and set up my own company. By the time I am 40 I will be a millionaire and I will retire to the South of France.

TASK 3 (Sample answers only)

2 we find a replacement.
3 his plane gets in.
4 I finish the project under budget.
5 the sales conference is over.
6 there's a suitable vacancy.

13 The future (2): present continuous and *going to*

Practice

EXERCISE 1

2 'm going
3 'm seeing
4 are you coming
5 'm not doing
6 'm seeing
7 's coming

EXERCISE 2

2 What are you going to do about it?
3 We're going to go ahead with clinical trials.
4 They aren't going to go abroad this year.
5 This is where we're going to build the new offices.

EXERCISE 3

2 The price is going to rise.
3 It's going to go bankrupt.
4 She's going to leave the company.
5 We're going to be late.

EXERCISE 4

2 will be 6 Will I need
3 're staying 7 'll phone
4 'll have 8 'll let
5 're seeing

EXERCISE 5

2 are you going to call
3 'm going to look
4 won't have
5 're going to cut
6 'll take
7 Will you carry
8 'll tell

Production

TASK 1 (Sample answer only)

The CEO is arriving at Heathrow at 9.00, and he's having a meeting with the Executive Vice Presidents at 10.15. He's having lunch with officials from the DTI, and in the afternoon he's opening the new office in Threadneedle Street. At 7.00 he's giving a speech on financial deregulation in the EU, and he's having dinner at the Guildhall at 8.00. He's flying back to New York the following morning at 11.30.

TASK 2 (Sample answers only)

2 We're going to bring out a new edition in February.
3 I'm going to buy a Dell laptop to use on the train.
4 We're going to recruit over 20 new sales reps next year.
5 I'm going to go to Paxos this summer.
6 We're going to run a $2million TV advertising campaign for the new car.

TASK 3 (Sample answers only)

2 They're going to cut overtime rates.
3 I'll come back later.
4 He's going to get a Lexus.
5 I'll let you know when I have made up my mind.
6 We're going to open up a branch there next year.

14 The future (3): other future tenses

Practice

EXERCISE 1

2 They were going to produce saloon and estate versions, but now they're only going to produce a saloon.
3 We were going to have $240,000 for the advertising budget, but now we're only going to have $180,000.
4 Jill was going to give a presentation on Tuesday, but now she's going to give it on Friday.

EXERCISE 2

Schedule B

10.00-11.30	have meeting with Mr Barber
11.30-1.00	see the Finance Director
1.00-2.00	lunch at Gee's restaurant
2.00-3.30	visit new warehouse
3.30-5.00	give presentation to IT department

1 He was visiting the warehouse at 10.00, but now he's visiting it at 2.00.
2 He was giving a presentation to the IT department at 11.30, but now he's giving it at 3.30.
4 He was having a meeting with Mr Barber at 2.00, but now he's having the meeting at 10.00.
5 He was seeing the Finance Director at 3.30, but now he's seeing him at 11.30.

EXERCISE 3

3 In August, we will be building the central hotel.
4 By the end of September, we will have built the central hotel.
5 In November, we will be putting up the 20 guest cottages in the grounds.
6 By the end of December, we will have put up the 20 guest cottages in the grounds.
7 In February, we will be finishing the golf course and the other sporting facilities.
8 By the end of March, we will have finished the golf course and other sporting facilities.
9 By the middle of April, the first guests will have arrived.

EXERCISE 4

2 a will take off
  b will be travelling
  c will have arrived

3 a will start
  b will be having
  c will have finished

Production

TASK 1 (Sample answers only)

2 I was going to go away this weekend …
3 We were going to upgrade our whole IT network …
4 She was going to give the keynote speech at the conference …
5 We were going to send five people to the conference …
6 I was going to get tickets for The Lion King …

TASK 2 (Sample answers only)

1 I'll probably be working for a larger company.
2 I'll be the Research Director.
3 I'll be managing large-scale research projects.
4 I'll already have developed several important new drugs.
5 I will have moved to a bigger house, and I will have had three children.

TASK 3 (Sample answers only)

1 I will have achieved as much as you have.
2 I'll be lying on a beach in Martinique.
3 it will have finished.
4 They will be holding it in Copenhagen instead of Hamburg.
5 I'll be giving my presentation.

15 The future (4): possibility and probability

Practice

EXERCISE 1

2 The euro probably won't rise against other leading currencies.
3 There definitely won't be a recession in Europe.
4 Maybe the stock market in Japan will recover.
5 There will probably be a fall in unemployment.
6 Overall taxation will definitely rise.
7 Exports to the US probably won't go up.
8 Exports from the Far East will probably increase.

EXERCISE 2

2 is certain to	5 is likely to	8 is unlikely to
3 are unlikely to	6 is certain to	9 is certain to
4 are unlikely to	7 are likely to	

EXERCISE 3

A

Definitely:
    I'm confident that
    I'm quite sure that
Probably:
    I should think that
    I expect that
    The chances are that

Probably not:
    I shouldn't think that
Definitely not:
    I'm quite sure + (won't)
    I doubt very much whether

B

2 e	6 b
3 a	7 c
4 f	8 d
5 g	

EXERCISE 4

2 Their new store is unlikely to attract many customers.

3 They probably won't give us better terms.

4 I'll probably be very busy early next week.

5 I shouldn't think that they'll deliver the equipment this month.

Production

TASK 1 (Sample answers only)

2 a I doubt very much whether I'll change jobs.

 b I definitely won't change jobs.

3 a I may get rich.

 b Perhaps I will get rich.

4 a I will probably get promoted.

 b I should think I'll get promoted.

5 a I shouldn't think I'll marry anyone English.

 b I'm unlikely to marry anyone English.

6 a I'm very unlikely to take control of my company.

 b I definitely won't take control of my company.

7 a I'm very unlikely to have to spend any time doing military service.

 b I definitely won't have to spend any time doing military service.

TASK 2 (Sample answers only)

2 I should think we will lose market share to some of our newer competitors, but we will probably still retain our position as the market leader.

3 New Internet services will probably reach schools and universities all over the country, and I should think that they will be integrated with mobile phone technology.

4 The countries of the Pacific Rim will definitely become more important economically, and I am confident that they will attract a lot of investment.

5 Genetic engineering will probably develop very quickly and I should think that there will be a vast range of medical advances in the next few years.

16 The passive (1): actions, systems and processes

Practice

EXERCISE 1

2	they're asked	7	is let
3	are left	8	are you asked
4	are not allowed	9	I'm contacted
5	is fitted	10	I'm given
6	are kept		

EXERCISE 2

2 are paid weekly.

3 is kept at Fort Knox.

4 are built in South Korea.

5 is grown on the Ivory Coast.

6 is stored underground.

7 are tested extensively.

8 are printed in Hong Kong.

EXERCISE 3

2	is built	11	are used
3	are made	12	are added
4	are put	13	are carried
5	are cut	14	are fitted
6	is bolted	15	are taken
7	are attached	16	are checked
8	are fitted	17	are cleaned and polished
9	is prepared	18	are despatched
10	is assembled		

EXERCISE 4

2 b

3 a

4 b

Production

TASK 1

2 is advertised in the papers.

3 are asked to send in their CVs.

4 are invited to an interview.

5 is drawn up.

6 are asked back for a second interview.

7 is chosen.

8 are checked.

9 is offered the job.

TASK 2 (Sample only)

The watches are manufactured in Singapore, and then they are shipped to our warehouse in Dresden. Next, they are transported to our distributors. After that they are sold on to retailers and finally they are sold to customers in stores all over the country.

The passive (2): other tenses

Practice

EXERCISE 1

A 2 are being carried out
   3 are being affected

   4 are not being taken
   5 are doing

B 1 were being displayed
   2 were waiting
   3 were standing
   4 were smashing

   5 were being kept
   6 were being taken
   7 was waiting

C 1 had been sold
   2 had been paid
   3 had received

   4 had been advised
   5 had visited

EXERCISE 2

2 'll be met
3 'll be driven
4 'll be
5 will last
6 'll be able

7 'll be taken
8 won't arrive
9 will be kept
10 won't be given

EXERCISE 3

2 has just been set up
3 've made
4 has been promoted
5 have been put

6 have they sent
7 's been demoted
8 has treated

Production

TASK 1

2 The Channel Tunnel was opened in 1994.
3 Radium was discovered by Marie and Pierre Curie.
4 The wireless was invented by Marconi.
5 Fiat SPA was founded in 1899.
6 The World Trade Center was destroyed on 11 September 2001.
7 President George W Bush was elected in 2000.

TASK 2 (Sample answers only)

2 It is being re-organized.
3 He was booed and shouted at.
4 They have all been sacked.
5 It has been cut
6 It has been sold.
7 It has been devalued.

TASK 3 (Sample answer only)

The company I work for was founded by two brothers, Jack and Daniel Partridge, back in 1866. They manufactured whisky, but only on a small scale. However, the whisky was well-produced and it soon became very popular. They got into difficulties when liquor taxes were raised, and the company was bought by a major brewer, who still owns it.

The passive (3): passive verbs and infinitives, *have something done*

Practice

EXERCISE 1

2 have a powerful graphics card added
3 have the programs loaded and tested
4 have a bigger hard disk fitted
5 have extra memory built
6 have them installed
7 have them delivered
8 have it repaired
9 have it fixed
10 have other things customized

EXERCISE 2

2 We get the floors swept every night.
3 We get the air conditioners serviced twice a year.
4 We get the indoor plants changed once a month.
5 We get the windows cleaned every six weeks.
6 We get the central heating system checked once a year.
7 We get oil delivered once every week or so in the winter.

EXERCISE 3

2 We are going to have 5,000 new catalogues printed.
3 When am I going to have my office redecorated?
4 They are having a new office designed.
5 I have had these figures checked.
6 Have you had your hair done?
7 You should have the photocopier mended.
8 We had the new furniture delivered yesterday.
9 I haven't had my car repaired yet.
10 Where did you have those t-shirts made?

EXERCISE 4

2 I'll have my PA set up a meeting.
3 I'll get the driver to come and collect you.
4 I'll get the canteen to send up some sandwiches.
5 I'll get Barry to come and have a look.
6 I'll have the personnel manager arrange an interview.
7 I'll have my secretary send you a catalogue.
8 I'll get the lawyer to check it carefully.

Production

TASK 1

1 You can have personal stationery made.
  You can have in-company magazines printed.
  You can have documents photocopied in colour.
2 You can have the outside of your office painted.
  You can have wallpaper put up.
  You can have your office maintained regularly.
3 You can have a passport photo taken instantly.
  You can have a black and white portrait taken.
  You can have old photos restored.

TASK 2 (Sample answers only)

2 On the Internet, you can have your own CDs made for you. You can select the tracks you want and you can have the files sent to you for a small fee.

3 In time, computers will be linked to machines that make clothes, so you will be able to have suits made for you in a fraction of the time it takes at the moment.

4 Online shopping is already becoming very popular because you can look at products online and can have them delivered to you at home.

5 Some car manufacturers allow you to have a new car customized according to your preferences. You start with the basic model and then you can have a particular engine fitted; you can have the steering wheel put on the left or the right, and you can have any extras such as air conditioning fitted at the factory.

TASK 3 (Sample answers only)

2 I have my secretary book me a ticket.

3 I get the IT department to give me a new one.

4 I get the garage to come and help me.

5 I have my accountant check the figures.

6 I get an interior designer to do it.

19 Conditionals (1): *if you go …*

Practice
EXERCISE 1
2 f		6 i	
3 g		7 c	
4 b		8 e	
5 h		9 a	

EXERCISE 2
1 b If the traffic is OK we'll get to the airport on time.

2 a If the weather is good they'll have the party in the garden.
   b If it rains they'll hold the reception in the marquee.

3 a If the play does well it'll open on Broadway.
   b If the play does badly it'll close after a week.

EXERCISE 3
1 if		4 when	
2 when		5 if	
3 if		6 when	

EXERCISE 4
2 tell		6 manage	
3 goes on		7 must	
4 can		8 may	
5 may		9 will want	

EXERCISE 5
2 right

3 wrong – *if it is*

4 wrong – *if I go*

5 right

6 wrong – *if everyone is still talking*

7 wrong – *if you go*

Production
TASK 1 (Sample answers only)

2 If we don't sell them, we can return them.

3 If you subscribe before 30 September, you'll save 33%.

4 If you don't like the car you can get your money back.

TASK 2 (Sample answers only)

1 I'll go over to Paris.

2 I'll spend some time in Greece.

3 I'll buy a better car.

4 I'll soon be brilliant at it.

5 I'll go crazy.

6 I'll go to bed early.

7 I'll visit some friends on the way home.

8 I'll get a place nearer work.

TASK 3 (Sample answers only)

2 I am sure that our market share will increase. If we cut our prices, more people will buy our products.

3 I think that several new competitors will emerge in the next few years. If they are successful, we'll lose some of our market share.

4 I think that technology may allow us to cut costs. If we can produce things more cheaply, we'll be able to sell more.

20 Conditionals (2): *if, unless*, etc.

Practice
EXERCISE 1
2 f		6 b	
3 h		7 g	
4 a		8 d	
5 c			

EXERCISE 2
2 unless we improve our offer.

3 unless it's an emergency.

4 unless demand increases soon.

5 unless you can cut your overheads.

6 unless I can have my job back when I return.

EXERCISE 3
2 in case he loses it.

3 in case he wants to hire a car.

4 in case the office needs to phone him.

5 in case he has to see a doctor.

6 in case it is cold.

EXERCISE 4
2 so that she doesn't have to find a bank.

3 so that she is able to change her flight times if necessary.

4 so that people are able to phone her.

5 so that she doesn't end up with a large hospital bill.

6 so that she is able to do some work on the plane.

EXERCISE 5

2 in case	5 in case
3 so that	6 in case
4 so that	

EXERCISE 6

2 as long as	5 Unless
3 unless	6 as long as
4 So long as	

Production

TASK 1 (Sample answers only)

1 I get a better offer from someone else.
2 the government manages to control inflation.
3 I can get the day off.
4 they will sell 50 of them to British Airways.
5 I'll see you at 6.30.
6 that you maintain our service standards.

TASK 2 (Sample answers only)

2 a I can change some at the bank.
  b I need to pay for a taxi.
  c I don't have to look for a cash machine.
3 a I go away next week.
  b I need to contact anyone.
  c I can note down any new contacts.
4 a they don't pay tomorrow.
  b they have forgotten about it.
  c they realize we haven't been paid.
5 a you're going abroad.
  b you get stopped by the traffic police.
  c you can hire a car if you need to.

21 Conditionals (3): *if you went …*

Practice

EXERCISE 1

2 wouldn't spend	6 would have
3 moved	7 started
4 would need	8 wouldn't get
5 went	

EXERCISE 2

2 if I had their address, I'd contact them.
3 if I didn't enjoy my job, I wouldn't work so hard.
4 if we didn't spend so much on R&D, we wouldn't be market leaders.
5 if I had the authority, I'd give you an answer.

EXERCISE 3

2 were, think	
3 change, spoke	
4 was/were, earn	
5 were, produce	

EXERCISE 4

2 'll meet, maintain	6 'd apply, had
3 was/were, 'd insist	7 'll be, isn't
4 wait, 'll give	8 would you change, were
5 ring, let	

EXERCISE 5

Questionnaire result

Write down the numbers you supplied for each of the questions.

Task questions	People questions
3 ___	1 ___
4 ___	2 ___
7 ___	5 ___
9 ___	6 ___
10 ___	8 ___
12 ___	11 ___
14 ___	13 ___
Total: ___	Total: ___

Add up your scores and put them on the diagram below. Draw a vertical line on the task axis and a horizontal line on the people axis. The point where the lines cross shows your leadership style.

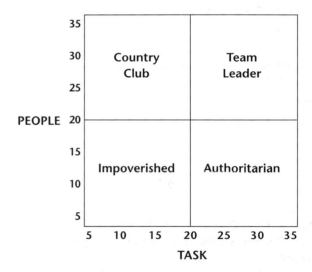

What the four styles mean:

Country Club leaders want everyone to like them, and are keen not to upset people. If you are a 'Country Club' leader you need to be more forceful with your employees.

Impoverished leaders are afraid of upsetting others and are not very capable of getting things done. If you are one of these, you need to re-evaluate your management style because at the moment you are not pleasing anyone or getting results.

Authoritarian leaders care very little about what people think of them. If you are one of these, you get results, but you should realize that they would be even better if you learned to deal with people more effectively.

Team leaders are the best type of leaders. If you are a team leader, you are good at managing people and at achieving results.

Production

TASK 1 (Sample answers only)

2 If I lost my job, I'd start my own business.

3 If I were offered a job in Saudi Arabia for five years, I'd seriously consider it.

4 If one of our competitors offered me a job, I'd turn it down.

5 If I lost all my money and credit cards, I'd be covered by my insurance.

TASK 2 (Sample answers only)

2 If I were you, I'd wait another day and then phone them.

3 If I were you, I'd get a Morgan.

4 If I were you, I'd get in touch with the Personnel Officer.

5 If I were you, I'd go to the Brasserie.

TASK 3 (Sample answer only)

… I'd award myself a large pay rise. Then I'd start looking at new areas of the world to do business, and would set up operations in Latin America. I'd spend more on new technology and I'd reduce the workforce.

 22 Conditionals (4): *if you had gone …*

Practice

EXERCISE 1

2 had made
3 would have gone
4 had been
5 had waited
6 would have moved
7 Would (you) have accepted
8 would have stayed

EXERCISE 2

2 hadn't had, would have come out
3 had been, would have fallen
4 hadn't started, wouldn't have seen
5 hadn't launched, would have gone down
6 hadn't received, wouldn't have reached

EXERCISE 3

2 wrong – *if there had been*
3 wrong – *if they had been able*
4 right
5 wrong – *if there hadn't been*

EXERCISE 4

2 d
3 g
4 f
5 a
6 h
7 e
8 b

EXERCISE 5

2 If we hadn't felt we could trust each other we wouldn't be partners.

3 If he hadn't lost his driving licence, he wouldn't have to take taxis everywhere.

4 If you had gone/been on the course, you would know how to operate the equipment.

5 If I hadn't gone/been to school in France, I wouldn't be bilingual.

Production

TASK 1 (Sample answers only)

2 If someone had stolen my credit cards and money, I'd have rung the bank.

3 If I had needed to contact the office urgently, I'd have used my mobile.

4 If I had fallen seriously ill, I'd have stayed in the local hospital.

5 If I had missed my return flight, I'd have bought another ticket.

TASK 2 (Sample answers only)

2 They shouldn't have hired so many people. If they hadn't taken on so many employees, they wouldn't have run out of funds so quickly.

3 They should have appointed a competent financial director. If they had had one, they wouldn't have wasted so much money.

4 Their website shouldn't have been so complicated. If it had been simpler, it wouldn't have been so slow.

5 They shouldn't have had such high prices. If they had had lower prices, they'd have sold more clothes.

23 Modal verbs (1): suggestions, advice, obligation and criticism – *shall I?, should, ought to*

Practice

EXERCISE 1

2 Shall we set up a meeting to discuss this?
3 Shall I call back later?
4 Shall I take the boxes down to the Post Room?
5 Shall we cancel this evening and meet up some other time?
6 Shall we stop now and carry on again tomorrow?
7 Where shall I put the new computer?

EXERCISE 2

2 How about waiting until the next financial year?
3 What about organizing a leaving party for Bob Simpson?
4 Let's share a taxi to the station.
5 Why don't we see if we can subcontract this work?
6 How about offering them a bigger discount?

EXERCISE 3

2 suggested that I should call back at 5.30.
3 suggested that I should check her references first.
4 suggested going together.
5 suggested that I should do some background research into the company.

EXERCISE 4

2 ought to be accompanied   5 should not be left

3 should report   6 should be deposited

4 ought not to bring

EXERCISE 5 (Sample answers only)

2 You should have tried to look more relaxed and confident.

3 You should have spoken more loudly.

4 You should have tried to stand still.

5 You should have tried to make eye contact with the audience.

6 You should have repeated the main points at the end.

7 You should have allowed time for questions at the end.

Production

TASK 1 (Sample answers only)

2 We ought to introduce flexi-time.

3 Why don't we set up a company crèche?

4 Let's give everyone incentives to reduce the cost of air travel.

5 How about splitting the company up into independent 'profit centres'?

6 I don't think we should stick to only producing the same old models.

7 Let's have a points system and a reward for the best performing managers.

TASK 2 (Sample answers only)

2 They should have spent much more time making sure it was reliable.

3 He should have saved it as he was going along.

4 They shouldn't have raised taxes.

5 We shouldn't have invested all that money in risky Central American companies.

6 She should have written down the date in her diary.

24   Modal verbs (2): ability, possibility and permission – *can, could, may*

Practice

EXERCISE 1

2 If you are decisive you can

3 If you are persuasive you can

4 If you are flexible you can

5 If you are numerate you can

6 If you are bilingual you can

7 If you are computer-literate you can

8 If you are logical you can

EXERCISE 2

2 can   4 been able to

3 can't   5 be able to

EXERCISE 3

2 could   6 could

3 managed to   7 could

4 managed to   8 managed to

5 could

EXERCISE 4

2 i   7 j

3 e   8 b

4 a   9 c

5 d   10 f

6 h

EXERCISE 5

2 a   6 b

3 b   7 b

4 b   8 a

5 a

Production

TASK 1 (Sample answers only)

2 I haven't been able to think of anything.

3 he can speak three languages fluently.

4 be able to give everyone a pay rise.

5 you can buy things over the phone.

TASK 2 (Sample answers only)

1 I could have been a famous actor.

2 you could have got an electric shock.

3 she could have got the top job.

4 could have saved a great deal of money.

TASK 3 (Sample answers only)

1 Could I have a glass of water, please?

2 Could I have a look at your magazine when you've finished with it, please?

3 Excuse me, could I get past, please?

4 Could I have the vegetarian meal instead, please?

25   Modal verbs (3): obligation and necessity – *must, have to, needn't, can't*, etc.

Practice

EXERCISE 1

2 can't   7 don't have to

3 mustn't   8 mustn't

4 needn't   9 don't have to

5 can't   10 must

6 must

EXERCISE 2

A 2 have to   6 can't

    3 have to   7 have to

    4 don't have to   8 can't

    5 have to

B 1 have to   5 can't
   2 don't have to   6 have to
   3 can't   7 have to
   4 have to

EXERCISE 3

2 We needn't discuss the matter any further.
3 We needn't order any more yet.
4 We must make sure we keep our market share.
5 You must call her right now.
6 I mustn't be late.

EXERCISE 4

2 had to   7 had to
3 couldn't   8 couldn't
4 had to   9 couldn't
5 didn't have to 10 had to
6 didn't have to

EXERCISE 5

1 didn't need to make   3 needn't have hired
2 needn't have spent   4 didn't need to

Production

TASK 1 (Sample answers only)

2 You must have a receipt if you want a refund.
3 You needn't pay into the fund every month.
4 You must think about what you are going to say beforehand.
5 You needn't save your work manually, because you can do it automatically.
6 You needn't arrange any insurance because all the staff are covered.

TASK 2 (Sample answer only)

visit client   oversee maintenance work   can't hire builders

I work for a property company. We have a large number of offices that we rent out, and I have to visit our clients on a regular basis to see if they are OK. I have to authorize repairs, but I don't have to oversee any of the maintenance work that gets carried out. I can't hire builders myself, as that is done by the Personnel Department.

26 Modal verbs (4): speculation – *may, might, must, can't*

Practice

EXERCISE 1

2 may strike   6 could have
3 might kill   7 could escape
4 may be able to   8 could still be
5 could prevent   9 might start

EXERCISE 2

A 1 might, might, can't
   2 must
   3 must, might

B The table should look as follows:

Mr Green	Mr Brown	Mr White
photocopier	computer	paper
20kg	22kg	18kg

EXERCISE 3

2 They must have moved to new premises.
3 The meeting must have been cancelled.
4 He might have gone to lunch.
5 She might have been phoning the Sales Department.
6 It can't have been repaired properly.

EXERCISE 4

2 must have been making long international calls.
3 can't be selling many cars.
4 must have lost a lot of money.
5 might be promoted at the end of the year.
6 can't have been expecting me.
7 can't have heard the announcement.

Production

TASK 1 (Sample answers only)

2 They might win the election.
3 It may do very well.
4 It could get into serious trouble.
5 It may be completed more that a year behind schedule.

TASK 2 (Sample answers only)

2 They must be coming to the end of a research project.
3 It can't be a genuine Rolex.
4 He must be ill.
5 She might tell you how to get hold of him.

TASK 3 (Sample answers only)

2 They must have overestimated the numbers of visitors.
3 The reviews might have been unfavourable.
4 It must have been badly managed.
5 It can't have appealed to people.
6 It might not have been advertised properly.

27 *-ing* and infinitive (1): verbs + *-ing* or infinitive

Practice

EXERCISE 1

2 going   6 writing
3 setting   7 getting
4 using   8 giving
5 doing   9 hearing

EXERCISE 2

2 to do   6 to take
3 to teach   7 to be
4 to finish   8 to meet
5 to go   9 to change

EXERCISE 3

2 to supply	8 getting
3 to go	9 having
4 to give	10 sending
5 to deliver	11 to be able to
6 to market	12 to contact
7 changing	13 to hearing

EXERCISE 4

3 to be paid	6 being taken over
4 being asked	7 to be sent
5 to be recruited	8 to be disturbed

Production

TASK 1 (Sample answers only)

A 2 I can't stand dealing with difficult customers.

  3 I dislike attending meetings.

  4 I really enjoy taking clients out.

B 1 I like meeting new people.

  2 I really enjoy travelling abroad.

  3 I dislike giving presentations.

  4 I don't mind commuting.

TASK 2 (Sample answers only)

2 is planning to expand its operation in the US.

3 threatened to take them to court.

4 she decided to set up her own business.

TASK 3 (Sample answers only)

2 to leave school and start working in a factory.

3 seeing my friends in the evening.

4 to buy another car.

5 starting on the new project.

6 to be able to run my own department.

7 restructuring the company completely.

28 -ing and infinitive (2): verbs and objects

Practice

EXERCISE 1

2 They persuaded the bank to finance the project.

3 The court ordered the company to pay compensation.

4 The fall in demand forced us to cut production.

5 They have invited me to speak at the conference.

EXERCISE 2

2 He encouraged me to apply for the job.

3 He advised me to make a formal complaint.

4 He asked me to finish the report as soon as possible.

5 He allowed me to leave early.

6 He warned me not to rush into a decision.

EXERCISE 3

2 They let us go out at the weekends.

3 They made us give a presentation every morning.

4 They made us speak English all the time.

5 They let us watch the TV.

EXERCISE 4

2 doesn't make (them) have

3 enabled (her) to increase

4 has persuaded (California and other US states) to ban

5 has invited (him) to talk

6 encourage (the government) to bring in

7 ask (their passengers) to put

8 lets (childminders) smoke

9 to force (other people) to breathe in

EXERCISE 5

2 I could smell something burning.

3 I didn't see her leave.

4 I heard him give a talk on 'Quality Control'.

5 The visitors watched some robots assembling cars.

Production

TASK 1 (Sample answers only)

1 to buy up some of our competitors.

2 to study at university.

3 to become plumbers and electricians.

4 to give a talk on the management of change.

5 not to walk in Central Park after dark.

TASK 2 (Sample answer only)

It probably won't be as bad as you think. They will make you get up early and they will make you take regular exercise. They won't let you drink alcohol of course, and they will probably put you on a special diet. They may let you have the evenings free, but they won't let you leave the grounds of the spa in case you are tempted to go to a restaurant or bar.

TASK 3 (Sample answers only)

1 I would ask them to explain what had gone wrong and I would tell them to pay the fine.

2 I would encourage her to do what she enjoys most and I would advise her to go to university.

29 -ing and infinitive (3): changes in meaning

Practice

EXERCISE 1

2 c	6 f
3 h	7 b
4 d	8 g
5 a	

EXERCISE 2

2 to look	6 to give
3 to send	7 resigning
4 hearing	8 to say
5 walking	9 to provide

EXERCISE 3

2 to arrange	5 working
3 working, commuting	6 to come
4 to have	

EXERCISE 4

2 sell	7 writing
3 seeing	8 offer
4 dealing	9 win
5 move	10 dealing
6 hearing	11 selling

Production

TASK 1 (Sample answers only)

2 to have a coffee break.
3 going to my first interview.
4 to make sure all my files are up to date.
5 running the Personnel Department, I am also in charge of our programme of social events.
6 going on my skiing holiday in February.
7 paying such high taxes.

TASK 2 (Sample answers only)

A 2 I prefer starting work early because I am better in the mornings.
3 I prefer working alone because I can concentrate better.
4 I prefer eating lunch out because it's good to have a change of scene.

B 2 I'd prefer to have a larger house because I am not interested in cars.
3 I'd prefer to work for a woman because they are usually better at managing people.
4 I'd prefer to have more time for myself because I have other interests.

30 -*ing* and infinitive (4): other uses

Practice

EXERCISE 1

2 to miss
3 to inform
4 to demand
5 to reduce
6 to increase
7 to attract
8 to prevent

EXERCISE 2

2 how to write
3 what financial institutions to approach
4 what to look out for
5 how to identify
6 where to manufacture

EXERCISE 3

2 b	5 a
3 f	6 d
4 e	

EXERCISE 4

2 After leaving university, she got a job with Microsoft.
or She got a job with Microsoft after leaving …
3 Instead of offering them a discount, we'll give them better credit terms.
or We'll give them better credit terms instead of offering them …
4 We managed to expand without increasing our debts.
or Without increasing our debts, we …
5 He worked in industry for many years before joining the government.
or Before joining the government, he …
6 The company became more profitable by making 700 workers redundant.
or By making 700 workers redundant, the company …

EXERCISE 5

2 to improve	7 to feed
3 Eating	8 to make
4 to mix	9 using
5 to make	10 to manufacture
6 trying	

Production

TASK 1 (Sample answers only)

2 to encourage the customers to see more of the merchandise.
3 to have a meeting with an important distributor.
4 to move house.
5 to see if I can change my ticket.

TASK 2 (Sample answers only)

1 Keeping up to date with all the developments in programming.
2 Doing the technical side – particularly systems analysis.
3 Seeing a project successfully to completion.
4 Travelling to the USA to attend major launches.
5 Finding people with not just the right technical qualifications but with the right attitude.

TASK 3 (Sample answer only)

After leaving school I went straight to university to do a degree in Electronic Engineering. Before graduating, I spent a few weeks every year with Olivetti, and after leaving university, I went to work for them full time.

31 Reported speech (1): statements, thoughts, commands, requests

Practice

EXERCISE 1

2 was	7 was taking
3 could take	8 wasn't
4 didn't have	9 had offered
5 would stay	10 had (never) seen
6 would be	

EXERCISE 2

2 d   6 b
3 g   7 h
4 f   8 c
5 a

EXERCISE 3

2 He told me to send the letter immediately.
3 He asked me not to mention the plans to anyone.
4 He asked me to return the form as soon as possible.
5 He told me not to put any calls through to his office.

EXERCISE 4

1 this afternoon   4 the previous day
2 the following day   5 here
3 there

EXERCISE 5

2 In 1899, Charles Duell said (that) everything that could be invented had been invented.
3 Thomas Watson said there was a world market for about five computers.
4 Leona Helmsley said (that) only the little people paid taxes.
5 J Paul Getty said the secret of success was to rise early, work hard and strike oil.
6 Bill Gates said (that) 640k ought to be enough for anybody.
7 Henry Ford said people could have any colour they liked as long as it was black.

Production

TASK 1 (Sample answers only)

2 I told him (that) it was a great place to work.
3 I told him (that) I was in charge of purchasing.
4 I told him I would need at least 30% extra to even consider moving.
5 He told me they were growing fast and wanted good people.
6 He told me it would be at a very senior level.
7 I told him I would think about it and get back to him.

TASK 2 (Sample answers only)

2 ... you were so old.
3 ... it would take so long.
4 ... he had gone back to Japan.
5 ... it would be so expensive.

TASK 3 (Sample answers only)

2 ... asked her to change our appointment to Friday.
3 ... told him not to drive home.
4 ... asked him to drop off a cheque for me.
5 ... asked them to replace it.
6 ... I asked him for an estimate before he started.

32 Reported speech (2): questions and reporting verbs

Practice

EXERCISE 1

2 They asked him how many people were going to lose their jobs.
3 They asked him where he could cut costs.
4 They asked him how much money the company had lost.
5 They asked him when the company would return to profit.
6 They asked him who was responsible for the figures.
7 They asked him what dividend the company would pay.
8 They asked him when he was going to resign.

EXERCISE 2

2 I asked her if they had signed the contract.
3 I asked her if she would need to go back again.
4 I asked her if the hotel had been any good.
5 I asked her if she had managed to have any time off.
6 I asked her if she was feeling tired.
7 I asked her if she had had any problems.
8 I asked her if they had liked the idea of a joint venture.

EXERCISE 3

3 how the negotiations are going.
4 if Peter's coming to the meeting?
5 when the talk is going to start?
6 if I should take the job.
7 where their head office is.
8 if they'll accept our offer.
9 if they've sent us an order form?
10 how they got this information.

EXERCISE 4

2 He encouraged me to give a talk at the conference.
3 He refused to give me a pay rise.
4 He denied leaving the office unlocked.
5 He warned me not to leave the hotel after dark (because it was dangerous).
6 He apologized for missing the meeting.
7 He advised me to get an agent.

Production

TASK 1 (Sample answers only)

2 That was Mr Davies from Moretons. He asked me if we could increase his discount to 20%, but I told him that 15% was the most we could offer.
3 That was Janet. She wanted to know when I would be able to go round and fix her computer and I said I would be there first thing on Wednesday.
4 That was Hanborough Chemicals – they asked me if I was certain that we had paid the invoice, and I said I was sure because I had written the cheque myself.
5 That was someone ringing about my car – they asked me how much I wanted for it and I told them I was selling it for $16,000.

TASK 2 (Sample answers only)

2 where the Post Office is.

3 if it has gone up or not.

4 when there is a suitable flight?

5 what she is talking about?

TASK 3 (Sample answers only)

2 refused to carry out the repairs for free.

3 offered to extend the guarantee.

4 apologized for any inconvenience they had caused.

33 Relative clauses (1): *who, that, which, whose, whom*

Practice

EXERCISE 1

2 who	7 who
3 which	8 which
4 who	9 who
5 who	10 which
6 which	

EXERCISE 2

2 that knows everybody.

3 that you interviewed?

4 that interviewed you?

5 that she doesn't like.

6 that runs on electricity.

In 1, 3 and 5 the word *that* can be left out.

EXERCISE 3

2 whose mother tongue must be English.

3 whose headquarters are in Helsinki.

4 whose car had broken down.

5 whose key competitors are Sony and Sanyo.

6 whose department was doing well.

EXERCISE 4

2 to whom

3 in which

4 with whom

5 to which

6 by whom

EXERCISE 5

2 invoice you were looking for.

3 customers I deal with are very pleasant.

4 we wanted to stay in was fully booked.

5 she works for has a very good reputation.

6 we went to wasn't very good.

Production

TASK 1

1 inVoice

2 cOntract

3 saLary

4 banK

5 subSidiary

6 laWyer

7 catAlogue

8 aGenda

9 collEague

10 telephoNe

Answer: VOLKSWAGEN

Clues (Sample answers only)

1 a document that asks for payment.

3 an amount of money that is paid to an employee.

5 a small organization that belongs to a larger organization.

7 a kind of brochure that lists what a company sells.

9 a person that you work with.

TASK 2 (Sample answers only)

2 who lets me work flexible hours.

3 that consists of twenty people.

4 who need advice on financial planning.

5 that I don't really want to.

6 who are intelligent.

7 who cannot make decisions.

8 that help me relax.

34 Relative clauses (2): *where, with, what* and non-defining clauses

Practice

EXERCISE 1

2 Would you like to visit the factory where we make the cars?

3 I recently went back to the town where I used to work.

4 Ivrea is the town where Olivetti has its headquarters.

5 This is the building where they filmed the Pepsi advert.

EXERCISE 2

3 with a DVD drive?

4 with a bit more experience.

5 that has a better view.

6 that has a lot of mistakes.

7 with a matching tie.

8 with a sense of humour.

EXERCISE 3

2 what you asked me to do.

3 can do what you want.

4 deliver what you need tomorrow.

5 hear what you said.

EXERCISE 4

2 The Oriental Hotel, where many famous people have stayed, is said to be the best in the world.

3 BMW's new Mini, which is built at Cowley in England, has been a great commercial success.

4 Exxon Mobil, which is the world's second largest corporation, is building a $3.5bn pipeline in Chad.

5 Their new range of cosmetics, on which they've spent €10 million, will be launched next month.

6 Mr Warburg, with whom I have discussed your proposal, would like to meet you next week.

EXERCISE 5

2 The room where we held the meeting was a little too small.

3 Brazil, which had high inflation in the 1990s, is now the leading economic power in South America.

4 The negotiators finally reached a formula on which everyone could agree.

5 I found it difficult to hear what the speaker was talking about.

6 Tim Lang, who only joined the company six months ago, is going to be promoted.

7 BMW, whose headquarters are in Germany, produces the new Mini in England.

8 I suggest we have a meeting in Romsey Street, where we rent a few offices.

Production

TASK 1

2 who were concerned about the growing number of addicts

3 which was at the centre of the opium trade

4 who had powerful allies in London

5 whose weapons were all old and outdated

6 which ended in 1842

7 which was signed the following year

8 which broke out in 1856

9 who were assisted by the French

10 which was signed in 1858

TASK 2 (Sample answers only)

2 My boss would like a Rolex watch with a gold strap.

3 My wife would like an Armani dress with a matching handbag.

4 My son would like a mountain bike with 27 gears.

5 My daughter would like a long coat with a high collar.

6 My niece would like an 'Executive Barbie' with a briefcase.

35 Countable and uncountable nouns

Practice

EXERCISE 1

2 a report	some news
3 a desk	some furniture
4 some accommodation	a hotel
5 a chance	some luck
6 some water	a litre
7 some equipment	a machine
8 a dollar	some money
9 a cheque	some cash
10 a letter	some correspondence

EXERCISE 2

1 is	5 are
2 is	6 is
3 are	7 is
4 is	8 is

EXERCISE 3

2 an
3 some
4 the
5 some
6 much
7 a few
8 much
9 a
10 a little
11 much
12 some

EXERCISE 4

2 a glass of wine
3 a barrel of oil
4 a kilo of sugar
5 a pint of beer
6 a tonne of coal
7 a sheet of paper

EXERCISE 5

2 a packet	5 a barrel
3 a pint	6 a litre
4 a tube	

Production

TASK 1

2 alcohol
3 time
4 weather
5 money
6 Spanish
7 meat
8 experience

TASK 2 (Sample answers only)

2 Time is money.

3 Meetings are designed to make idle people look busy.

4 Work is the new opium of the people.

5 Men are from Mars.

6 Women are from Venus.

7 Experience is only valued by the person who has it.

8 Productivity can be measured but satisfaction cannot.

36   Articles: *a/an, the* or Ø (no article)

Practice

EXERCISE 1

2 a	7 an
3 a	8 an
4 a	9 an
5 an	10 a
6 an	

EXERCISE 2

1 A: the
   B: a
2 A: a
   B: the
3 A: the
   B: a
4 A: the
   B: a
5 A: a
   B: the

EXERCISE 3

2 Ø	12 the
3 the	13 Ø
4 Ø	14 the
5 the	15 Ø
6 a	16 Ø
7 the	17 Ø
8 the	18 Ø
9 the	19 the
10 the	20 the
11 the	21 Ø

EXERCISE 4

Haiti	2	the
	3	Ø
	4	the
	5	Ø
Zimbabwe	6	Ø
	7	Ø
	8	the
Somalia	9	the
	10	the
	11	Ø
Tajikistan	12	the
	13	the
	14	Ø
	15	Ø
	16	Ø
North Korea	17	Ø
	18	Ø
	19	Ø
Mongolia	20	the
	21	the

Production

TASK 1 (Sample answers only)

2 We will ensure that the poor get equal access to education.
3 We will make sure that the rich pay a fair share of tax.
4 We will give new hope to the unemployed.
5 We make a promise that the sick will get free medical treatment.

TASK 2 (Sample answers only)

1 Médecins Sans Frontières is an international aid organisation that works in over 80 countries. It provides emergency medical assistance and often operates in countries where there is a war. In addition, the organization trains local personnel and uses the media to raise awareness of countries that are in crisis.
2 The World Food Programme is a branch of the United Nations and is based in Rome. It provides emergency food aid and, for example, it supplied emergency food to Mozambique after the recent floods. In addition, the organization helps to provide long term economic and social development. It is funded by governments, and the largest donors in 2000 were the United States, Japan and the European Union.

37   *Some* and *any*

Practice

EXERCISE 1

2 a	6 some
3 a	7 any
4 any	8 some
5 some	

EXERCISE 2

1 any	6 some
2 some	7 some
3 any	8 any
4 any	9 any
5 any	10 any

EXERCISE 3

2 right
3 wrong – some letters
4 right
5 wrong – any major orders
6 right
7 wrong – some problems
8 right

EXERCISE 4

2 somewhere	5 anyone
3 something	6 anywhere
4 someone	7 anything

EXERCISE 5

1 anyone	4 anything
2 anywhere	5 anything
3 anyone	6 anywhere

EXERCISE 6

2 a lot of	7 a lot of
3 much	8 much
4 a little	9 a lot of
5 many	10 a few
6 a few	

Production

TASK 1 (Sample answers only)

2 I needed some legal advice.

3 Yes, they've moved somewhere outside Madrid.

4 No I haven't said anything to anyone.

TASK 2 (Sample answers only)

2 No, you can discuss it with anyone you like.

3 No, you can sit anywhere you like.

4 You can store anything you like.

TASK 3 (Sample answers only)

2 Well, we didn't meet many of the people we wanted to see. A lot of them were too busy to see us, and a few people were away on holiday because it was August. I suppose we got a little business out of it but it wasn't really worth it.

3 Yes – I think I made a lot of progress. There weren't many people on the course so we all got a lot of attention. The only problem was that we didn't have much free time at the end – I saw a few famous places like Buckingham Palace, but I would have liked a lot more time off.

38 Adjectives and adverbs

Practice

EXERCISE 1

2 quarterly	6 heavily
3 punctually	7 patiently
4 late	8 silently
5 publicly	

EXERCISE 2

2 recovered briefly

3 collapsed dramatically

4 fell considerably

5 fell slightly

6 improved steadily

7 improved gradually

EXERCISE 3

2 surprisingly good

3 commercially viable

4 totally illegal

5 badly designed

6 terribly quickly

EXERCISE 4

2 excellent	7 nicely
3 soft	8 competitively
4 raw	9 specially
5 fresh	10 widely
6 tough	

EXERCISE 5

2 well	5 good
3 well	6 well
4 good	7 well

Production

TASK 1

2 properly

3 badly

4 fine

5 noisy

6 ineffective

7 immediately

8 grateful

9 warm

10 strong

TASK 2 (Sample answers only)

2 I complained to the bank because they had processed the cheque very <u>slowly.</u>

3 I bought a laptop that was very <u>disappointing</u>.

4 I had a <u>horrible</u> meal in that restaurant last week.

5 The holiday was ruined by the <u>terrible</u> weather we had from start to finish.

6 The trains are so <u>badly</u> run that almost nobody uses them.

TASK 3 (Sample answer only)

I would like to tell you about a major opportunity that we are currently offering to our most valued customers. We are launching a brand new share dealing service that will let you buy and sell shares instantly. Please read through the enclosed leaflet, and if you would like to know more, phone me on 0007 232 2288.

39 Comparison (1): comparing adjectives

Practice

EXERCISE 1

expensive	more expensive than	the most expensive
good	better than	the best
wealthy	wealthier than	the wealthiest
big	bigger than	the biggest
narrow	narrower than	the narrowest
cheap	cheaper than	the cheapest
bad	worse than	the worst
profitable	more profitable than	the most profitable
long	longer than	the longest
interesting	more interesting than	the most interesting

EXERCISE 2

1 larger	7 newer
2 more competitive	8 better
3 more expensive	9 more important
4 cheaper	10 older
5 competitive	11 wealthier
6 more popular	12 more lucrative

EXERCISE 3

3 Norway has the longest life expectancy.
4 Mexico has the shortest life expectancy.
5 Norway has the highest GDP per capita.
6 Mexico has the lowest GDP per capita.
7 Mexico has the best unemployment rate.
8 Poland has the worst unemployment rate.

EXERCISE 4

2 the most boring presentation I have ever heard.
3 the most difficult customers I have ever dealt with.
4 the best product we have ever produced.
5 the simplest program I have ever used.

EXERCISE 5

2 the second most profitable company in Korea last year.
3 the third wealthiest person in the world.
4 the fourth biggest killer in the world.

Production

TASK 1 (Sample answers only)

2 The job I do now is harder than my last job.
   The job I do now isn't as easy as my last job.
3 Inflation this year is higher than it was last year.
   Inflation this year isn't as low as it was last year.
4 Our company isn't as large as our major competitor.
   Our company is smaller than our major competitor.

TASK 2 (Sample answers only)

2 The most interesting course I've ever been on was at MIT.
3 The best computer I've ever used was a Mac.
4 The nicest country I've ever visited is Argentina.
5 The most expensive hotel I've ever stayed in is the Oriental in Bangkok.
6 The fastest car I've ever driven was a Ferrari.
7 The most reasonable boss I've ever worked for was Robin Vernede.
8 The worst job I've ever had was filing dividends in the bank.

TASK 3 (Sample answer only)

I work for a local radio station in the south of England and I sell advertising. Our radio station is smaller than the main national stations, but we have a larger local audience base, so our local clients are very interested in our services. It's cheaper than advertising on TV, and we get lost of repeat business because our ads are more effective than newspaper adverts.

40 Comparison (2): comparing adverbs and nouns

Practice

EXERCISE 1

2 faster	5 more rapidly
3 more reliably	6 better
4 more quickly	7 more clearly

EXERCISE 2

2 the most extensively tested
3 best selling
4 the most efficiently managed
5 the most rapidly developing
6 the most heavily guarded

EXERCISE 3

A	B
1 the most	1 more (value) than
2 the fewest	2 less (value) than
3 more (shares) than	3 as much (value) as
4 the most	4 the least
5 as many (customers) as	5 the most

EXERCISE 4

1 more	4 much
2 many	5 less
3 fewer	

Production

TASK 1 (Sample answers only)

2 I don't go abroad as regularly as I used to.
3 I work harder than I used to.
4 I stay at work later than I used to.
5 I don't speak English as well as I used to.
6 I don't live as far from work as I used to.

TASK 2 (Sample answers only)

2 the hardest	5 the fastest
3 the most often	6 the most appallingly
4 the best	

TASK 3 (Sample answers only)

2 I don't have as much free time as I used to.
3 I go to more dinners than I used to.
4 I don't go on as many training courses as I used to.
5 I get less sleep than I used to.
6 I don't buy as many books as I used to.

41 Degree: too, not enough, so, such

Practice

EXERCISE 1

2 too (high)	5 too (much work)
3 (clearly) enough	6 enough (money)
4 too (late)	

EXERCISE 2

2 We don't have enough food.
3 We haven't brought enough warm clothes.
4 They make us walk too far.
5 We're having too many arguments.
6 We're disagreeing too much.
7 The weather isn't good enough for this kind of exercise.
8 The instructors don't help us often enough.
9 We aren't sleeping enough.
10 We're carrying too much equipment.

EXERCISE 3

2 Your products are too expensive for us to stock.
3 This contract is too complicated for me to understand.
4 My fax wasn't clear enough for him to read.
5 Your quotation wasn't low enough for us to accept.
6 The project was too risky for them to go ahead with.

EXERCISE 4

2 such good graphics; so fast; so user-friendly (software)
3 such a good idea; so clever; so useful (an invention)
4 so tasty; so nicely presented; such good value (a meal in a restaurant)
5 so light; so modern; decorated so beautifully (an office)
6 such good food; such style; such friendly staff (a hotel)
7 so illogical; so useful; so easy to learn (a language)
8 so fair; such a support; so conscientious (a colleague)

EXERCISE 5

2 d The company was in such a bad financial state that they called in the receivers.
3 f Frankfurt was so busy during the book fair that we couldn't get a hotel room.
4 b They treat their employees so well that nobody ever wants to leave.
5 g My laptop is so unreliable that I don't like to use it.
6 a The new drug was so successful that the factory couldn't meet the demand for it.
7 c He had such a good CV that we decided to interview him.

Production

TASK 1 (Sample answers only)

2 He hasn't got enough experience.
3 It isn't big enough for all of us.
4 I find him a bit too demanding.
5 I simply haven't got enough time.
6 I thought it would take up too much of my time.

TASK 2

2 a Their forecasts are too inaccurate for us to use.
   b Their forecasts aren't accurate enough for us to use.
3 a Our tax laws are too complicated for most people to understand.
   b Our tax laws aren't simple enough for most people to understand.
4 a Rents in the city are too high for us to have an office there.
   b Rents in the city aren't low enough for us to have an office there.
5 a The town is too small for us to have a branch in.
   b The town isn't big enough for us to have a branch in.

TASK 3 (Sample answers only)

2 I am so tired.
3 You speak it so well.
4 She seemed to be so happy.
5 She gets such a lot of money.
6 He tells such good jokes.

42 Adjective + preposition combinations

Practice
EXERCISE 1

1 foR
2 About
3 With
4 siMilar
5 suitAble
6 relaTed
7 opposEd
8 Rich
9 afraId
10 capAble
11 guiLty
12 intereSted

Answer: RAW MATERIALS

EXERCISE 2

2 moving
3 taking
4 running
5 hiring
6 manufacturing

EXERCISE 3

2 good with
3 responsible for
4 responsible to
5 annoyed with
6 sorry about
7 bad for

EXERCISE 4

2 proud
3 accustomed
4 capable
5 aware
6 rich
7 famous
8 popular
9 interested

Production

TASK 1

2 I don't think she is capable of doing the work.
3 Everyone knows that Bordeaux is famous for its fine wines.
4 Mr Renaldinio is responsible for hiring new staff.
5 The Industrial Society is opposed to higher taxes.
6 Would you be interested in arranging a meeting?

TASK 2 (Sample answers only)

2 I'm answerable to the Director of Medical Research.
3 I'm good at executing complex projects.
4 I'd be capable of running any of the research departments.
5 I'd be satisfied with an extra 20%.

TASK 3 (Sample answers only)
2 I'm very interested in antique furniture.
3 I'm different to my brother in a lot of ways.
4 I'm not afraid of taking risks.
5 I'm proud of the work that I've done for the company.
6 The work I'm doing now is similar to what I did in my last job.

43 Noun + preposition combinations

Practice
EXERCISE 1
2 request for
3 advantage of
4 reply to
5 cheque for
6 experience of
7 price of
8 difference between
9 trouble with
10 solution to

EXERCISE 2
1 in
2 of
3 in
4 of
5 of
6 in
7 of

EXERCISE 3
A 2 by
  3 out
  4 by

B 1 on
  2 in
  3 on
  4 on
  5 at
  6 in

EXERCISE 4
1 to
2 of
3 for
4 On
5 of
6 to
7 at
8 of
9 to
10 in
11 by
12 of

Production
TASK 1 (Sample answers only)
2 between what you do and what I do.
3 in crime in inner cities?
4 to the political problems in the Middle East.
5 for coal rises dramatically.

TASK 2
2 ... in a hurry.
3 ... at a loss.
4 ... by car.
5 ... on time.
6 ... for sale.
7 ... in debt.
8 ... on order.

TASK 3
2 out of hand
3 by hand
4 on hand
5 in the hands
6 On the other hand

44 Verb + preposition combinations

Practice
EXERCISE 1
2 of
3 on
4 of
5 on
6 to
7 on
8 from

EXERCISE 2
2 hear about
3 write to
4 wait for
5 think of
6 look at

EXERCISE 3
1 blaMe
2 provIde
3 Congratulate
4 tHank
5 insurE
6 suppLy
7 divIde
8 speNd
Answer: MICHELIN

EXERCISE 4
2 for
3 to
4 ✗
5 about
6 for
7 ✗
8 ✗

Production
TASK 1 (Sample answers only)
2 I'd talk to a friend about it.
3 I'd write to the Investor Relations Department.
4 I'd think about it for a few days.
5 I'd rely on my lawyer's advice.

TASK 2 (Sample answers only)
2 He provided me with the information.
3 She thanked me for helping her.
4 He asked me for my opinion.
5 They congratulated us on solving the problem.

TASK 3 (Sample answers only)
2 invest it in the stock market.
3 spend it on a new suit.
4 insure it against theft.

45 Phrasal verbs

Practice

EXERCISE 1

3 PV   6 PV
4 OM   7 PV
5 OM   8 OM

EXERCISE 2

2 a You should never throw away receipts.
   b You should never throw them away.
3 a They've closed down the factory.
   b They've closed it down.
4 a We've managed to keep down inflation.
   b We've managed to keep it down.

EXERCISE 3

1 put me through   3 put it off
2 cut us off   4 pick him up

EXERCISE 4

2 look into   7 turn up
3 do without   8 look after
4 taking up   9 hold on
5 run out of   10 call on
6 checked in

EXERCISE 5

1 d   4 d
2 a   5 a
3 d

Production

TASK 1

2 up   5 out
3 into   6 through
4 forward

TASK 2 (Sample answers only)

1 *come across:* He comes across as being a rather aggressive person.
2 *come down:* The price of DVD recorders will come down as they become more common.
3 *come up with:* He thought about the problem and came up with a brilliant solution.
4 *come down with:* Have tomorrow off – you sound as if you are coming down with a cold.
5 *come on:* Come on, we have to leave now or we'll be late.
6 *take over:* I lost my job when our firm was taken over.
7 *take on:* They are expanding fast and want to take on 500 new staff.
8 *take up:* The charity work she does takes up a lot of her time.
9 *take to:* I'm surprised you liked him; I didn't take to him at all.
10 *take in:* There's too much information to take in all at once.
11 *get on:* I like my boss – we get on very well.
12 *get through:* I've been ringing her all day but I haven't managed to get through yet.
13 *get by:* I don't need much money; I can get by on very little.
14 *get down:* The thought of having to do all that filing is really getting me down.
15 *get in:* Do you know what time Mr Carlton's flight is getting in?

Progress tests

(total = 20 marks)

QUESTION 1 (10 marks)

Fill in the blanks in the following email. Put the verbs in brackets into the present simple (e.g. *he works*) or the present continuous (e.g. *he's/he is working*). See the examples.

Dear Jim

Thanks for your message, and yes, I'm back at the ski resort for the next three months. I'm working (work) for Snowtravel again and I know (know) a couple of the other instructors from last year.

At the moment I ^{1}.......................... (sit) in the new Internet Café in the village, which is great to have. It ^{2}.......................... (open) at 6 a.m. and ^{3}.......................... (not/close) until midnight, so it's very convenient, and it ^{4}.......................... (mean) you can contact me any time.

The job is great – at the moment I ^{5}.......................... (teach) a family – they're just here for a week and I ^{6}.......................... (give) them private lessons. The three children ^{7}.......................... (make) good progress, but the mother and father are a disaster.

The weather isn't very good – in fact right now it ^{8}.......................... (rain) a little, so there's no snow in the village. But it ^{9}.......................... (get) colder, and by next month there will be plenty of snow. ^{10}.......................... (you/want) to come over some time? Please let me know and I'll find you a place to stay.

All the best
Nancy

QUESTION 2 (10 marks)

Complete the following sentences. Put the verbs in brackets into the present simple or the present continuous.

1 A: Where .... (you/come) from?
   B: I'm Indian – my home town is Mumbai.

2 I'm in the pharmaceutical research division. Currently we .... (develop) a new drug for heart disease.

3 I'm afraid Mr Brasseler is out – he .... (have) lunch with a client.

4 As a rule, cuts in interest rates .... (help) companies to create jobs.

5 TJR Systems is a small company that .... (produce) software for engineering firms.

6 I .... (use) a company car this week because mine is at the garage.

7 As a rule my manager .... (go) abroad once or twice a month.

8 Because of global warming, sea levels .... (rise) slowly.

9 I'm on the 18.30 flight that .... (get) in at 21.25.

10 I'm sorry this is a bad line – where .... (you/call) from?

(total = 20 marks)

QUESTION 1 (10 marks)

Complete the following text. Put the verbs into the past simple (e.g. *he worked*) or the present perfect (e.g. *he's/he has worked*).

James Dyson, one of the UK's most successful inventors, began his career when he ^{1}.......................... (be) a student at the Royal College of Art. He ^{2}.......................... (launch) the Sea Truck in 1970, and a few years later he ^{3}.......................... (think) up the award-winning Ballbarrow.

In 1978, he ^{4}.......................... (build) a new kind of machine for removing dust, and this ^{5}.......................... (lead) to the idea of a new kind of vacuum cleaner. It ^{6}.......................... (take) him 15 years to finish, but when the first DC01 vacuum cleaner ^{7}.......................... (come) out in 1993, it ^{8}.......................... (become) an instant success.

Dyson's company is inventing products all the time, and they ^{9}.......................... (just/develop) a new kind of washing machine which ^{10}.......................... (already/have) considerable commercial success.

QUESTION 2 (10 marks)

Complete the dialogues. Put the verbs into the past simple or the present perfect.

1 A: .... (you/ever/be) to Singapore?
  B: Yes – in fact I .... (live) there for two years, from 1997 to 1999.
2 A: I .... (not/receive) your report yesterday – could I see it now?
  B: I'm sorry, but I don't know where it is – I .... (lose) it.
3 A: I can't find Mrs Langer – .... (she/go) to lunch?
  B: Yes, she .... (leave) about 10 minutes ago.
4 A: .... (John/send) you those figures yet?
  B: Yes, he .... (email) them to me last night.
5 A: How many units .... (we/sell) last year?
  B: 8,500 – and so far this year we .... (sell) over 10,000 and it's only May.

Test 3 Units 7–9 (total = 20 marks)

QUESTION 1 (10 marks)

In each of the following sentences, fill in the blanks with ONE word only.

1 We haven't had any new orders .... over a month.
2 We have been producing cars at the Oxford factory .... nearly 80 years.
3 It's several weeks .... I was last at the office.
4 My boss went on a course .... September last year.
5 How long .... did Mr Koczka leave?
6 The last meeting took place .... 18 July.
7 A lot of the factories here were shut down .... the 1980s.
8 I got my first proper job .... 1992.
9 I haven't been feeling well .... I went to that fish restaurant.
10 My colleague worked in Hong Kong .... five years before coming back to Hamburg.

QUESTION 2 (5 marks)

Read the newspaper article. Put the verbs in brackets into the past simple (e.g. *he worked*) or present perfect continuous (e.g. *he's/he has been working*).

The smash musical *Mamma Mia* [1] .... (entertain) audiences at London's Prince Edward Theatre since it [2] .... (open) on April 6th 1999. The show is full of energy and features the music of Abba, the Swedish band who [3] .... (win) the Eurovision song contest in 1974. The story concerns Sophie, who [4] .... (try) for a long time to find out from her mother, Donna, who her real father is. The cast are extremely good, and Louise Plowright, who [5] .... (act) in the production since the beginning, is very strong as Sophie's mother.

QUESTION 3 (5 marks)

Rewrite the following sentences using the verb in brackets. See the example.

The last time I heard from her was months ago. (hear)
I haven't heard from her for months.
1 How long ago did you come to England? (be)
  How .... England?
2 The last time I updated the web page was on 11 June. (not/have)
  I .... 11 June.
3 It's not a new car – I bought it over a year ago. (have)
  It's not a new car – I .... over a year.
4 I've rung them again and again, but they won't answer. (ring)
  I .... all day, but they won't answer.
5 The last time they invested in any new equipment was years ago. (have)
  They .... years.

Test 4 Units 10–11 (total =30 marks)

QUESTION 1 (20 marks)

Put the verbs in brackets into the past simple (e.g. *he worked*), the past continuous (e.g. *he was working*) or past perfect (e.g. *he'd/he had worked*).

1 I .... (not/pay) the cheque in because the bank .... (already/shut) by the time I got there.

2 Anja .... (not/pick up) the phone because she .... (deal) with another customer when it rang.

3 While I .... (travel) in South America, I .... (get) the idea for my new business venture.

4 I .... (take) the car to the garage this morning because it .... (make) a strange noise.

5 They .... (still/not/pay) their bill, so we .... (send) them a second reminder.

6 When I .... (reach) the airport, the flight .... (already/close), so I waited for the next one.

7 Jason .... (be) worried about last week's presentation because he .... (not/prepare) his talk.

8 Sheila was very happy when I last .... (see) her because she .... (just/get) a raise.

9 He .... (lose) his passport while he .... (travel) to the conference.

10 While I .... (check) the figures, I .... (notice) a couple of mistakes.

QUESTION 2 (10 marks)

Complete these sentences. In each one, put one verb in the past simple (e.g. *he worked*) and the other verb in the past perfect continuous (e.g. *he'd/he had been working*).

1 When he finally .... (retire), he .... (work) for the company for 20 years.

2 We .... (wait) for over five hours by the time the plane finally .... (leave).

3 When they .... (make) the breakthrough, they .... (try) to solve the problem for two years.

4 He finally .... (decide) to see a doctor because he .... (not/feel) well for months.

5 When the accident .... (happen), he .... (drive) the lorry for 13 hours without a break.

Test 5 Units 12–15 (total = 25 marks)

QUESTION 1 (5 marks)

Change the verbs in brackets using *will* (e.g. *he'll work*) or *going to* (e.g. *he's going to work*).

1 A: Did I see Cathy driving into town just now?
   B: Yes, she .... (get) some cash from the bank.

2 A: I need to see the price list soon – today if possible.
   B: OK – give me your address and I .... (email) it to you now.

3 A: I'm afraid that we've sold out of the green folders.
   B: I see – OK, I .... (take) the blue ones instead.

4 A: Are you sure to get your money back?
   B: Yes – the guarantee says that they .... (give) you a refund at any time for any reason.

5 A: Have you seen their new plans for the Sports Centre?
   B: No – What .... (they/do)?

QUESTION 2 (8 marks)

Read the dialogue. Change the verbs in brackets using *will* (e.g. *he'll work*) or the present continuous (e.g. *he's working*).

A: I think I'd like to go now – I've got a busy weekend ahead.

B: Really? What [1] .... (you/do)?

A: Well, tonight I [2] .... (have) dinner with the Jamiesons, and then tomorrow morning I [3] .... (drive) to Bristol with Frau Müller for a conference.

B: That's quite a journey – how long [4] .... (it/take)?

A: About six or seven hours. Of course it means we [5] .... (need) to leave early because the conference starts at 11.

B: Do you plan to drive back tomorrow night?

A: No, I've booked a hotel – we [6] .... (stay) at the Intercontinental, which [7] .... (make) things easier.

B: So when do you suppose you [8] .... (be) back?

A: Late Sunday night I suppose. And in time for work on Monday.

QUESTION 3 (6 marks)

In each of the following sentences, choose the correct answer.

1 Monsieur Dégas .... this afternoon, but he rang to change the appointment to next Thursday.
   a would come
   b was coming
   c is going to come
   d will have come

2 We .... our normal suppliers, but we have changed our minds because we have found some new ones that are cheaper.
   a will use
   b are going to use
   c will be using
   d were going to use

3 Could you look after Mrs Cervenkova tomorrow – I can't do it because I .... back from the conference when she gets here.
   a will have travelled
   b was travelling
   c was going to travel
   d will be travelling

4 If sales continue to do this well, we .... our target by the end of next month.
   a will have reached
   b are reaching
   c will be reaching
   d were reaching

5 Ring Rodrigo and see how the interview went – I'm sure he .... by now.
   a will be hearing
   b is going to hear
   c will have heard
   d is hearing

6 I'm off on holiday on Saturday, so this time next week I .... on a beach in Barbados.
   a will lie
   b will be lying
   c will have lain
   d am going to lie

QUESTION 4 (6 marks)

Re-write the following sentences using the words in brackets. See the example.

There's a very good chance that we will win the contract. (probably)
We'll probably win the contract.

1 The chances are that there will be more redundancies soon. (likely)

....

2 I doubt that Tamas will want to come to the meeting. (shouldn't think)

....

3 I don't imagine I'll get a pay rise this year. (probably)

....

4 The new IT system is certain to improve our efficiency. (definitely)

....

5 There's a chance that Signor Lupelli will come in tomorrow. (might)

....

6 I shouldn't think that he will get the job. (doubt)

....

Test 6 Units 16–18 (total = 20 marks)

QUESTION 1 (10 marks)

Read the newspaper article. Underline the correct form of the verb in *italics*.

The telecoms regulator Oftel [1] *has released/has been released* figures showing that broadband [2] *is taking up/is being taken up* rapidly by British households and businesses. The statistics, which [3] *published/were published* yesterday, [4] *show/are shown* that over 30,000 subscribers a week [5] *are turning/are being turned* to high-speed Internet services. The main advantage of broadband is that files [6] *can download/can be downloaded* by users up to 40 times faster than with a dial-up modem, and the connection [7] *can leave/can be left* open all the time. Broadband services [8] *have reached/have been reached* most major towns and cities, but customers in more remote areas [9] *do not know/are not known* whether the phone lines in their areas [10] *will upgrade/will be upgraded*.

QUESTION 2 (10 marks)

Re-write the following sentences so that they have the same meaning.

1 A local firm is redecorating our offices.
   Our offices .... a local firm.
2 They grow a lot of the world's tea in India.
   A lot of .... in India.
3 I'll have the interviews conducted by my assistant.
   I'll get .... the interviews.
4 His suits are all made in Savile Row.
   He has .... in Savile Row.
5 Two brothers founded the company in 1896.
   The company .... in 1896.
6 Nobody has paid the bill yet.
   The bill still ....
7 They reorganized the department last year.
   The department .... last year.
8 An Italian designer updated our winter range.
   We had .... by an Italian designer.
9 You will be collected from the airport.
   Someone .... from the airport.
10 I'll ask Accounts to send you another copy of the invoice.
   I'll have .... another copy of the invoice.

Test 7 Units 19–22 (total = 30 marks)

QUESTION 1 (5 marks)

Complete the sentences with *if*, *when*, *unless* or *in case*.

1 Please don't disturb me in the meeting ....
   something really urgent comes up.
2 M Dubarry is coming in today – please give me a ring
   .... he gets here.
3 .... everything goes according to plan, we
   will meet our targets easily this year.
4 The flight is full, so I can't get a confirmed seat
   .... there is a cancellation.
5 I always take a spare battery for my laptop
   .... the main one runs out.

QUESTION 2 (10 marks)

Complete the sentences by putting the verbs in brackets into the first conditional or the second conditional.

1 If I .... (be) you, I .... (ring)
   them and see what's happened to the order.
2 I'm worried that unless sales ....
   (improve), they .... (close) the factory.

3 I've had a long career in the law, but if I
   .... (have) the chance to start all over
   again, I .... (study) medicine.
4 Take the receipt with you – if you ....
   (not/have) one, they .... (not/give) you
   your money back.
5 What products .... (you/develop) if you
   .... (be) the head of a company like
   Microsoft?

QUESTION 3 (5 marks)

Re-write the sentences below using a conditional form so that they have a similar meaning. See the example.

He didn't do well in the final interview. He didn't get the job.
If he had done well in the final interview, he'd/would have got the job.

1 You checked the invoice. We didn't make an expensive mistake.
   If you ....
2 Fiona didn't come to the meeting because she was in London.
   If Fiona ....
3 We didn't realize interest rates were going to rise so quickly. We took out a big loan.
   If we ....
4 I didn't know you were planning to leave. I promoted you.
   If I ....
5 They didn't give a good presentation. They didn't win the contract.
   If they ....

QUESTION 4 (10 marks)

In each of the following sentences, choose the correct answer.

1 I think I'll check my emails, just .... Kostas has sent me a message.
   a if
   b unless
   c so that
   d in case
2 My flight gets in at 9.30, so I'll call you .... I get there.
   a when
   b if
   c unless
   d in case

3 Neil's a good administrator, but if he deals with customers, he always .... problems.

a is creating

b creates

c created

d would create

4 If that package from Neilson's arrives this afternoon, ... it up to my office immediately.

a you are bringing

b you would bring

c bring

d you brought

5 If you .... tomorrow, you'll have problems because of the strike.

a will travel

b travelled

c would travel

d travel

6 It's got a year's guarantee, so you can bring it back if anything .... wrong.

a will go

b would go

c goes

d had gone

7 You can go ahead and order the parts as .... as you get permission from Accounts.

a long

b high

c far

d many

8 It was clear that the strike would go ahead .... there was a last-minute breakthrough.

a unless

b as long as

c so that

d if

9 If I .... a bit more experience I'd be in a position to apply for that job, but they need someone more senior.

a have had

b would have had

c will have

d had had

10 I .... the contract if I had read it properly.

a will have signed

b wouldn't have signed

c didn't sign

d signed

QUESTION 1   (5 marks)

Rewrite these suggestions using the word in brackets.

1 Shall we go out to the new Italian restaurant? (Why)

....

2 Let's set up a meeting to discuss this. (How)

....

3 What about finishing this off tomorrow? (Shall)

....

4 Why don't we have a word with the boss? (Let's)

....

5 Shall we send them another email? (What)

....

QUESTION 2   (10 marks)

A Complete the text with *have to*, *don't have to* or *can't*.

Capital cities around the world are trying to tackle the problems of busy roads and pollution in different ways. In Athens, on certain days of the week, you can drive if your car number plate ends in an even number, but on the other days, you ^{1} .... drive and ^{2} .... find some other way of getting to work. In London there is a congestion charge, which means that you ^{3} .... drive through central London for free any more – you ^{4} .... pay about £5 to take your car into the city centre. There are some exceptions – people with electric cars ^{5} .... pay the charge because they don't cause any pollution.

B Complete the email message with *had to*, *didn't have to* or *wasn't/weren't allowed to*.

Thanks for your message. Yes, Peter and I both went on that course last year. We ^{6} .... work from 9 to 1, and 2 to 4.30, but the rest of the time we were free (apart from the homework assignments that we ^{7} .... do every night). It was a residential course – and in fact we ^{8} .... leave the campus for any reason – they said participants ^{9} .... take every opportunity to exchange ideas. At first it felt a bit like being locked in, but it wasn't too bad, and we found we had a lot more time because we ^{10} .... travel to and from home every day.

QUESTION 3 (10 marks)

In each of the following sentences, choose the correct answer.

1 The files aren't here – I .... them back at the office.
  a may leave
  b must be leaving
  c should have left
  d must have left

2 If the meeting goes well, they .... award us the contract.
  a ought
  b shall
  c need
  d might

3 I haven't seen Simone for ages – she .... in a different department.
  a should work
  b needn't have worked
  c must be working
  d ought to have been working

4 It's a pity we sold the shares when we did – we .... them for another couple of months.
  a should keep
  b should be keeping
  c should have kept
  d should have been keeping

5 Sorry, but .... you give me a hand with these boxes? They're very heavy.
  a might
  b may
  c would
  d shall

6 He worked until 10 p.m. and .... finish the proposal in time.
  a managed to
  b was able
  c could
  d succeeded

7 We had to get an interpreter in Japan because none of us .... speak Japanese.
  a knew
  b were able
  c could
  d succeeded

8 We were lucky that the security guard put out the fire in time – we .... the whole warehouse.
  a were able to lose
  b managed to lose
  c could lose
  d could have lost

9 The CEO is confident that we will .... increase sales by 10% next year.
  a can
  b ought
  c be able to
  d manage

10 We .... them the reminder on Monday morning because the cheque arrived in the post that afternoon.
  a needed to send
  b needn't send
  c needed to have sent
  d needn't have sent

Test 9 Units 27–30 (total = 25 marks)

QUESTION 1 (10 marks)

Complete the dialogue. Put the verbs in brackets into the infinitive (e.g. *to work*) or the *-ing* form (e.g. *working*).

A: How can we justify [1] .... (spend) so much money on advertising? We agreed [2] .... (try) and cut down expenditure, but this proposal of yours means [3] .... (use) even more resources than last year.

B: I realize that, and I would like [4] .... (make) cuts, but we can't afford [5] .... (lose) any market share at the moment. If we are hoping [6] .... (increase) sales, we've got to carry on [7] .... (advertise).

A: Maybe, but I can't help [8] .... (feel) that there's a better way. For a start I'd suggest [9] .... (get) some other advertising agencies to give us some quotes.

B: OK, I'll arrange [10] .... (see) some others and I'll let you know what they say.

QUESTION 2 (5 marks)

Re-write these sentences using the verb in brackets.

1 He said to me: 'Go on, apply for the job!' (encourage)
  He .... the job.

2 He said to me: 'Don't drive too fast – there's a speed camera ahead.' (warn)

He ....
because there was a speed camera ahead.

3 He said to me: 'Could you put the offer in writing?' (ask)

He ....
the offer in writing.

4 My boss said: 'You have to stay until the project is finished.' (make)

My boss ....
until the project was finished.

5 He said to me: 'You ought to see a lawyer.' (advise)

He .... a lawyer.

QUESTION 3   (5 marks)

Complete the following sentences. Put the verbs into the infinitive or the -ing form.

1 I forgot .... (take) my mobile phone charger with me on my last trip, so I had to buy a new one.

2 A: Anna, did you remember .... (send) that contract off to Licia?

B: Yes, I did it yesterday.

3 These figures need .... (check) – they don't look right to me.

4 I regret .... (say) that we will not be able to offer you the job, but we would like to thank you for your interest in the company.

5 When interest rates rise, consumers usually stop .... (spend) and start saving.

QUESTION 4   (5 marks)

Complete the text. Put the verbs in brackets into the infinitive or the -ing form.

After [1] .... (leave) university in 1986, Luis Miguel knew that he wanted a career in travel. However, before [2] .... (start) his own business, he got a job with a local travel firm, where he quickly learned how [3] .... (operate) a small agency. A year later, he left [4] .... (set up) his own company, Travelextra, which grew rapidly by [5] .... (concentrate) on giving excellent value and top class customer service.

QUESTION 1   (10 marks)

Re-write these sentences by filling in the gaps.

1 'Please don't smoke in front of the customers,' he said to me.

He asked .... in front of the customers.

2 It's an American company, but I had no idea.

I had no idea .... an American company.

3 'I've been working very hard all week,' she said to me.

She told me .... very hard all week.

4 'Don't send those invoices out without checking them,' my supervisor said to me.

My supervisor told me .... the invoices out without checking them.

5 'I haven't had much experience of retail,' he told the interviewer.

He told the interviewer that he .... much experience of retail.

6 'I'm calling on behalf of SGE Electronics', the man said.

The man said .... on behalf of SGE Electronics.

7 'I don't want the job,' I said to them.

I told them .... the job.

8 Maria told me they had given her a pay rise.

Maria said to me: 'They .... a pay rise.'

9 Last week Jack said: 'I'm seeing Angela tomorrow.'

Last week Jack told me .... day.

10 He said he was afraid he couldn't come to the meeting.

He said to me: ' I'm afraid .... to the meeting.'

QUESTION 2   (10 marks)

In each of the following sentences, choose the correct answer.

1 I asked Martha .... the conference had gone well.
   a what
   b did
   c if
   d that

2 The Manager asked me .... of the new proposal.
   a what did I think
   b if I thought
   c that I did think
   d what I thought

3 At the meeting the shareholders asked how the company .... in the previous year.

a did

b had done

c have done

d has done

4 I couldn't find Mlle Arnoux, so I asked her secretary ....

a was she there

b where was she

c where she was

d where she was being

5 He rang to ask .... we were still interested in the site or not.

a whether

b when

c where

d that

6 I didn't receive the ticket, so I rang the travel agent to ask if they .... it.

a sent

b had sent

c have sent

d sends

7 My boss was very supportive and .... me to apply for the promotion.

a refused

b threatened

c apologized

d encouraged

8 He apologized .... at the meeting late.

a to arrive

b that he arrived

c of arriving

d for arriving

9 It's a nice car but I wonder ....

a what it costs

b what does it cost

c how much does it costs

d if it costs

10 I rang to ask when they ...., but in fact they had already relocated.

a are moving

b will move

c shall move

d were moving

QUESTION 1 (10 marks)

Complete the text with the words in the box.

who what whose where which

In the corporate market, apartment hotels are rapidly becoming popular with executives [1] .... travel a great deal. Apartment hotels, [2] .... share some of the features of traditional hotels such as a reception desks, can be hired for a single night or for several weeks. They are ideal for anyone [3] .... job takes them away from home for a month or so at a time, because [4] .... they provide is a space that is much more like home, with a bathroom, sitting room, bedroom and working area. Apartment hotels also come with a kitchen, [5] .... executives can make meals, and they have laundry facilities as well, [6] .... helps to keep costs down.

Dominique Villon, [7] .... consultancy company DSD International advises clients on corporate travel, says they are a welcome development but are not ideal for everyone: 'Apartment hotels are great in places like London, [8] .... traditional hotels are extremely expensive, but [9] .... they lack is room service, and that can be a problem for executives [10] .... don't have the time to cook for themselves.'

QUESTION 2 (10 marks)

Complete the following sentences with a relative pronoun. Sometimes there is more than one correct answer.

1 I have to share an office with a colleague .... smokes.

2 Passengers without a valid visa will be sent back to the country from .... they have come.

3 Do you have the number of that hotel .... Mrs Serdar is staying?

4 What was the name of that man .... came in yesterday?

5 Manuel's father, ... set up the company in 1965, has handed control to his son.

6 Can you find out what has happened to the shipment .... we sent them?

7 We need a translator .... mother tongue is Icelandic.

8 In 1987 he moved to Seoul, ... he set up the Asia division.

9 .... I am looking for is a job with more responsibility.

10 Please show Mr Kiedrowski to the room .... they are holding the meeting in.

Test 12 Units 35–37   (total = 20 marks)

QUESTION 1   (7 marks)

Complete the sentences with *a*, *an* or *some*.

1 Take .... cash with you for the taxi from the airport.

2 Do you know .... hotel in the centre of Istanbul?

3 I've got .... money invested in the stock market.

4 He has ordered .... new furniture for the office.

5 I'd like .... litre of water please.

6 I've got .... interesting news for you.

7 In this department they are doing .... research into new heat-resistant materials.

QUESTION 2   (7 marks)

Complete the dialogue. Fill in the blanks with *a/an*, *the* or *ø* (no article).

A: How long have you been in engineering?

B: About twenty years. Just after I graduated, I went to work for ¹ .... small company in ² .... Lille.

A: So you haven't always been your own boss?

B: No – I worked there for about five years, but then ³ .... company got into trouble and closed down. I had to find ⁴ .... new job, and decided to set up ⁵ .... business of my own. Now we have one hundred employees and specialize in projects in ⁶ .... Middle East, and it's those projects that are ⁷ .... most valuable to us.

QUESTION 3   (6 marks)

Complete the dialogue with the words in the box.

a lot	much	many	a little	a few

A: Is the project still on schedule? We haven't got ¹ .... time left, you realize.

B: Yes, everything's fine – the site manager has had ² .... of experience with building projects like this, so we haven't had ³ .... difficulty getting things done.

A: What about the budget?

B: The clients have made ⁴ .... changes to the original plans, but nothing major, and we've managed to save ⁵ .... money by leasing equipment from a local supplier.

A: So how ⁶ .... weeks do you think you will need to finish?

B: Two at the most, so we're nearly there.

Test 13 Units 38–41   (total = 30 marks)

QUESTION 1   (8 marks)

Complete the sentences with a suitable adverb or adjective based on the word in brackets. See the example.

The stock market has fallen dramatically (drama) over the last few weeks.

1 The new model has excellent sound insulation and runs almost .... (silent).

2 I have just received the latest .... (quarter) sales report.

3 I have had .... (consider) experience of working in the private sector.

4 You'll like working here, and everyone is very .... (friend).

5 What's the matter with Stefan? He looks very .... (anger) about something.

6 The bank was not convinced that the new business would be .... (commerce) viable.

7 It's an excellent Chinese restaurant and the food tastes really .... (authenticity).

8 We ought to look into Mika's proposal; it sounds very .... (interest).

QUESTION 2 (7 marks)

Complete the extract from a presentation. Put the adjectives in brackets into the correct comparative or superlative form.

The shop in Alan Street has some advantages. For a start, it is in [1] .... (busy) street in the town, so there would be a lot of potential customers. As it is the town centre, it would be [2] .... (convenient) than going out to the Retail Park for a lot of people. As far as the rent is concerned, they're both about the same – in fact Alan Street is a little [3] .... (cheap).

However, if we now take a [4] .... (close) look at the Retail Park outlet, you'll see that it also has a number of advantages. Firstly, it was only built last year, so it feels much [5] .... (modern) than Alan Street. It's also in the [6] .... (good) position of all of the shops there, which would be very helpful. So all in all, although the Retail Park outlet is [7] .... (not/easy) to get to as Alan Street, I think it would meet our needs.

QUESTION 3 (5 marks)

Complete the sentences by changing the words in brackets to comparative or superlative adverbs.

1 The new temp types .... than my usual secretary, but she's not as good at shorthand. (fast)

2 The original Barbie was a great success and quickly became the .... selling toy in the USA. (good)

3 Car engines run .... if they use the correct grade of motor oil. (efficient)

4 I did .... in the exams than I had expected. (bad)

5 As he arrived ...., he had to unlock the office and turn on the lights. (early)

QUESTION 4 (5 marks)

Complete the dialogue with the words in the box.

many	less	fewer	much	more

A: How do you find the new car compared to the old one?

B: Well, the Audi got through [1] .... petrol – it only did about 20 miles a gallon, but it was quite old. The Citroën is better and uses [2] .... fuel, but of course it doesn't carry as [3] .... people – it's just a normal five-seater, but that's all I really need.

A: What about luggage space?

B: The Citroen doesn't have as [4] .... room as the Audi, but that doesn't really matter as I don't set up exhibitions myself any more, so I take [5] .... cases than I used to.

QUESTION 5 (5 marks)

Re-write the sentences.

1 I couldn't carry the boxes. They were too heavy.
  The boxes were .... lift.

2 The bill was too high. I refused to pay it.
  The bill was .... that I refused to pay it.

3 He can't join the Army. He is too young.
  He isn't .... to join the Army.

4 The design was so good that everyone copied it.
  It was .... that everyone copied it.

5 We couldn't take on the project. It was too big for us.
  The project was .... to take on.

Test 14 Units 42–45 (total = 30 marks)

QUESTION 1 (10 marks)

Complete the puzzle opposite to find the missing word.

1 What are the main differences .... the two offers you have received?

2 Southern Africa is rich .... minerals such as gold.

3 She's very enthusiastic .... the new project and is really looking forward to starting.

4 I enclose a .... for $300 made payable to Lawsons Inc.

5 We had to sell all our stock at .... notice, so we didn't get the best price.

6 I am writing in .... to your letter of 18 November.

7 A further rise in interest rates would be bad .... business.

8 I complained to the manager that I was not satisfied .... the service I had received.

9 Yes, I can confirm that the house is for ...., and the asking price is $950,000.

10 There have been no delays so we expect the flight to arrive on ....

```
1  [ ][ ][ ][ ][ ][ ][ ]
2  [ ][ ][ ][ ][ ][ ]
3  [ ][ ][ ][ ][ ][ ]
4        [ ][ ][ ][ ][ ]
5     [ ][ ][ ][ ][ ]
6        [ ][ ][ ][ ][ ]
7     [ ][ ][ ][ ][ ]
8        [ ][ ][ ][ ][ ]
9     [ ][ ][ ][ ][ ][ ]
10    [ ][ ][ ][ ][ ][ ]
```

QUESTION 2 (5 marks)

Complete the sentences with a suitable word.

1 Mr Salepçioglu is very keen on the venture, but I'm not sure that I agree .... him.
2 The correct mixture consists .... 25 parts of petrol to one part of oil.
3 I may be able to come on Friday – it depends .... how work goes this week.
4 You can always rely .... Laura for good advice.
5 How much do you pay .... electricity per quarter?

QUESTION 3 (5 marks)

Re-write the following sentences using the verb in brackets.

1 Could you give us tea and coffee at 11 a.m.? (provide)
Could you .... tea and coffee at 11 a.m.?
2 He said thanks because I came to the meeting. (thank)
He .... coming to the meeting.
3 An airbag stops you hitting the steering wheel in an accident. (protect)
An airbag .... hitting the steering wheel in an accident.
4 What is your clothes expenditure in a year? (spend)
How much .... clothes in a year?
5 The bank will lend us $2 million. (borrow)
We can .... the bank.

QUESTION 4 (10 marks)

Re-word the verbs in *italics* using a two- or three-part phrasal verb based on the verb in brackets. See the example.

It's a binding contract, and that means we can't *withdraw from* it now. (back)
It's a binding contract, and that means we can't back out of it now.

1 I'm calling to see if we can *delay* the tour. (put)
I'm calling to see if we can .... the tour.
2 Someone needs to *tidy* this office. (clear)
Someone needs to .... this office.
3 I want you to *discover* what is going on in the sales department (find)
I want you to .... what is going on in the sales department.
4 The man who came for an interview got lost and eventually *arrived* two hours late. (turn)
The man who came for an interview got lost and eventually .... two hours late.
5 It's not a very reliable scanner – it seems to *stop working* all the time. (break)
It's not a very reliable scanner – it seems to .... all the time.
6 Leave the problem with me and I'll *investigate* what has gone wrong. (look)
Leave the problem with me and I'll .... what has gone wrong.
7 The loss of the order is a serious blow, but we will *recover from it*. (get)
The loss of the order is a serious blow, but we will .... it.
8 I'll call you as soon as I've *registered* at the hotel. (check).
I'll call you as soon as I've .... at the hotel.
9 I'm very lucky because I *like* my boss. (get)
I'm very lucky because I .... my boss.
10 Martine Sanchez is the Head of Personnel, and she'll *take care of* you during your visit. (look)
Martine Sanchez is the Head of Personnel, and she'll .... you during your visit.

Progress tests – Answer key

Test 1

QUESTION 1

1 'm/am sitting
2 opens
3 doesn't close
4 means
5 'm/am teaching
6 'm/am giving
7 are making
8 's/is raining
9 's/is getting
10 Do you want

QUESTION 2

1 do you come
2 're/are developing
3 's/is having
4 help
5 produces
6 'm/am using
7 goes
8 are rising
9 gets
10 are you calling

Test 2

QUESTION 1

1 was
2 launched
3 thought
4 built
5 led
6 took
7 came
8 became
9 have just developed
10 has already had

QUESTION 2

1 Have you ever been, lived
2 didn't receive, 've/have lost
3 has she gone, left
4 Has John sent, emailed
5 did we sell, 've/have sold

Test 3

QUESTION 1

1 for
2 for
3 since
4 in
5 ago
6 on
7 in
8 in
9 since
10 for

QUESTION 2

1 has been entertaining
2 opened
3 won
4 has been trying
5 has been acting

QUESTION 3

1 long have you been in
2 haven't updated the web page since
3 've/have had it for
4 've/have been ringing them
5 haven't invested in any new equipment for

Test 4

QUESTION 1

1 didn't pay, had already shut
2 didn't pick up, was dealing
3 was travelling, got
4 took, was making
5 still hadn't paid, sent
6 reached, had already closed
7 was, hadn't prepared
8 saw, 'd/had just got
9 lost, was travelling
10 was checking, noticed

QUESTION 2

1 retired, 'd/had been working
2 'd/had been waiting, left
3 made, 'd/had been trying
4 decided, hadn't been feeling
5 happened, 'd/had been driving

Test 5

QUESTION 1

1 's/is going to get
2 'll/will email
3 'll/will take
4 'll/will give
5 are they going to do

QUESTION 2

1 are you doing
2 'm/am having
3 'm/am driving
4 will it take
5 'll/will need
6 're/are staying
7 will make
8 'll/will be

QUESTION 3

1 b   3 d   5 c
2 d   4 a   6 b

QUESTION 4

1 There are likely to be more redundancies soon.
2 I shouldn't think that Tamas will want to come to the meeting.
3 I probably won't get a pay rise this year.
4 The new IT system will definitely improve our efficiency.
5 Signor Lupelli might come in tomorrow.
6 I doubt if/whether he will get the job.

Test 6

QUESTION 1

1 has released
2 is being taken up
3 were published
4 show
5 are turning
6 can be downloaded
7 can be left
8 have reached
9 do not know
10 will be upgraded

QUESTION 2

1 are being redecorated by
2 the world's tea is grown
3 my assistant to conduct
4 all his suits made
5 was founded by two brothers
6 hasn't been paid.
7 was reorganized
8 our winter range updated
9 will collect you
10 Accounts send you

Test 7

QUESTION 1

1 unless
2 when
3 If
4 unless
5 in case

QUESTION 2

1 was/were, 'd/would ring
2 improve, 'll/will close
3 had, 'd/would study
4 don't have, won't give
5 would you develop, were

QUESTION 3

1 … hadn't checked the invoice, we'd/would have made an expensive mistake.
2 … hadn't been in London, she'd/would have come to the meeting.
3 … had realized that interest rates were going to rise so quickly, we wouldn't have taken out a big loan.
4 … had known you were planning to leave, I wouldn't have promoted you.
5 … had given a good presentation, they'd/would have won the contract.

QUESTION 4

1 d   4 c   7 a   9 d
2 a   5 d   8 a   10 b
3 b   6 c

Test 8

QUESTION 1

1 Why don't we go out to the new Italian restaurant?
2 How about setting up a meeting to discuss this?
3 Shall we finish this off tomorrow?
4 Let's have a word with the boss.
5 What about sending them another email?

QUESTION 2

A
1 can't
2 have to
3 can't
4 have to
5 don't have to
B
6 had to
7 had to
8 weren't allowed to
9 had to
10 didn't have to

QUESTION 3

1 d	4 c	7 c	9 c
2 d	5 c	8 d	10 d
3 c	6 a		

Test 9

QUESTION 1

1 spending
2 to try
3 using
4 to make
5 to lose
6 to increase
7 advertising
8 feeling
9 getting
10 to see

QUESTION 2

1 encouraged me to apply for
2 warned me not to drive too fast
3 asked me to put/if I could put
4 made me stay
5 advised me to see

QUESTION 3

1 to take
2 to send
3 checking/to be checked
4 to say
5 spending

QUESTION 4

1 leaving
2 starting
3 to operate
4 to set up
5 concentrating

Test 10

QUESTION 1

1 me not to smoke
2 (that) it was
3 she'd/had been working
4 not to send
5 hadn't had
6 he was calling
7 I didn't want
8 've/have given me
9 he was seeing Angela the following
10 I can't come

QUESTION 2

1 c	4 c	7 d	9 a
2 d	5 a	8 d	10 d
3 b	6 b		

Test 11

QUESTION 1

1 who
2 which
3 whose
4 what
5 where
6 which
7 whose
8 where
9 what
10 who

QUESTION 2

1 who/that
2 which
3 where
4 who/that
5 who
6 which, that, or ø (no relative pronoun)
7 whose
8 where
9 What
10 which, that, or ø (no relative pronoun)

Test 12

QUESTION 1

1 some
2 a
3 some
4 some
5 a
6 some
7 some

QUESTION 2

1 a
2 ø
3 the
4 a
5 a
6 the
7 the

QUESTION 3

1 much
2 a lot
3 much
4 a few
5 a little
6 many

Test 13

QUESTION 1

1 silently
2 quarterly
3 considerable
4 friendly
5 angry
6 commercially
7 authentic
8 interesting

QUESTION 2

1 the busiest
2 more convenient
3 cheaper
4 closer
5 more modern
6 the best
7 not as easy

QUESTION 3

1 faster
2 best
3 more efficiently
4 worse
5 the earliest

QUESTION 4

1 more
2 less
3 many
4 much
5 fewer

QUESTION 5

1 too heavy for me to
2 so high
3 old enough
4 such a good design
5 too big for us

Test 14

QUESTION 1

1 betwEen
2 iN
3 abouT
4 chEque
5 shoRt
6 rePly
7 foR
8 wIth
9 Sale
10 timE

Key word = ENTERPRISE

QUESTION 2

1 with
2 of
3 on
4 on
5 for

QUESTION 3

1 provide us with
2 thanked me for
3 protects you from
4 do you spend on
5 borrow $2 million from

QUESTION 4

1 put off
2 clear up
3 find out
4 turned up
5 break down
6 look into
7 get over
8 checked in
9 get on with/ get along with
10 look after

Index

References are to unit numbers (e.g. Unit 36) and page numbers (e.g. 152).